FOOTY ROCKS!

The 50 Best Rants and Dribbles

JOHN NICHOLSON
Edited by Sarah Winterburn

FOOTY ROCKS!
www.northernmonkeypublishing.co.uk

ISBN 0-9554029-0-5
ISBN 978-0-9554029-0-6

First Published 2006 by
Northern Monkey Publishing

Printed in Great Britain for Northern Monkey Publishing

...for Beer Pigs and freaks everywhere!

CHAPTER	**CONTENTS**		PAGE

	Prologue		III
	Introduction		VII
	THE 50 BEST RANTS AND DRIBBLES		1
1	The Barnsley Surrealist Collective	*28/11/2001*	3
2	LSD Football	*02/12/2001*	9
3	The Berwick Alternative	*09/01/2002*	12
4	The Manchester Hedonists	*24/09/2002*	17
5	Chelsea: The Shaven Haven	*06/10/2002*	22
6	Newcastle: That's Living Alright	*12/11/2002*	28
7	Guns and Poses	*26/11/2002*	33
8	Significant Shrinkage	*11/12/2002*	37
9	A Very 1970's Xmas	*19/12/2002*	42
10	Its A Spurs Thong	*14/01/2003*	47
11	Souey Made My Mate Gay!	*20/01/2003*	52
12	Metal Mick's Madness	*29/04/2003*	56
13	Football Nutters Unite!	*04/08/2003*	59
14	I Swear. It's The Truth	*11/08/2003*	65
15	"Why is Ian Rush Between Your Legs?"	*27/08/2003*	70
16	"Wax My Anus!"	*21/09/2003*	74
17	My Drug Hell	*08/10/2003*	79
18	Dressing Inappropriately	*10/12/2003*	85
19	A Hard, Hard Christmas	*18/12/2003*	89
20	Two Red Setters In Jedburgh	*22/01/2004*	96
21	Ciao Edie	*01/04/2004*	100
22	Stairway To Boro Heaven	*05/02/2004*	104
23	Plastic People Oh Baby Now You're Such A Drag	*08/03/2004*	108
24	Kidnapping Women In Tewkesbury	*08/04/2004*	114
25	Notes From Another Continent	*06/07/2004*	120
26	Sex And The Single Manager	*03/08/2004*	125

27	The Sound Of Silence	09/09/2004	130
28	Turn Off Your Mind, Relax And Float Downstream	29/09/2004	135
29	How I Lost My Pain	14/12/2004	139
30	The Vegas Imperatives	27/12/2004	143
31	Where There's Blame, There's A Claim	18/01/2005	148
32	Are We Not Men?	02/02/2005	154
33	Lick My Love Pump	23/02/2005	158
34	Bring On The European Super League	21/03/2005	162
35	Bank Holiday Madness	28/03/2005	166
36	The Bloated Boy's Club	31/03/2005	171
37	Pissing In Sinks: Lads	13/04/2005	175
38	One Long Bacchanalia Of Materialism	07/06/2005	179
39	Anthem Schmantham	05/09/2005	184
40	"Yoo-Weff-Oww"	30/10/2005	189
41	Stand Up If You Don't Want Piles	08/11/2005	197
42	George Best: Rebel Spirit	24/11/2005	204
43	A Minute's Silence For The Death Of The Minute's Silence	28/11/2005	208
44	The Mystery Of The Stewards	05/12/2005	212
45	Falling Out Of Love With Boro's Slappers	11/01/2006	216
46	The Media Are From Mars	17/01/2006	224
47	Red Nev Incites A Riot	23/01/2006	230
48	Ossie Ossie Ossie	01/03/2006	235
49	Pissing In Sinks: Lasses	15/05/2006	238
50	Fear And Loathing In England	26/06/2006	243

NEW WRITINGS   249

| 1 | What's What: A Rock 'n' Roll Granddad | 250 |
| 2 | Code Of The Road – *an excerpt* | 272 |

When I started writing for Football365 in November 2000, Terry Venables had just taken on the job of Bryan Robson's assistant/dad/red wine taster at my club, Middlesbrough. Now, six years later, in one of those strange twists of fate the universe occasionally throws up, Terry Venables has just taken up the position of assistant to Robson's successor at Middlesbrough, Steve McClaren, only this time for England. So, with the universe apparently briefly in harmony with my life, now seems like a good time to publish a book of fifty of my favourite columns of the last six years.

There's also a big new piece called 'What's What' here which might go some way to illustrating how I ended up like this and there's a taster from my next project; a rock 'n' roll road movie of a book called 'Code of the Road'.

It always seemed to me that when writing for what I consider to be the biggest, most important football website in the world, it was a bit pointless to approach the gig as though I was a proper, trained journo. There were, after all, plenty of them around already and I had got the job of columnist largely by writing in long letters about how Alan Shearer should join folk group The High Level Ranters, how Glenn Hoddle will eventually evolve into pure white light and how great I thought Steely Dan, Rick Wakeman's silver capes and Jerry Seinfeld were.

Back in 2000 all things interwebby were still new and revolutionary. So I wanted to bring an equally new kind of attitude to this new, liberating media that didn't have to rely on many of the old values and attitudes; this new media that could respond within minutes to breaking stories, that was more democratic and instinctively rebellious.

My favourite writers have always been the whack-jobs who went about their work with a wanton disregard for convention.

People like Lester Bangs, Hunter Thompson, Jack Kerouac and Allen Ginsburg.

But being a very self-consciously proud Northern lad, born in Hull, Yorkshire and growing up in Stockton-on-Tees, on Teesside (I could never bring myself to call it Cleveland) I also liked that whole gritty, northern tradition of writing that was embodied in the books of Alan Sillitoe, Keith Waterhouse, John Braine, Stan Barstow and even Alan Bennett.

Then there's my deep and life long passion for noisy electric guitars and for the purveyors of the riff. It's been my religion. I even bleed in E major. The Holy Rock 'n' roll in all its forms is always with me and informs everything I do.

So I poured all these influences into one big mental bucket, added a lot of strong drink and a passion for football that borders on the clinically obsessive and sat back to see what came out.

Instead of just offering up my opinions on the current issues of the day, I thought it would be far more interesting to try and make bizarre, often tortuous analogies between my own anecdotes and whatever was pressing my football buttons at the time.

Thus was born my now infamous style of 'a long story with a bit of football tagged on at the end'.

And thanks to the liberal, creative and open-minded editorship of F365 over the years, I have quite literally been given my head to go on about anything I want to go on about, in any manner I want, even if it involves all things seedy, druggy and downright dirty and barely any football at all.

So a massive thanks must go out to editors past and present, Steve Anglesey, Sarah Winterburn and Pete Gill for letting me do what I wanted to do for all these years.

Thanks also to the other F365 luminaries along the way such as Lord Howard of Johnson, Tarby, Alan Tyers, Philip Cornwall, Neil Rowlands and these days Sheridan Bird, Tim

Stannard, Rob McNicol and Adam Fraser for continuing to make the journey so enjoyable.

Sarah Winterburn deserves a special mention for being my glamorous northern bird of an editor for this project and for knowing which commas go where. No man could have a finer woman in charge of his syntax. Or indeed his sin tax.

Back on the ranch, all the Members of the Rock Family Tree and Sponge Family Cork who continue to make life good; you know who you are - this is for all of youse lot as well. We'll enjoy spending the money.

Finally, thanks to you lot out there who read my stuff, who write to me and who continue to make this all such an interesting adventure. I'd buy you a drink if I could.

Cheers.
Now, let's get down to it baby.

John Nicholson, Edinburgh, September 2006

INTRODUCTION

Sometime in the mid-1970's, a group of Fleet Street's finest headed into southern France to report on a London club's UEFA Cup tie. The match over, they repaired to their hotel bar for the traditional post-match warm-down, where one of their number became so completely relaxed the others left him slumbering in a corner booth as they stumbled off to bed.

He was still there the next morning as his giggling colleagues crept past him as they left for the local airport. There, each was met with a telex from his offices back in London. A plane carrying British holidaymakers had crashed in mountains near the very hotel they had left earlier that day and since they were under three hours away, could they divert to the scene of the accident and pick up whatever information they could find until the real news reporters arrived?

Back in the hotel, our sleepy hero awoke to find his companions gone and the barman sadly tutting over TV coverage of the tragedy. Seizing his moment, the errant hack leaped into his rental car and headed for the crash site.

But the combination of twisting hillside paths and flesh-crawling hangovers is a dangerous one. As he attempted to navigate one switchback bend, our hero lost control of his vehicle, sending it spinning down through the trees and bushes towards the valley below.

Time passed. Our man awoke in a snow-covered forest, bloodied and with his clothes tattered, but miraculously thrown free of the wreckage of his car.

Reasoning that his life had been spared to he could bring home the story; he began to stagger back up the mountainside.

Finally, dizzy, disorientated and bitten through by the cold, another miracle occurred. Through the trees, our man spotted unmistakably human figures and rushed towards what turned out to be a thoroughly startled group of nuns.

Speaking no French, he stuck out his arms and mimed a plane crashing as an indication that he wished to be taken to the scene of the accident. The sisters seemed to understand all this perfectly and led him back to their nunnery where, presumably awaiting his transport, he was given a brandy and a handful of painkillers and settled back into an armchair for a quick nap.

And so it was that some hours later, having arrived at the crash site to hear that a survivor had been found and an English one to boot, the redeployed football reporters filed into a tiny cell in a mountainside nunnery, where they were greeted by the site of their colleague in repose, snoring loudly.

This story, 100 per cent true, by the way, has nothing to do with John Nicholson. And in a way it has everything to do with him.

Not long ago, men like that plane crash survivor were the only people in Britain who had the ability to relay their opinions about football to more than four or five people at a time. A group of middle-aged white men who drank like lions and occasionally wrote like them too, their job was to hand down the received wisdom about football in print every morning. We had no choice but to be grateful even if their similar backgrounds and the pack mentality meant that received wisdom tended to be somewhat uniform, echoing the same old tenets and prejudices, praising the same heroes and excoriating the same hate figures through the years.

Now, three decades on, a few minutes browsing the internet will reveal countless opinions on countless footballing issues from countless fans in countless countries throughout the world. Some of these voices are entertaining or important and some are not but they are all there and our enjoyment and understanding of football are stronger for their diversity.

And few of those voices are more entertaining and diverse, and maybe even as important, than that of my friend John Nicholson.

He first came to us at Football365.com as an email apparition every bit as miraculous as those nuns on the mountainside; great screeds of text always signed 'Johnny, Malton, The North'. You clicked them open to find detailed explanations of why Norwich City were the Van Der Graaf Generator of football, or a discussion of the relative penis sizes of Captain Beefheart and Leeds United's David Harvey.

We gave him a column, of course. And thus were able to bring you some of what I think is the best and funniest writing about football ever composed by a Teesside guitar hero and T-shirt salesman with a screen press by his side, a riff in his heart and a head full of Sun-in, fly agaric and the far-off memory of disturbing a friend in the act of masturbating while staring at a photograph of the young Graeme Souness.

John is often compared to Hunter S Thompson, to Vivien Stanshall and to Bill Bailey and that is not bad company to keep. But comparisons are erroneous if they suggest that he is anything other than a 100 per cent original.

He writes like that plane crash survivor should have written: Careering half-naked through the snowy forests of football, leaving a bloody trail behind him as he presses on for the mountaintop.

Steve Anglesey, (Editor Football365.com 1999 – 2002)
Canary Wharf, August 2006

The 50 Best Rants and Dribbles

1. THE BARNSLEY SURREALIST COLLECTIVE

28/11/01

Using mind-expanding hallucinogenics isn't for everyone. And going to a game under their influence is not something to be recommended if it's your first time. You may freak out and think you have been kidnapped and forced to live in an ant colony.

As a Yorkshireman by birth I have a deep fondness for the county and its bizarre folk. Some areas of the country have a naturally poetic way of talking where expressions of opinion or perceptions are all made through off-the-wall analogies or images. In most of Yorkshire, such observations are made with a dour, unexpressive face which somehow makes them all the more funny.

All my family come from Yorkshire and some thought that laughing was a character weakness. "What's he got to laugh about?" they'd say in an accusatory tone at someone sharing a joke with a friend in the street. Laughing meant you were unreliable, flighty and probably lacking in moral fibre. I had an Uncle Len who had a hair-lip, which meant he was permanently doing an Elvis lip sneer. I never saw him laugh. Not once.

I knew it would be interesting going to Barnsley while out my brains but I had not expected the locals' South Yorkshire way of speaking to seem so profound and I have never listened to them in the same way again. And it all comes so naturally to them.

Clubs like Barnsley are the very bedrock of football. They're a world away from places like Old Trafford but have a gritty, low-rent kind of glamour all of their own – with or without mind-altering drugs.

This week's column is about Barnsley, but it could equally be about any of the clubs from obscure or unfashionable towns that litter this small island - clubs adored by the locals that the rest of the country couldn't even find on a map.

Barnsley, before and since their season-long excursion into the Premier League, have an underwhelming history. An FA Cup win in 1912 and a few lower-league promotions are the meagre rewards of the last 100-odd years. And it's more than likely that success will continue to elude them. So be it.

Given that Oakwell is one of the coldest grounds you can go to watch football and, I believe, one of the highest in the country, it's worth considering why exactly an impressive average of 14,500 people currently turn up to see Barnsley kick a ball around.

This question has puzzled me for years. Not just in relation to Barnsley but to all clubs who go decades with little success and little quality football.

Anyway, with this mystery in mind, many years ago I decided to undertake an experiment into this mysterious phenomenon. The experiment was conducted at Barnsley F.C. on a cold November afternoon and in order to gain a deeper perspective and insight, involved the consumption of a good handful of fungi that tabloid newspapers would call, accurately enough, Magic.

I just happened to be in South Yorkshire that weekend but what better place to marry the worlds of post-industrial northern culture, sport and transcendental psychedelia than Barnsley?

It was icy cold and windswept as I took my seat on the half-way line. The mushrooms began to kick in. The tannoy was playing The Smiths' 'What Difference Does It Make?' I had to disagree with Morrissey that 'it made none'. Indeed, the difference was remarkable.

A slow, sweeping, buzzing sensation began passing through my body from right to left and back again like the sweep of a photocopy machine's light. It was not unpleasant. The players ran out to a cacophony of noise that was almost primeval. Fans reacted to the players' presence as though they were long-lost friends who'd turned up with a bag of gold in one hand, some expensive vodka in the other and a loose woman on each arm.

The noise phased around my ears like one of those late 60's singles by the Small Faces and then mutated into wow and flutter as though it was being played on a cheap, worn-out C60 cassette.

After kick-off the buzzing, sweeping feeling became somehow synchronised with the ebb and flow of the match. It was as though the energy from the game was being mirrored in my own body. It tingled for a while and I briefly thought I may be sick. However, after years of watching the Boro this was not an unfamiliar sensation and it soon passed. As I opened and closed my eyes I was certain I was actually taking photos of the action with my pupils for future reference and I became briefly concerned that I might actually begin to emit the photos from an orifice.

The players moved across the pitch leaving a gaseous rainbow trail behind them. It looked like they were farting colour.

More profound still was the energy coming from the lumpy, gnarled crowd of bluff ex-miners and steel workers. Their deep voices resounded like a tuba playing brass band music. Their words were words of philosophers and mystics.

One bloke handed his mate a cup of tea.

"I think I'd die without tea," he said gratefully and drank it as though it was indeed the elixir of life, his hands cupped around the polystyrene as though worshipping the hot liquid. The steam drifted up in a dance of infinite complexity.

Another, in a resonant muffled voice that sounded as though it actually was coming from underground, shouted,

"Come on lads, give it double Giro."

I swear he did. I wasn't sure he was speaking English but it seemed to make sense so I wrote it down. He may have been speaking in tongues.

Nearby someone declared of a wayward striker,

"He couldn't boil a kettle in our house."

All his mates agreed.

Wow it was weird. He must be useless to not have the ability to put a kettle on. I wondered why the bloke would even let a footballer he didn't know come into his house specifically to boil a kettle. It didn't make sense and I felt that this was all some sort of code they were talking. A code I wasn't able to decipher.

Another animal, I couldn't think of them as human now, let out a howl of pain or delight, it was hard to tell which, and shouted at a painful volume,

"Ey up lads, they're playing with the rubber ball again."

Unwittingly, I appeared to have entered the world of the little-known Barnsley Surrealist Collective. Almost no comment was passed in a literal way. It was all done via tangential metaphors in a range of expressive grunts.

The Tykes' red shirts began vibrating violently; so violently that the players themselves became invisible behind the blinding, oscillating colour. I turned to the bloke sitting next to me and said,

"Those are amazing shirts they're playing in."

"Should hope so for the money they cost," he replied in a voice carved in equal measure from oak and tar

"Fifteen quid they are!" He said in a tone of depressed amazement.

A quid sounded like some kind of tropical gourd to me but even so it was hard to believe you could buy a wearable vibrating ball of colour so cheaply and I made a mental note to try and exchange some other kind of fruit or vegetable for one before leaving.

During the half-time interval I got confused between the concept of sexual intercourse and the consumption of a hot dog while watching a blonde woman sharing one with her boyfriend. I was probably staring in a socially unacceptable manner, but no-one seemed to care.

A bloke came back with a bag of Pontefract cakes and offered one to a small boy. I couldn't stop laughing at the small black liquorice sweets. They'd been fooled into thinking these were cakes! Ha! Should I tell them what a cake really was?

I chuckled to myself but before I could tell them my mind was taken by a few pigeons flying off the top of the stand behind the goal. Pigeon lofts! There must be pigeon lofts up there. Wow how brilliant! Maybe there were allotments up there as well full of old men like my Uncle Fred, who wasn't really my uncle but my step grandfather, all dressed in old waistcoats, collarless shirts and coal dust embedded into his hands. I suddenly felt so happy at this notion of people growing fruit and veg on the top of a football stadium.

When the players came back out the blinding red shirts had calmed down a bit but kept dripping like red mercury onto the pitch. I did wonder if it was me who was making this happen but decided it was probably just the cold weather.

People seemed distracted and were not even looking at the game half the time and during the latter stages of the second half I realised that the only thing in the world that didn't matter at Oakwell that afternoon was the football, and this was the big lesson I took away with me.

The football match was clearly just the excuse all these thousands of people came together and there seemed to be hundreds and thousands of them to me. The real reasons they were there was to have laugh, express their brilliant subconscious poetic talents, share floppy hot dogs with lovers and to reinforce their view of the world and more importantly of Barnsley. It was wonderful. I felt like a Psychedelic Yorkshire God who should really be called Herbert.

I think it was a goalless draw and on reflection an uneventful one, but it didn't seem important. As I walked away still in a state of euphoria, people seemed to be wallowing in the bleak tedium of the game, played out in a cold wind on a dark day. It was as though they were only happy when they were sad and yet they had an almost post-coital contentment.

In the next few weeks I shall be revisiting Barnsley for the first time since that memorable afternoon and expect to find the same mixture of phlegmatic resignation and below-average football. And I trust the Barnsley Surrealist Collective is still going strong.

In a moment of clarity, Eric Cantona said, "Acting is a drug, but football is a big, big drug like LSD" It's not hard to imagine King Eric dropping acid. In fact, it would explain a lot. And as a bit of a fan of all things psychedelic, it naturally fell to me to show for those who had not seen it for themselves just how uncannily like being out of your brains on mind-expanding psychotropics football is; all in ten easy-to-read bullet points as was the fashion at the time.

There are some cultural references here that have since dated. Goalkeepers don't wear garish, psychedelic shirts any more but there was a time when every season seemed to bring more outlandish vomit-inducing patterned shirts. Luke Chadwick's skin seems to have cleared up as well.

Intense Colours

Seeing a miasma of swirling kaleidoscopic three-dimensional shapes and colours is a common-enough experience while staring at a typical goalkeeper's shirt. However, you will need chemical assistance to attain the ability to actually taste and feel the colours. Sucking the goalie's shirt will not bring about enlightenment and may result in hassle - or even arrest - at the hands of 'very uncool pigs'.

My Body Is Melting!

We've all felt this one. Your once-solid form seemingly begins to dissolve into a molten lava flow. Melting from the inside out, you feel you will never be the same again. You are forever changed. Your form has altered. That's what a polystyrene cup of piping hot Bovril can do for you at half-time. LSD isn't nearly as good.

The Acid Test
The legendary acid-dipped Merry Pranksters who travelled all over America in a psychedelic school bus (well, we've all done it) used to say: 'You're either on the bus or off the bus.' Well, let's face it, if you're off the bus, you're not going to get to the match are you? Warning: You are unlikely to have books written about you by Tom Wolfe if you are just on the number 19 double-decker into town.

The Unravelling Of Time
Anyone who has watched football at Old Trafford will know this feeling only too well. Unusual ways of experiencing space and time are not uncommon, especially if Manchester United are losing. Do not panic, you are not on LSD; it's just an extended period of injury time.

Seeing The Light
If all around you is light and all you can see is a trillion atomised crystals shimmering in a blinding incandescence, do not be concerned. You are not God; you may not even be tripping. The floodlights have just had some new bulbs fitted.

Everything Is Everything
The LSD user often engages in mythic episodes, senses a unity of all peoples and a convergence of time and space and has an impression that everything is happening all at once in a non-linear manner. This is precisely the same feeling you get watching a side managed by Kevin Keegan.

Reality Gap
Ever had the feeling of being separate from the rest of society? Does everyone seem to exist in a different world to you? Are you concerned for your sanity? If the answer to these questions

is 'yes', you have either taken LSD or you are a supporter of Hartlepool United.

Apparently Meaningless Activities Acquire Great Profundity

Trying to get a ball into a net is, when all is said and done, a fairly pointless activity - but we all know how desperately we want our club to do it. Indeed, most of our waking lives are geared around those rare and elusive moments. To non-fans of the game, it's as incomprehensible as someone on acid telling you how God lives in the folds of his trousers or that he can paint the air with his 'magic finger'.

Horrific Visions And Delusions

A bad trip - a seemingly interminable experience where all before you is incomprehensibly ugly and threatening. Terrifying creatures will appear before your eyes. This same experience can be had by visiting Middlesbrough or watching Luke Chadwick at close quarters.

Transcendent Ecstasy

Tough one this. Ascending to a higher spiritual dimension and feeling a oneness with God is a rare feeling at the football - though Southampton fans used to feel something similar when in the proximity of Matt le Tissier. It is because of this he has copied the physique of the Buddha.

Back in 2002 I wrote about various lower-league football clubs from Exeter City to Queen of the South, whoever he is. There is something thoroughly satisfying about the low-rent, downbeat feeling you get standing on a crumbling terrace with 195 other people, watching 22 chunky men sponsored by the local pig factory.

It is the very grass roots of football and shows just how deeply entrenched and important the game is in our everyday culture. It's rarely impressive football and it's usually not very exciting, but it's usually a good laugh and you can get to the bar at half-time for a couple of pints and it doesn't cost you a week's wages to get in either. That's why clubs like Berwick still exist. No-one anticipates much or any success but it's somewhere to go and something to do on a Saturday afternoon that doesn't involve shopping or DIY.

And if you think about it, a lowly club like Berwick on a good day might get a crowd of 1,000. If any other gigs in town got that many people through the doors, it'd be considered a roaring success. It's only because football is so vastly popular at higher levels that it seems like a paltry number.

The autumn and winter of 1979 was my first year at the grandiose educational establishment that was Newcastle Polytechnic, which is now, bizarrely as far as I'm concerned, called Northumbria University, presumably because they always had an inferiority complex about being a poly and not a university. Like a degree from a poly wasn't 'worth' as much as one from a university. I don't know whether it was or whether it wasn't and I have no idea why anyone would even worry about something so bloody trivial, but worry they did.

Snobbery knows few boundaries in Britain. I do know though that my English Lit degree has been of no use or value to me as a qualification and I'm probably not alone in that. Mind you, I've never had a job interview in my life so maybe I've got a warped impression of the lack of importance of these things.

However, the drugs I took and the life I led while at college has been of immeasurable worth and for that reason alone I'm glad I did it. I might never have seen Berwick Rangers otherwise.

I had been drunk for approximately four months. I was itching in places that it's bad to itch. I smelt of stale patchouli and spilled snakebite. It was that most self-indulgent first taste of freedom that is your first term at college. As an English Lit student I had just seven hours of lectures a week, all of which were easily negotiated - and for the most part improved - while pissed. The rest of my time was my own to go and find myself in the canyons of my mind and in the pubs on Percy Street. I set about the task with some gusto.

The first term at college is a time you will never forget, roaming around the town off your head on strong drink and dodgy narcotics, being driven on by a nuclear-powered libido and the knowledge that your mam won't see the state of your sheets.

But everyone needs some sort of balance in their lives, something to take the edge off the excess and indulgence. I realised this after staying up for over 65 hours during which I saw Thin Lizzy, met Phil Lynott, had my first ever blow job (not from Phil Lynott I hasten to add), bought 23 second-hand albums in one afternoon on Newcastle's Westgate Road and ate pie and chips eight times consecutively from the semi-legendary 'Hairy Pie' on Percy Street as part of a diet that otherwise included only four foodstuffs - Ryvitas, marmite, thin slices of hazlet and bags of Wheat Crunchies, all washed down with pints of Exhibition Ale.

This was about as high on the hog as I could live at the time on a full grant, which you didn't have to pay back in those days. It was only a couple of thousand quid in a year but it was a ton of money to me. Beer was only around 30p a pint back then so for two quid you could get wasted and still have enough for chips.

Not wanting to burn out too soon, I decided to take some time away from this scorched earth lifestyle to go and see Berwick Rangers with a mate called Richard who was always up for a bit of alternative living. Get the blood pressure down, get chilled out. Literally.

Stepping from the train onto Berwick Station in 1979 was like stepping back in time 20 years. Windswept does not do it justice. It felt like a nuclear power station had just blown up, so bleak and desolate was it.

With eyes watering, we walked into a head wind in search of the stadium of footballing excellence that played host to Berwick's own curious brand of football.

Now the Borderers are a peculiar club. There's the 'English but playing in the Scottish league' business that's a bit strange for a start. Shielfield Park was less like a football ground and more like a cabbage patch surrounded by allotment sheds and, despite being in existence for 121 years, their only honour is a Second Division title in 78/79.

So in the winter of 79/80 I caught this newly-triumphant promotion side.

It wasn't immediately obvious. But seeing anything at all was a bit difficult because of the searing cold wind blowing off the North Sea that made your eyes water so profusely. In fact it appeared fans were actually weeping at the quality of the football on show, which frankly would have been an appropriate reaction. I imagined this was what it'd be like to be in a Siberian gulag on a Saturday afternoon.

At one point a large slavering doberman ran onto the pitch and tried to eat some of the players before being captured by a Will Hay look-a-like club official using a piece of steaming pie as bait. After such stunning entertainment the football seemed far less interesting.

From Berwick's current status as bottom club of Division Two, it would appear that little has changed at Berwick since those halcyon, dog days of the late 70's.

The club is sponsored by something called Marlborough Unit Trusts. Perhaps some sort of cigarette investment trust. The kit sponsor is apparently Paul Smith - nice of him to take time away from the catwalks of Milan to look after the Borderers, eh. Perhaps it's his influence that leads the Rothmans football bible to so specifically state that their shirts are 'Black: with four-inch gold stripes.' Details darling; they're everything.

Berwick has not produced a wealth of footballing talent, unless you include Trevor Stevens, who once spent an hour in town buying socks on his way to Glasgow.

But that's not really the point of Berwick Rangers. There are more people in your local pub at this moment than regularly turn up to see Berwick. Last season they attracted a staggering 402 to see Stenhousemuir.

The football at Berwick is doubtless utterly appalling. But in a vaguely masochistic way, there is much pleasure to be gained from suffering the torture every Saturday at one of the coldest grounds in the country. Not unlike picking a scab off your knee, you know you shouldn't but it's irresistible.

With the cup games with Rangers still to come and dreams of repeating their historic cup win of 35 years ago, football fever is running high in the town. Estate agents are putting poor-quality photocopied sheets of A4 in their windows which read 'Come on Berwick'. Yes, it's that thrilling. The local folk are being vox-popped by Tyne Tees television and asked what the score will be and the mood is resolutely upbeat. The scent of victory is in the air. Except for one gaunt youth with spots who looked high on glue who replied, "Rangers v Rangers?! That's too confusing that is."

So if you're in need of a break from the mundane, workaday routine of life, take a trip on the East Coast mainline to Berwick. I recommend the beer in the White Horse and the toasted tea cakes in the Rooftop Cafe overlooking the river. The football is rotten but hey, you can't have everything.

4. THE MANCHESTER HEDONISTS

24/09/02

Manchester City estimate they have a two million-strong global fan base. If this is true, there are a lot of dangerous lunatics and hedonists on the loose. It's more than likely that the maddest person you know will support City. They attract rhinos, winos and lunatics. If you see a man in the street running away from a team of doctors and nurses with a swimming hat on, shouting wildly, "Nurse, where are the bifocals for the puppies?"- he'll be a City fan.

Remember in the 80's when they all started taking inflatable bananas to games? That was all something to do with Imre Varadi mutating into Imre Banana. Aye. Right. It's stoner talk man. When they went down to the third tier of football, they still got over 30,000 of them turning up to sing Blue Moon, which in itself is a weird but appropriate song to have as your 'anthem'. It's a song of loss, a song quite literally of the blues, but even if it was Son Of My Father by Chicory Tip or they hummed the riff from P.F.M's classic Italiano prog rock album Chocolate Kings, I wouldn't be surprised. It's what City is about.

The two words 'typical City' have a unique resonance in English football, expressing as they do the ability to achieve greatness one week and humiliation the next. It is as though the club is imbued with a kind of manic depression as it veers from highs to lows, sometimes within a few minutes.

When this column was written, the mighty surrealist Kevin Keegan was in charge. Since then he's been replaced by another of football's rock 'n' roll crazies. Stuart Pearce is the latest inheritor of the City insanity. Which other club would have a manager called Psycho?

It's so City it's scary. The Gods are playing dice with them again. Other clubs spend years just being plodders, anonymous deliverers of success or mediocrity, but not for City this pedestrian life; for City it's glory or heartache all the time. Long may it be the case. In an era of corporate blandness on and off the pitch we need the rebel spirit of City to survive. We need them to let their freak flag fly.

I write a lot of stuff like this while not sober. When I look at it the next day, it's often a lexicon of random letters. This is partly because obviously my hand-to-eye co-ordination has been fractured. But it is also because I type on a keyboard that is blank. There are no letters on my laptop, the vicious, bitter acid that exudes from my fingers has cleaned all the letters away. So though I've been typing for 35 years, I still miss keys and it all ends up as a jumble that no spell-check can decipher. The secret is not to think about it. As soon as I start thinking about where a key is, I miss it. There I just did, only you'll never know because I went back and corrected it while sober. Hah!

I am very drunk.

What you are reading now will have been tidied up and spell-checked before publication so it's readable, but I can assure you, I am totally shit-faced. I can't stand up and soon I will have passed out. The monitor is moving slowly from right to left and my fingers are currently owned by a green-faced troll that is scratching at the window.

Now, there's a reason for this - and not just the usual need to exchange the usual dull half-tones of reality for something more vivid. I had to get utterly slaughtered in order to talk to you about Manchester City, because Manchester City in my world are a byword for intoxication.

Everyone I know who supports Man City is a hedonist. All of them crazy people for whom supporting a 'normal' club would be like living life in monochrome. I've never met a City fan who wasn't warped or wild in some way. They're all oddballs. Like they've been to the edge and seen too much truth. Wild-eyed and gregarious mixed with acrid, bitter cynicism. They usually take drugs, listen to weird music and have a unique outlook on life.

And it's always been that way.

Back in the late 70's I used to drink in a pub called The Talbot in Stockton-on-Tees. The Talbot was a fantastic place full of messy, hairy people, bikers and other peripheral members of society. In the windowless, downstairs cellar, you could sit in a fug of patchouli and fags, listen to Frigid Pink, have a few beers and learn how to take drugs. So there I was, a wide-eyed innocent 16-year-old boy enjoying an under-age pint or four before going to see the Boro play Man City.

A dishevelled regular with an explosion of hair called Shorty sat down next to me. Shorty was an acid casualty. His whole body gently oscillated to its own private, shaky rhythms. His mind was fried like a transport cafe egg. He was a gentle soul but totally away with the fairies.

"Hey, what you doin' man?" he asked, trying to roll a fag with wobbly hands and imprecise fingers.

I explained I was off to see Boro play City.

He looked at me with expressionless interest as though I were a television, doubtless watching unholy images appear and disappear on my face. Then his faced turned to a smile and he laughed silently and nodded.

"City yeah? City are the colour of the sky," he said blissfully and went back into his head for another long and winding journey.

It was a boring nil-nil. At the time Boro were going through a Mogadon phase. The idea was apparently to send fans to sleep quickly so they wouldn't have to sit through the boring football.

I couldn't help thinking that the game would have looked much better through Shorty's rainbow eyes.

God may actually be a Man City fan, not because the sky is the same colour as City's strip, though that's an interesting theological notion, but because Kevin Keegan is their manager, so all is therefore right with the universe. Never was any man so suited to the surreal intoxication of Maine Road than Kevin.

He's the Rene Magritte of football, with wisdom beyond knowledge. This is a bloke who has said:

"I know what is around the corner - I just don't know where the corner is. But the onus is on us to perform and we must control the bandwagon."

And,

"I'd love to be a mole on the wall in the Liverpool dressing room at half-time."

And,

"I've had an interest in racing all my life, or longer really."

These are not slips of the tongue. These are statements of an alternate, eccentric reality. It's as though he's the living embodiment of City's innate surrealism.

Maine Road has always been this way.

City holds the record for scoring most goals and still being relegated. In the early 1930's, they scored more than the team that won the league but still went down. That's a very City thing to do.

From 1968-76 they won the league and a League Cup and would have won the league again in 71/72 if they hadn't signed Rodney Marsh. He was worth the money on his own. Full of 'fuck you' rock 'n' roll attitude, outrageous skill and long hair, Marsh was signed to be the icing on the Championship cake - in fact, he disrupted a winning side and they ended up letting a title slip that they should have easily won. Again, that was a very City thing to do.

City hold the record for a player scoring most penalties in a season. Francis Lee scored a huge 13 - and he won most of them himself with laughable belly-flop dives. How City is that?

No-one can tell what will happen to City this season. Perhaps the only team in the land that could beat Real Madrid and lose to Swansea, it's as though City have stolen an infinite improbability drive and do not obey any known laws of the universe.

Just a couple of weeks ago I was sitting at the bar of the Hard Rock Cafe in Manchester. I was doing time in the universal mind, I was doing alright. It was full of Oasis fans from all over the country for the next day's gig. A Scotsman from Dundee introduced himself to me.

"I fuckin' love those Gallagher boys - ye cannae see them supporting United can ye - it'd have to be City." He swirled a finger round in the air next to his temple and pulled a mad face.

"Fucking crazy, eh."

Of course he was right and I for one wouldn't have dared suggest otherwise.

Yes, City's rock 'n' roll heritage is alive and well.

Come the end of the season I fully expect Kevin Keegan to have played at least one horse as a midfielder, appeared on Sky Sports muttering Haitian voodoo curses, revealed Shaun Goater to be his very own chimera and announced to the world that Manchester City are relocating to a new planet and the Commonwealth Stadium is actually a spacecraft specially designed to take them there.

And now my friends, I must lie flat for ten hours and dehydrate.

5. CHELSEA: THE SHAVEN HAVEN
06/10/02

This was written half-way through the Claudio Ranieri reign at Chelsea, which is now looked back on with some glassy-eyed fondness by everyone who thinks the club has since become a vehicle for the devil to manifest his work on earth. Ken Bates was still chairman, the club was deep in debt and players like Winston Bogarde were milking £40k a week out of the club for doing not much at all. I thought they were a disgraceful bunch of wasters.

Do you remember how bloody terrible Manu Petit was for them, hoovering up a load of cash in one last gorging on football's tit? They drove me mad. Oddly enough, I feel differently about them now. At least they deliver the goods and get kicked by Jose Mourinho if they don't. Back in 2002/3 they were overpaid under-achievers who were frankly taking the piss. Naturally, I found a way to connect this to lasses who have shaved all their pubes off. That's why I'm here.

I read a recent statistic that said that over 50% of women are now 'shaved' - they've had all of the front bottom thatch ripped out. How you collate figures like that is open to question. It's not the kind of thing you go up to people in the street to survey now, is it?

And even if you did, you can hardly ask to have a quick look just to make sure. You'd have a lot of people off the dole volunteering for the work though, eh. Now, call me an old fashioned hippy if you like, but I like hair. I draw the line at a full beard on a woman or a handle bar moustache but other short and curly regions that naturally sprout hair are not rendered any more attractive to me by making them smooth and hairless. I don't even like those hairless dogs. It looks wrong to me. It's like there's been a massive radiation leakage and everyone's hair has fallen out.

And let's be honest, it's already like a day out at the butchers at the coal face of the lady front bottom isn't it? Who needs to see all that?

This was Hairy Tony's first of many appearances in my columns. All you need to know for now is that he's a Geordie, he looks like a hairy biker and he plays the bass. Oh and he's a legendary shagger.

He reckoned the shaving gave you a better look at what you're aiming at, but his eyesight is destroyed by years of self-abuse and, let's face it, as complicated a construction site as it is for us blokes to find our way around, there's not that many places to get lost, are there? You'll eventually find where you need to put whatever it is that's in your hand by a process of elimination I would have thought. So to me, it's all a waste of time unless you are simply a pervert and like shaving things - in which case, please feel free to indulge yourself. Live like you want to live, baby.

Hairy Tony came running into our kitchen. He looked wasted - long, matted blonde hair and dark rings around his glassy eyes. He looked like he'd seen a ghost.

"Hey Nic, you know that lass I met last night?"

He had copped off with a girl wearing a tight Black Sabbath t-shirt, stretch jeans and crimped hair in the City Tavern, which was a hairy pub in Newcastle where legions of denim and leather-clad rock 'n' roll types used to drink. Back in '79 this was a tremendous achievement. Women who liked heavy rock were a highly-prized rarity, even in the heavy metal capital of Newcastle. Finding women who liked heavy rock, looked human and would sleep with you was an even more difficult, almost impossible task.

"Aye, what about her?" I said, as I prepared my Sunday lunch of Ryvitas, Marmite and Brown Ale.

"She was shaved!" he shouted with shock and awe. ".....fuckin' shaved man!"

"Well you wouldn't want to snog a lass with a beard, would you?" I said sarcastically.

"Nah man, not up top, I mean shaved, y'knaw, down below."

This was astounding news. You have to remember that in 1979, working-class lads like us were culturally and sexually extremely unsophisticated. Pizza was genuinely considered fancy foreign food to us. Kebabs were impossibly exotic and upmarket. I can still vividly recall the taste sensation of my first kebab consumed in Newcastle's Bigg Market after a skin full of drink. Not only delicious, it also served as a powerful emetic the following day, thus handily allowing you to keep your weight down despite consuming 7,000 calories in one evening.

Back then, drinking beer out of the bottle was only done by street-dwelling alkies and we were brought up with the notion that sex was for men to enjoy and for women to endure. Women who shaved their pubic hair was the stuff of our elder brothers' Scandinavian porno mag fantasies. Waxing bikini lines was considered to be some sort of totalitarian-regime-style torture.

"So what was it like?" I asked with dry-throated anticipation.

He picked up and bit into one of my buttered Ryvitas and thought about it, clearly re-living the experience,

"Not much different really - except you could see what you were aiming at, like. And there was some stubble growing back, so it was a bit like stroking a hedgehog. Apart from that it was the same as usual."

For Tony this meant the same as the other woman he had slept with.

"How many hedgehogs have you stroked then?" I enquired.

24

"Enough. A man can get cold and lonely up here in the winter y'knaw. Men have been known to shave a badger and call it Susan."

This only serves to illustrate how appearances can be deceptive; the apparently exotic can turn out to be mundane.

And nowhere in football is this truer than at Chelsea.

Stamford Bridge in the 70's was possibly one of the worst places to watch football.

You were miles from the pitch and many of the local fans were housed in a creaking, woodworm-ridden old wooden shed at one end of the ground, looking like it was the last building standing after a nuclear explosion. Honestly, if you never saw it, you wouldn't believe how crap it was.

These days Stamford Bridge is a 21st century modern stadium and indeed, so is the team. However, this is not a good thing. Chelsea FC is a manifestation of everything that most genuine fans of football hate.

The club is shallow, image and money-obsessed and, most important of all, treats its fans as a cash cow to be milked furiously in order to fund the lavish wages of piss-poor players. Almost all of the players don't give shit about the club and are only there for the money. While this is true at most clubs to some degree, at Chelsea it has become the dominant culture.

Last week's shocking performance in Europe was just the latest in a line of humiliating defeats by part-time footballers from distant lands and terrible performances against 'small' clubs.

Well, I say 'humiliating', but the truth is that this group of arrogant players is not in the slightest bit humbled by their shambling, passionless display, with the exception of the honourable Gianfranco Zola. I watched a side that frankly took the piss out of the many fans that had made a long and expensive journey. I saw a once fearsome player in JFH playing so terribly, I can only assume he was trying to get himself the sack.

Chelsea are now the thick end of £100m in debt but are still paying Winston Bogarde £40,000 a week to not play football. They're paying a similar amount to a giant blob of nature known as Mark Bosnich. Can anyone, anyone at all, tell me why Bosnich was signed? Was it just to pay him the chunky end of £2million a year to get him bloated? The money would have been better used if the club had hung 400,000 fivers a year on a nail in the bogs instead of buying toilet paper. This kind of financial indulgence is obscene and we all know it - everyone except those who run Chelsea.

Most Chelsea fans that I've talked to who didn't want to kick my head in for being a northern monkey (which, incidentally, is a fine thing to be) blame this culture squarely on Ken Bates. Bates of course is never slow to tell everyone else how to run the game, while his own club is going down an expensive gold-plated toilet.

Chelsea, like many others, tried to buy success. It worked for Blackburn and Arsenal and to a degree it's worked for Chelsea with their cup wins, but the Premiership has always been well beyond them, not due to lack of talent but to lack of basic guts, attitude and application.

That's what is so unforgivable. It's one thing to fail because players aren't good enough, but it's a kick in the dangly bits to fans when failure is simply because the players can't motivate themselves to play against so-called 'lesser' teams.

It was hard to dislike Gianluca Vialli with his watery, almost-stoned eyes, and he did bring the club five trophies (only three proper ones though 'cos you can't count Charity Shields can you?). By contrast, Raneri has won the club nothing and his post-match comments after the Viking game suggest he's gone as mad as a mongoose. Bi-lingual confusion may be his best option in dealing with the media given the appalling nature of his team.

"How did you think it went today Claudio?"

"Good although ginger hamsters are eating my mother."

"Are you disappointed to lose the game?"

"Yes, my yellow matter custard parachute is stuck on your javelin."

Mind you, Bates has just extended Raneri's contract, presumably with the sole intention of bankrupting the club when he sacks him later this season and has to pay off his contract in full. Why did he do that? Does he think there are any other clubs who want Raneri as their manager?

Personally I think Ken Bates was the victim of one of those early 60's covert CIA experiments with LSD. It may explain his madness.

Now Chelsea are the worst club in west London with Fulham ahead of them - how much more can Chelsea fans take? How long will they pay big money just to see disgraceful players like Petit and his breed take the piss out of them?

'Cos that's what they're doing. They don't care about the fans. Not even 0.1%.

They don't even care about the club being successful unless there's more money in it. Just look at them squabbling about their £20,000 bonuses for beating a lowly Norwegian club rather than concentrating on actually beating them.

It's despicable and frankly, it would do the whole of football good if Chelsea went bust as soon as possible.

It's been several years since I wrote this, but still nothing has changed in Newcastle. It's the same as it ever was. The Quayside has been totally and splendidly revamped since my glory days but it's still jam-packed with scantily-clad lasses and lads all on the piss and on the pull. Geordies still have the instinct to live now for tomorrow we may die and you know if you think about it, it's really the only way of life that makes any sense in a fragmented, chaotic world of trouble and strife.

The football club is still in chaos with managers coming and managers going. The place is run more like a Working Mens Social Club than a PLC. There's a touch of low-rent pissed anarchy about the place. And still the fans come in their 50,000s and more. The ground just keeps getting bigger and bigger and is more like an intergalactic spacecraft than ever. There's still a revolving door of players coming and going every year and they still haven't got near winning anything. The day that happens you'll hear the noise from outer space.

If you've never been to Newcastle and have grown up somewhere respectable and quiet in Northamptonshire, Surrey or Wiltshire, it will scare the bollocks clean out of your pants. It's full on, in your face and won't be taking no for an answer, so get ready to party. The pubs in Newcastle are fucking huge - great big palaces dedicated to inebriation full of hundreds of drunken punters. You've never seen drinking like you see on Tyneside. They go about it en masse with a professional dedication to the job.

It was also the primo town in Britain for heavy rock. Newcastle City Hall and the Mayfair were temples dedicated to worshipping the art of bludgeon riffola. For a heavy-riffing lad like me it was like one big extended family of denim and leather acolytes all around the hairy pubs; The Percy Arms, The Haymarket - before the cunts knocked it down - the Farmers, the City Tavern and the Market Tavern. If you're of a certain age and grew up on that music, you know who you are. It was you and me and our mates who put Freebird on the fucking jukebox, man.

I once said living in Newcastle for five years was like living in almost any other town for 20. It can use you up and wear you out, but what do you want from life? Do you want a good time? Do you want the adrenalin to race through your veins? If so, then you owe it to yourself to spend some time by the Big River. It will tattoo itself on your soul and that tattoo will say 'haddaway & shite' and also 'lie down, I think I love you'.

Think you're working-class? Yeah well, wait 'til you go to Newcastle...you'll realise you're middle-class.

I'd like to claim this joke as my own, but it's a Dick Clement/Ian La Frenais classic used in at least five different TV series (three Auf Wiedersehens, Porridge and The Likely Lads if you're interested).

However, it expresses something core about Newcastle and the way people see the place.

I lived in and around Newcastle for many years in some of the dodgiest parts of the city. It was great. Not that we considered ourselves unsophisticated. We had a self-cleaning oven - which in 1980 was a very advanced thing. It was somewhat organic in nature, being as it was several hundred highly-trained mice. They also did a very good job of keeping the floor clean.

We also had powerful air-conditioning. This was courtesy of a large hole in the kitchen wall through which the neighbourhood cats would enter the flat and eat the mice that were by then fat and juicy after feeding heavily on left-over pieces of Goblin Meat Puddings, Crackerbread and Abbey Crunch biscuits.

Remarkably, we survived the winter of 1981/2 with this hole - the result of laughable attempts at DIY by our fantastic landlord Mr Rudki. Mr Rudki was a man full of good vibes and vodka but absolutely no idea how to maintain buildings. After disconnecting a gas grill he promised to "tie the gas pipe in such a way as it will not leak". We managed to persuade him to cap it instead, though a pipe burning with a constant flame in your kitchen is a nice talking point for dinner parties and handy for lighting joints.

That winter temperatures dropped to -23, snow was frozen into solid ice on the ground. The buses weren't running because the diesel had frozen in the tanks, and yet, I swear this is true, there were lads going out drinking dressed only in capped-sleeve t-shirts and women would try walking in stilettos and mini skirts across long sheets of ice, their legs mottled pink with the cold.

This area of Walker (salubriously located beside the Tyne) housed many people who had been living in the Men's Palace. You might think the Men's Palace sounds like a gay nightclub, but in fact it was sheltered accommodation for people who had a bit of trouble dealing with reality. Although these were often scary people, they seemed to like our band of raggle-taggle urban warriors, even though our band spent most evenings and weekends playing an ear-bleeding version of rock 'n' roll in the attic, out of tune and out of our minds.

One particular 6' 4" bloke with candyfloss curly hair would stand at the bus stop, stripped to the waist, shouting at the local women who were dressed up for a night out on the town,

"Youse are all fucking tarts, aye, you and your muthas! Tarts!"

Then there was our next-door neighbour Mary. She drove the men wild. She was a wizened woman of indeterminate age

30

who, we suspected, sold sexual favours for cash. One Sunday morning we awoke to the sounds of a man beating his fists on her front door bellowing, "No man could stand it! No man Mary! I'm away." He was in his mid 50's and dressed only in a yellowing old vest and a pair of ragged comedy shorts - the sort worn in 70's situation comedies by Terry Scott.

The local offy, which in reality was no more than four bare walls and a couple of wooden shelves, actually served Armadillo which, if you don't remember, was a British sherry sold on draught in off licences! Better still, you could take any receptacle in and they'd fill it up with the sweet booze. We used milk or Tizer bottles. Now that's sophistication in my book.

Every area of the country boasts of having the friendliest folk, except perhaps North Yorkshire, which is full of miserable, tight-fisted farmin' folk who see being warm and friendly as political correctness gone mad.

But Newcastle is a simply extraordinary place. Regularly voted as one of the best places for a night out, the locals are genuinely welcoming and open, while also being some of the most wild and intimidating.

I thought I was no stranger to debauched living when I arrived on Tyneside after an upbringing on Teesside. However, even I was surprised to see lads walking from pub to pub down the Bigg Market, casually putting their fingers down their throat and throwing up beer while still walking, in order to make room for even more ale. It was casually and professionally done.

And even I was surprised to see a man doing it doggy-style to a woman down a dimly-lit Quayside alleyway while all her friends stood around cheering and clapping along with every thrust.

It was as though people were living every day as though it was their last, and I bloody loved it. Life lived with passion and without caution befits a place founded on Viking and Celtic rebel hearts and it's no surprise that that's exactly how the Toon Army like their football as well.

Back in the 70's there was a time when they had that vibe. Jinky Jimmy Smith and Terry Hibbert mesmerised defences, while Supermac and big John Tudor banged in the goals. It's hard to convey just how massive Supermac was back then. Still the only England player to score five in a match, he was the living embodiment of the 1970's; messy hair, big burners, bandy legs and built like a brick shithouse. He was as gloriously unsophisticated as the city itself.

The 80's team of Keegan, Beardsley, Gascoigne and Waddle had the same good vibrations. Let's not forget, Keegan left St James' Park in a helicopter that landed on the pitch! This is a place that implicitly understands rock 'n' roll football.

Then came the Keegan years as manager. Anyone who went to St James' Park in that era will never forget it. It was like going to see Motorhead live. The noise was incredible, the crowd were going apeshit and the players played like the possessed. Even if you didn't support them, it was spine-tingling, goosebump stuff, the apex of which was the 5-0 defeat of Man United. When Philippe Albert lobbed in the last goal, Tyneside had a single collective orgasm.

St James' Park dominates Newcastle city centre. It looks like an alien spaceship has landed. You can't ignore football in Newcastle. It's not a marginal activity, it's right at the heart beat of the place, unlike anywhere else I've ever been. It's almost as if the collective mood is predicated on the success or failure of the team.

You owe it to yourself to at least once in your life, get yourself to Newcastle, have a lot to drink, watch a 5-3 home win, have a lot more to drink, pull a lass called Julie for a one-night stand and finish it all off with a curry. The classic quartet. That's living alright.

This piece originally had a throwaway paragraph about Everton tacked on the end – which was me at my most tenuous - but even I have to admit that the Toffees have very little connection to gun-toting nutters in Southern California.

This was the first piece in which the band appeared. The Beer Pigs were me, Hairy Tony, Lenny and Hunter. We played messy old school R & B. We never made any money, any records or achieved anything at all of any note. We did it for the life on and off for five years in the late 80's and early 90's until we got sick of it all and sick of each other. We spent a lot of time in California and Nevada playing gigs and this tale comes from our first 'tour'.

I think this was the first time I'd ever actually seen a proper handgun. It scared the living jobbies out of me I don't mind admitting. It looks so relatively innocuous. It could just as likely be some sort of glue gun or a toy but it isn't. It'll kill you right there and right then. The power of the thing is out of all proportion to the size of the actual tool. If you've got something so deadly, I think it should at least have some decent size and weight and possibly have a flashing red light on it.

If there's any argument for restriction of handguns then this is it. Someone pisses you off, you're in a stinking mood or a bit depressed, and if you have a gun in the house you might start waving it around just to threaten people and, in the heat of the moment, shoot them. But if you don't have a gun, probably the worst thing that might happen is a fistfight.

This argument doesn't cut much ice with a lot of Americans, who rather like their guns. I know it always seems so alien to us in the UK that you might want a rack of guns in the house, but a lot of Americans see it as part of their sense of freedom and independence. To them it's a way to keep the bad guys at bay and to be honest if I lived there, I'd probably have a range of semi-automatic weapons too. It still really is the Wild West and you can't underestimate that.

I often wonder what ever happened to this bloke, if it was a one-off bit of craziness or if he ended up actually killing someone. This would not be the only time Hunter bailed us out of trouble, but it was probably the most dangerous situation we ever found ourselves in. I'm just glad I kept control of my bowels.

So there I was in the famous City Lights bookstore in San Francisco, waiting in line to get my copy of Maybe The Moon signed by Armistead Maupin.

I really like Armistead Maupin, especially his idea in Tales Of The City idea that women could carry around specially-shaped funnels to allow them to piss like men. Genius.

So I get to the front of the queue and he says,

"Who shall I make it out to?"

"Just put something profound in it," I said in my usual cheeky stoned way. And what does he write?

'Watch out for the quiet ones'.

As it turned out, he was absolutely right, because only a few days later I was almost shot dead by a very quiet man during an argument in an apartment on Bundy Drive in West LA.

The evening had started well enough. The band and a couple of other ex-pats were drinking, smoking and trying to work out how many pairs of knickers you'd need to make a quilt for a bed. Clearly it depends on the size of the garments in question so we'd decided upon what were known back then and probably still are as Tanga knickers. Not tangy knickers, they're something else. I think we arrived at the figure of 386, though you may want to work it out for yourself.

However, while we were engrossed in this important debate, outside LA was still smouldering. This was not long after the riots and people were still a bit jumpy. Everyone had been buying up guns and learning how to shoot them in order to protect their crappy stucco apartments from being looted by Ice T wannabes. Car-jacking was a new and popular sport. Indeed, it was on TV every night. Whitey was taking a beating.

Having shared some serious bong, we felt obliged, the way the British do, to make light of danger by taking the piss remorselessly out of the situation. To me, it didn't seem worth killing someone just to save your TV from ending up in some fat burrito-munching guy's home in South Central.

There was much debate amongst us Brits about the pros and cons of owning a semi-automatic pistol or a hunting rifle, the pros being largely based around the fact that you could get served a lot quicker in the pub if you waved a .22 Smith and Wesson around. Plus; there was the chance to torture games teachers for humiliating us. Bastards. They even shagged the good-looking fourth-year girls.

The cons, of course, were life in prison for murder, the consequent anal prolapse due to severe and persistent buggery, and also doing anything Ted Nugent would think was cool.

What we hadn't reckoned on was how this piss-taking would affect our American host. He was an apparently quiet, unassuming man who worked in an art gallery in Newport Beach. He'd invited us round after an acoustic gig in a coffee shop in the San Fernando Valley. We didn't know him very well but didn't suspect he was a nutter.

That is, not until he got up and went to a small cupboard under his stairs, took out a leather case and unveiled a really big fuck-off handgun, Obviously, the first thing I did was laugh and say that if he wanted to have sex with me all he had to do was ask.

35

"I'm not a fucking queer and do not insult me or my country you muthafucker," he said very quietly, picking up the gun. Trust me to get an American who didn't understand irony. What were the chances? He suddenly looked like a vicious dog who stares at you silently, doesn't bark at all, then savages you.

We couldn't believe he was serious, but then he began loading it with bullets.

At this point, naturally, we legged it out of the door and off down South Bundy, all except for Hunter who was rather typically pissed off that this bloke was threatening him at all. We begged him to leave the bloke alone but we could hear him shouting, "Think you're fucking hard do you - you soft fuckin' shite; just 'cos you've got a fucking gun! Too scared to use your fists are you?"

We called the cops from a phone box, expecting at any moment to hear the gun go off. The police took about ten minutes to arrive, but by the time they pulled up, Hunter had disarmed the man and was sitting on his sofa, smoking a fag and pointing it at his erstwhile assassin, who was now bleeding from the nose and protesting that he'd never intended to shoot anyone.

It turned out Hunter had leapt at him in a sort of Middlesbrough version of kung-fu, kicked the gun out his hand and then applied a similar kick to the bloke's face. "I had to pacify him like," he said to the cops, who thought he was stupid, but you could tell they admired his bravery.

So if you ever get invited to a quiet man's house on South Bundy, don't diss his guns dude - not unless you've got a psychopath mate with you, anyway.

This was another early piece written about life on the road in California with a small bit of football stuck on the end, which has accidentally become a bit of a trademark.

Don't get me wrong, it's not like I was Jim Morrison. I never even wore leather trousers, though I did on occasion sport tight velvet pants. I had a go at the tight black plastic pants too but they make you sweat so much it feels like you're permanently incontinent.

They were good times though and if there was a hog around to live high on, we did our best to climb aboard. I never planned to write so much about it all, but there seemed to be so many parallels between that life and football, I just kept raiding my diaries for more tales.

This was written in the middle of an 11-match run in the Premiership without a win for Liverpool stretching from 9 November 2002 to 29 January 2003 during which period they dropped out of the Champions League as well. It was back when some people were still prepared to give Emile Heskey the benefit of the doubt as a striker, which proved to be very badly misplaced faith. They were managed by that nice - recently recovered from a heart condition - Mr Houllier and this run was perhaps the start of the end for him, instilling in some fans a lack of faith in his abilities.

To understand this you need to know about shrinkage. You do know about shrinkage, right? Well if you're a Seinfeld nutter like me you will. I still find it amazing that some people have never even heard of Jerry, let alone watch the show. I've seen him twice in Las Vegas and he was weepingly good both times. Not least because Caesars Palace lets you buy a bucket of beers all crammed into ice in the foyer and take it to your seat to drink during the show. I had eight bottles of Coors in two hours to celebrate this most civilised practice. Well you would, wouldn't you?

Anyway, this night was, on reflection, a pretty wild night and this was just one incident in 72 hours of serious debauchery. One of those nights where you try to pretend you're cool about it all and it doesn't faze you but inside you're thinking, 'bloody hell'. We all behaved like it was our last day alive. It's amazing what you can do to your body and it still keeps going.

I mean, even the idea of having a pool party when you come from the north-east of England is pretty amazing to start with (I thought for years it was a party at which you played pool), but one that takes place by the ocean in sweltering Santa Barbara seems especially glamorous. And believe me, it was. At this party full of beautiful rich Californians we must have looked like four scarecrows that got up and walked out of the field. This party went on for three days without stopping. Wave after wave of new guests seemed to keep arriving and the band played on. We were that band. I think we played Roadhouse Blues for two hours at one point. I was higher than God for more than two days and all bets were off....this is just a scene or two.

Lads, if you've ever been to a pool party, the story I'm about to tell you will strike a resonant chord. Now, this wasn't a Michael Barrymore kind of pool party, underwater buggery being something I've always tried to avoid on account of the trouble with lubrication.

This particular pool party took place in Santa Barbara, California. If you grew up like me, in the windswept cold grey north of England, Santa Barbara is like paradise. Surrounded by shockingly beautiful hills and coastline, balmy temperatures all year and upmarket Spanish-style houses. Only the beggars that are hassling for change remind you of home. But even they have great tans and teeth.

So what was a hairy-assed northern git like me doing there? Well, we'd been invited to stay with a bloke called Fonzy. It wasn't Henry Winkler sadly, but a man called Fred Onslow, which on reflection sounds like a character in Coronation Street. But in real life Fred owned a bar and restaurant somewhere in Santa Barbara County. The deal was free doss, free food and drink for a couple of days in return for playing a gig at this guy's party. No brainer, eh.

We turned up at 7pm at this big house set back from the ocean in its own grounds. It looked like the kind of posh expensive gaff at which crimes were committed in Columbo. There was a small stage and we faced right out to the shoreline. There's nothing like hearing your music in the open air. It feels infinite somehow. There was a big swimming pool and even a temporary bar with optics and a barrel on tap. Fred was rich and this must have cost him a small fortune. The whole event was catered by a team of impossibly good-looking out-of-work actors all dressed in white jeans and t-shirts.

We bashed out a few tunes for a couple of hours, just jamming mostly. I remember someone came up and requested we play a song by Men Without Hats - seeing as we didn't usually play anything recorded after 1968, this was never going to happen. We seemed to be going down well even without playing Safety Dance, and a drumstick was nearly inserted up the sphincter of the chap that suggested we should.

It was mid-way through an oddly out-of-key version of Wild Thing that I noticed that people were jumping into the pool naked. Unfortunately, it was mostly middle-aged stodgy executives and not curvy good-looking women.

We took a break, some amphetamines and vodka, and not having any standards of either taste or decency ourselves, we stripped off and dived into the pool.

As all British men tend to do, we found a ball and began a high-speed hybrid game of our own invention which was part football, part volleyball.

I had just hauled myself out of the pool to retrieve the ball when a woman, who I later learned was called Rudy Trudy, came up to me swaying gently. She had a massive rack on her like two Asda bags full of custard crammed into a bikini. Clearly she was as mortally drunk as anyone could be. I shook her outstretched hand. She was probably in her late 40's and had the leathery skin of a woman who had spent too much time in the sun.

"Ah, you are the English boys," she said in a curious slur.

Hairy Tony emerged naked from the pool, his long blonde hair plastered down his back, his white, white skin glowing in the gloaming and stood beside me:

"Hey, I'm not just an Englishman, I'm a Geordie, me!"

She had no idea what a Geordie was of course and was probably too drunk to even know where England was but she took a drink from a large glass of something fluorescent and pink which on reflection, was the first time I'd seen a strawberry daiquiri. Her eyes dropped to his crotch and she raised her eyebrows,

"My dear, you are barely a man at all."

And on that bombshell she spun on her heels and walked away. It was true. He appeared to be a woman; admittedly a hairy woman.

This was before Seinfeld coined the expressed 'significant shrinkage', but significant shrinkage was exactly what it was.

For the uninitiated, significant shrinkage is the physiological condition that the male genitals undergo after swimming in a pool. Essentially your tackle tries to crawl back up into your pelvis. And unless you are the kind of guy with a foot-long swinging there, you're left looking as though everything down there is not as it should be, when it is in fact all it should be and more.

However Trudy, like most women, was probably not aware of the significant shrinkage effect. Let me tell you, if we'd had a reputation as rock 'n' roll studs, we'd have been ruined. But we didn't. And in fact, no-one gave a shit.

It was watching Liverpool recently that made me recall that memorable night. Because if there is any side currently suffering from significant shrinkage it's Liverpool. Although capable of being the biggest and the best, they're currently looking shriveled and impotent.

Players having trouble with form shrinkage are Gerrard, Owen, Dudek, Riise...the list goes on and on.

They're still playing as narrow as a tom cat's cock. Earlier in the season I suggested they had to sell Heskey and buy top-quality defenders as back-up to Henchoz and Hyppia. Probably the majority of Liverpool fans agree Heskey should be on his way out of Anfield despite cheeky Rivaldo's surely ironic comment that only Heskey could get into the Brazil team.

Liverpool are so frustrating - they promise so much, but deliver so sporadically. Many people are beginning to wonder if Houllier will ever deliver the title, whether he's taken them as far as he can. Strange team choices, the Gerrard incident, players bought and rarely played. Perhaps it is his reputation that has suffered the most significant shrinkage of all and this season could quite easily turn out to be a load of old cock.

I'm often labeled as a bit of a 70's nostalgia junkie but to me, it's not about being nostalgic, it's just about celebrating great times and great music and great football whenever it happened; but the 1970's were special even if for most of the 80's they were derided as the decade that fashion forgot.

It's always got on my tits that music goes in and out of fashion. I remember in the 80's when Steely Dan were derided as old hippies and tired self-indulgent rubbish, as indeed were Zeppelin just shortly before becoming cool again. And now thankfully they're just classic. It's the same with the football. Kids think the 70's was full of hairy fat blokes kicking seven shades out of each other - like that's a bad thing. In fact it was full of aggression but also loads of skill by players who could take a knock and could get up and beat a defender on a pitch made of glue and sand. It was more edgy and yes, it was a bit scary, but you felt alive. It was in a pure way very rock 'n' roll. Going to the football now by contrast is smooth jazz. It's still good but it too often lacks that edge that makes the good great.

As a teenager for most of the decade, it seemed to go on forever. Now ten years pass by in an afternoon's snooze but back when you're young, time runs at a different pace.

Christmas was always a time to go to the match, even for people who didn't go at any other time of the year. We seemed to live in very small houses that were always full of unpleasant relations with malfunctioning digestive systems brought on my massive consumption of sprouts and thinly-sliced haslet. What haslet was exactly I've been unable to discover but it was my mam's idea of a cold meat. I suspect it was pressed eyes and arseholes or anything nasty cut off a creature that had once had parents.

After I initially wrote this I had a lot of e-mails from Teesside asking who the people in question were. Everyone seemed to think they knew them. In fact, both of them now live in Australia and the girl still looks like Suzi Quatro, which is no bad thing. You can never see too many women in zip-up leather jumpsuits can you?

Everything in the 1970's was better than today; the massive sideburns, the mad, unconditioned hair, kipper ties, the three-day week, high-waist three-button trousers, WonderBras (the first time round), stack-heeled platform boots with metal segs in, Ziggy Stardust, chopper bikes, The Sweeney and progressive rock. We all smelled of Brut, carried around albums by King Crimson and Black Sabbath and going abroad meant a day out to Carlisle. It did. Honest.

A 70's Xmas was full of unchanging certainties. These were, in no particular order, Double Diamond beer, Slade, a bottle of Advocaat for the over-60's, a box of dates with a wooden fork that only your dad would eat, radioactive orange-coloured cheese balls that made small children hyperactive and eventually vomit.

Of course there was Morecambe and Wise, The Great Escape, a box of liquid centre fruit jellies and laughing at your granddad trying to open walnuts with a hammer on the hearth because you'd lost the nutcracker. You'd always get several pairs of large brown nylon Y-fronts with contrast trimmings which could be pulled up to your neck. You'd usually be given soap on a rope by your grandma, a copy of the Joy of Sex from one of your older brother's daft mates and a Magpie annual from one of your aunties who still thought you were ten. This happened every year.

By Boxing Day you were on the verge of insanity after being crammed into a small room with eight people, all of whom you're related to and not one of whom you liked in the slightest. The windows would be flooded with condensation and the room choking with the smell of sprout farts and Embassy No. 7s.

This explained why Boxing Day matches always got such massive crowds. Even people who loathed football went just to get out of the house. Darlington would get 37,000 turn up to see them play Rochdale, or at least it seemed like it. Thousands of fans crammed onto terraces all over the country to see football played by overweight men in heavy 100% cotton football shirts. It was always freezing cold and frosty and it was the law that you had to wear a Parka or, if you were a bit older and had long hair, a Great Coat.

Great Coats were rightly named. The really were great. They were either old army coats or were styled on trenchcoats. They were huge and were almost floor-length and made of 100% heavy-duty wool. They were compulsory clothing if you were going to see Jethro Tull or The Groundhogs, even in the summer. They soaked up loads of ale and were so heavy you could sleep warm in a ditch after too much beer at a Fairport Convention reunion gig in a field somewhere in Oxfordshire.

The best Xmas present a man ever got was given to a mate of mine in 1975. The location was Ayresome Park, Middlesbrough and it involved one such huge army-style trenchcoat. You might want to ask your loved one to give you the same present this Xmas. However, you may well be spending Xmas sleeping on the sofa if you do, so beware.

You have to remember that sex in the mid-Seventies was still a relatively harmless occupation. Anything you caught could be cured with penicillin, a pink cream or by wearing loose underwear.

The lad in question had a brilliant girlfriend. We all thought she was brilliant anyway. She looked like Suzi Quatro and though only 16, could drink us all blind. She was the sort of girlfriend your grandma would call 'a bit loose', which was rarer and more keenly desired than you might imagine for most of us.

So when she asked what he wanted for Xmas he naturally wanted, as any 16-year-old would, to combine football and sex. Having it off while Match of the Day was on in her parents' back room was pretty good as long as Jimmy Hill wasn't on screen, but he wanted to go one step further.

And so it came to pass that his Xmas present was to be orally pleasured live at Ayresome Park in the middle of a match. Try sticking wrapping paper round that.

This is where the Great Coat came into the equation. She was a small girl. Small enough to crawl under a big coat and huddle under there undiscovered. Or so she thought.

We stood right at the back of the Holgate so no-one was behind us. Fans stood either side but the football was really good (it was the 70's) so they were all distracted. Half-way through the first half she bent down as though to fasten a shoelace. He opened the coat for a moment and then fastened it around her.

We'd thought it would be easy to hide her but we were wrong. He looked like he was holding an angry otter under his coat as she unzipped him and got to work.

When you're 16 you're pretty much ready for red-hot action every hour of the day and things reached a critical point within two minutes. But even in this short space of time, everyone around us had become aware of something odd going on under his coat, despite his best attempts to look casual.

He was sure he'd be able to keep a straight face. But evidently nothing can prepare you for the sensory delights of a blow job during a football match and his face was a contorted mixture of pleasure and embarrassment.

Soon everyone had sussed what was going on, especially as her legs were sticking out of the bottom of his coat. It was pretty obvious to all when she'd reached 'the end game', by which time there were general cries of encouragement and requests that she perform similar service to other fans.

It was a classic very 70's moment. Even more so because afterwards we went and drank lager and lime and ate Tudor beef crisps - crisps so pungent and strong that they stained your fingers for days and you couldn't lose the smell until you dipped your hands in bleach.

So now you know what to ask for next Xmas. And I don't mean Tudor beef crisps.

10. IT'S A SPURS THONG

14/01/03

Back in the winter of 2003, Spurs were in the middle of Glenn Hoddle's reign at the club. A lot of Spurs fans were already discontented. The side wasn't playing well and though when I wrote this they'd just beaten Everton 4-3 with new boy Robbie Keane scoring three, Spurs were about to get very useless and only won four more matches that season. It was all supposed to be so different under The Messiah. Surely Hoddle would bring back the old flair and swagger of Spurs sides of old, they thought. They were wrong. They played some dire stuff. Even Boro put five past them that year.

But Spurs' history of playing with flair and a bit of culture always seemed like a good thing and I still like to see them winning, as does the Jenna of this story. If you want to know what she looked like, picture Joan Jett in 1978 - that was the cool rock chick look for anyone with a bit of edge. Forget Debbie Harry; that was pop. Forget Kate Bush; that was hippy. Joan was the girl, despite being called....er...well, Joan. Joan is an auntie's name, isn't it? But Joan Jett was a rock chick who, as it turned out, was also interested in rock chicks. Well, who can blame her?

So to me, Spurs will always be a rock 'n' roll club and no matter how many trophies or titles Arsenal win, for that reason alone, they still seem like a bigger club. And yes, I know that's nonsense. I don't care.

Would you tattoo your groin or any other part of your body for your club?

The first woman I ever knew who was tattooed was called Jenna and she was from Leighton Buzzard and she was a Spurs fan. The tattoo was at the top of her inner right thigh and was of the Spurs badge. This was 1979 and it was considered radical body art for a woman.

For a while, Jenna was in a Runaways-style punk band called The Not Nice. All thick eyeliner, messy short hair and skimpy trashy lurex clothing, she played a low-slung white Flying V guitar and made barking noises that might not be filed under singing by traditionalists, but which sounded great nonetheless. She was partial to blackcurrant snakebites and wearing black G-strings, which at the time was impossibly glamorous, lowdown and dirty. She loved her rock 'n' roll and she was determined to make it big.

I also had dedicated my life to the riff and though I some how doubted my future as the saviour of rock 'n' roll, to me it was the only thing that meant anything in the late 70's winter of discontent. You can't explain how important the dirty skinny ass rock 'n' roll is to people who never felt it. It's not just music, it's like blood in your veins. It is literally everything. It is what feeds and sustains and I fucking love a bit of sustain. It goes beyond what regular members of society think music is. It's a whole life. It was a place to live and it felt like home. It was the only home I had.

She was doing one of those courses at college that are invented for kids who are a bit crap at academia. Like Business Studies or Psychology. I mean, I don't care, it's cool, but don't pretend it,s high intellect. It's a skive off of real life and to me, that is one cool skive.

Her slutty rock chickness was the best thing I'd seen. I was glommed on her from the get-go from the way she pushed her groin forward on the two and the four to the pouty rock 'n' roll poses she threw while playing E major. I was a walking, talking erection. And the Gods were smiling on me right then, well it was about fucking time son. Turns out, she loved her football. Oh baby.

I couldn't imagine her being a Boro fan. She was too glam, too classy. We used to lie in bed for days smoking crap dope, as you do when you're a student with seven hours of lectures a week, talking about music and football and all the while her white Flying V was resting against the wall. It made me feel like I'd grown up overnight. We'd sit up and try and work out the chords to Whitesnake songs. We fucking loved Whitesnake. A band named after the lead singers cock. How brilliant. And let me tell you, if you want some music to fuck to, Whitesnake will do it every time for you.

She saw supporting Spurs and playing in a glam punk band as a perfectly-matched pairing.

Spurs were glam, a bit rock 'n' roll. A bit posey. Flashy Argies played for them. They were a shirts out, socks rolled down side. They always seemed to win a cup - which was always a more glamorous thing back then; more glamorous than winning the league even. How times have changed.

A couple of years later we were down in London to see a Neil Young gig and I ran into her again. Spurs had recently won the cup again by beating Manchester City. Her glam punk band was now a NWOBHM (New Wave Of British Heavy Metal) band called something like Iron Bitch, or Metal Mother - something like that. She had grown her hair, was still playing the white Flying V, was in love with Ricky Villa and was raving about how brilliant Spurs were. That night, for old times' sake, we got wrecked on snakebites and I joined her band on stage to play Whitesnake's hit Ready 'n' Willing, which is a dirty-fuck-me riff in excelsis. Sweet satisfaction.

After five minutes crowd participation "C'mon let me fucking hear ya!"......I took the solo home. It was one of those nights, you know. Somewhere, somehow, it's all still happening. Then we finished it all of by doing Aint No Love In The Heart Of City, which wasn't strictly true. That night and maybe only that night, that song was a lie.

Boro were in Division Two, Spurs were riding high, it seemed like it would always be that way.

I got an e-mail out of the blue from her recently. She's now living in a quiet town in the Home Counties and works part-time in a bank. She doesn't drink blackcurrant snakebites any more or play in a band, or wear G-strings (they gave her terrible yeast infections). Life is no longer dedicated to rock 'n' roll but she is still dedicated to Spurs. Her comment on the current team: "Where have my real Spurs gone? Whatever happened to my rock and roll?"

I bow to no man in my dislike of London teams. Indeed, I've vented many thousands of words on the subject, and by doing so attracted much loathing from southerners who, to a man, appear to believe that I live in a hole in the ground somewhere 'up north' with whippets knawing at my filthy, undernourished and withered corpse. Of course, the truth is I live a life of opulence and luxury. Okay, living in an abandoned Ford Capri in a lay-by on the A19 isn't everyone's idea of glamour, but it suits me fine.

However, in my league table of southern loathing Spurs are for some reason at the bottom. I've never even disliked Spurs.

Now, you will think this the ramblings of a madman, but in my mind Spurs are really a bigger club than Arsenal. Clearly a cursory glance of the facts today show you that this isn't the case. Arsenal are sadly streets ahead of them, but the really big issue here isn't the facts, it's the feeling, the history and the legend of the club. Being a big club is nothing to do with a bank balance, or even to some degree success, in the same way that social class is nothing to do with money.

Since the war, Spurs have been a byword for class, skill and entertainment. Gilzean, Greaves, Ardiles, Villa, Hoddle, Waddle and Gascoigne, even Klinsmann. Spurs have boasted some of the best, most skilful flair players this country has ever produced or imported. They've also had a bit of steel to them with hard men like Mackay, England, Roberts and, in Gary Mabbutt, a real hero, albeit one with an own-goal-prone pie arse. But for the duration of the Premiership they seem to have been stuffed with ordinary journeymen.

At least Keane is Spurs class. What a brilliant hat-trick against Everton. A bit of the old flash. Even Gus Poyet, as old as he is, has that old top-notch South American vibe about him. Surely Spurs want more of their class in the side and less of the Iversen, Sherwood, Perry, Thatcher type players. Good, but not special, players have cluttered the Spurs squad for too many years.

Maybe it went wrong under Venables. Did Sugar wreck or save the club? What the hell were they doing employing George Graham? I don't know but one thing I do know is Spurs have the tradition and the support to be that flashy rock 'n' roll glory, glory team again. Do it. Do it for Jenna.

As unfashionable as it might seem, I am a big fan of Graeme Souness. As a player he had few equals, but as a manager his record is patchy to say the least. Four SPL titles and four cup wins is more than most men can claim to have won but his tenure at Liverpool, although he won the FA Cup, was largely a disaster, and you can forget about the months at Southampton.

When he took over Blackburn he won the League Cup and for a season it looked like Rovers were going to be a top side - but then it all went downhill and he left for Newcastle just before he was pushed. At the Toon he quickly spent a lot of money, fell out with lots of players, failed to make the team consistent and inevitably got the push again.

He has a distinctive style of management that he deploys at every club; he turns players against him by abusing or even fighting with them. He throws his weight around and demands that men be men. He sells really good players who he can't control and buys worse players who he can. Back in the Rangers days this obviously worked well, but that was the end of the generation of footballers that Souness understood; the end of the era when you could terrorise a player into playing better out of fear and respect. It's still really the only way he knows how to manage. It is who he is; an old school hardman. That's what I like about him.

But in these days when all the power lies with multi-millionaire players, if they don't want to play for you they won't and you can't do much about it. You can insert an air pump into them and threaten to inflate their lower bowel and they still won't perform.

This new era demands new approaches and styles but Souey can't adapt. It's sad really. I know how anachronistic he looks to those who have grown up in the lavender-scented, delicate modern era but to me, he will always be a bit of a hero for playing the game with total commitment and aggression that was awesome and frankly thrilling.

But when I say 'thrilling', I don't mean in quite the same way he moved my mate Frankie.

Graeme Souness Made My Mate Gay.

This would be the tabloid headline if the story I'm about to tell you happened this week and not 25 years ago.

Yes, Graeme Souness - a volcano wrapped in a full-length coat; his anger always ready to erupt like molten lava over an Italian village. 'Twas ever thus.

Souness played for Boro from '73 to '78. I first saw him in 1974. Throughout his playing career he was always liable to give you a good kicking, but in his early days at the Boro under Big Jack Charlton, he was simply vicious. If he could have worn boots with rotating razor blades he would have jumped (two-footed) at the chance.

Souey didn't just tackle firmly, he mowed ruthlessly into opponents, savaging them and then emerging without a scratch. But despite his ferocity, by mid-70's standards he was always well turned out. He was neat, he was tidy, he had a substantial moustache, a big disco perm and he was lean and muscular.

In short, he looked very gay, though not for one moment did Souness - as a man with an unblemished record of heterosexuality - think that himself. However, Souey's mixture of on-pitch violence and muscular good looks awakened the latent homosexuality in one Teesside boy.

Frankie was a regular 70's Teesside lad. He liked drinking Cameron's beer, wore Brutus fader jeans with huge 24" flares, listened to Cockney Rebel and enjoyed going to Ayresome

Park. The '74 Second Division-winning side was a killer team and we all enjoyed our football that season. I hadn't noticed at the time that Frankie was more passionate in his love of Souness than the rest of us and of course we had no idea our hero looked like the sort of bloke you might meet in a San Franciscan bath-house.

Remember, it was the 70's, and none of us thought we even knew anyone who wasn't straight. Such things were a mystery to us. Somehow we had got the idea, probably through watching Dick Emery, that being gay involved mincing around with a pink handbag and calling everyone 'Ducky'. We were very naive. We thought doing it doggy style would involve the participation of a real dog. We thought blow jobs involved actual blowing - "Wouldn't it inflate your balls?". I remember being told categorically that oral sex just meant talking dirty. If someone had told us Cunnilingus was an Irish airline we would have believed them.

Our only exposure to sex was Page Three in the Sun and hoping your mam and dad were out when A Bouquet of Barbed Wire was on the TV. So we didn't spot the signs. We didn't see that Frankie wasn't just a fan of Souness; he was actually in love with him.

Frankie's devotion to Souey continued even after his transfer to Liverpool. He kept several scrapbooks about him. Scrap books are an old fashioned concept in these digital cut-and-paste days, but by any standards Frankie's scrapbook was a work of art. Newspaper cuttings and magazine posters were all neatly clipped and placed chronologically in big thick books.

We all started to grow up and football had to compete with the lure of girls, booze and rock 'n' roll. Frankie had been going out with Janice for a few months when one day she went round his house after school. She knocked on the back door as usual but there was no reply. She knew he would be in and presumed he was just listening to music on his headphones so let herself in.

She put her head around his bedroom door and was confronted by the vision of Frankie standing completely stark-bollock naked in front of a full-length mirror, vigorously pleasuring himself while staring intently at, appropriately enough, a Shoot poster of Souness in full Boro kit.

There was nothing much he could say was there? He simply gave a sheepish grin and continued until the job was done. Janice fled without saying anything at all.

Naturally, it wasn't long before the girlfriend had told her best friend about this naked encounter with a mad masturbating teenager and she may as well have taken out a full-page ad in the Evening Gazette to advertise Frankie's persuasions. Soon everyone knew.

These days Frankie is cool about it all but people tell me he still has a special gleam in his eye every time he sees Souness - it's a love whose light has never really gone out. You never forget the first person who makes you stand stark-bollock naked in front of a mirror, even if it is a gruff curly-haired Scot who's now a rubbish manager.

One of the great delusions of the average football fan is how attractive his club is to potential new signings. But of course players don't care about your club like you do; it means nothing to them unless they've been brought up through the youth team. As much as fans wish it wasn't, it's just a job to most players. They just play football, take their money (your money) and go home to their fake Georgian mansions until something better turns up or their contract runs out. I wish it wasn't true, but it is.

Every season you'll hear all sorts of speculation about the big names on the verge of signing, but of course they never do. Around the time of this article, Spurs were signing anyone with a V in their surname and all of them were rubbish, while they were rumoured to be about to sign Rivaldo for months but it was all delusion. I got a couple of predictions wrong in this but the principle remains as true now as it did then - fans over-rate the attractiveness of their club and can't see any reason why anybody would reject a move there. This is especially true of clubs who are in theory big and important (like Man City), but always find it difficult to attract top-rank players no matter how much cash they've got to spend.

Not long after this was published Mick gave up his pursuit of the lesbian in question and settled for a nice lass from Redcar. I assume she is not of the sapphic persuasion. Though she does smoke a pipe. And has a beard.

My mate Metal Mick fancies a lesbian.

He wants to 'convert' her to heterosexuality.

He thinks he's irresistible. He thinks it's only a matter of time.

He is, of course, crazy

Mick isn't at all familiar with the 'nature or nurture' debate. In fact, when I raised the issue of sexual politics, he thought I was talking about 'MPs having it off'.

Middlesbrough isn't exactly a vortex of sexual enlightenment, even if the local lasses do bang like a steam hammer after a few drinks. But Mick's convinced that the woman in question (imagine if Nicole Kidman had grown up on the dole in Teesside) just hasn't met the right bloke yet. It's that simple to Mick.

I told him he's got no chance - she'd no more go out with him than he'd go on a date with Michael Ricketts.

"Nah, I'll get in her pants yet man," he said last weekend.

"No chance," I said. "Even if you did, you're on a hiding to nothing. Straight blokes can't compete with lesbians, man. They're professionals. They've got access to all that complicated 'down below' equipment every hour of the day. They know which bits do what and how quickly. She's used to someone who knows what they're doing - not some bloke like you who thinks a clitoris is a new Renault hatchback."

"Aye, I bet she's got a hot hatch, like," said Mick, not listening to me at all.

He's still convinced that the sight of his hairy arse and dubiously-proportioned genitalia will be enough to melt the heart of any woman.

And in his way Mick is like a lot of football fans, who can't bring themselves to believe that their club isn't as irresistible as they think it is.

This is how we arrive at the ridiculous situation of Man United thinking that they can attract Ronaldo. It's why Spurs fans expect to sign some big player every summer, even though every year they end up with someone called Crapovicomov from Upper Volga reserves. It's why fans whose teams get relegated think their players will still be loyal. Hammers fans think Joe Cole's heart is tied to Green Street - he wouldn't leave would he? Yup he would and he will. Just like Beckham will go to Real, Paul Robinson to Man United and Alan Smith to Liverpool.

Loads of us suffer from such delusions, we can't believe that players see our club as a going-nowhere shit-hole, less a Theatre of Dreams and more like a Bog of Despair.

Admittedly, Leeds fans this season may have had their eyes opened, as might Sunderland. Being a Boro fan however, I've never suffered any delusions that anyone recently came to play for us for any other reason than great thick, donkey-choking wads of cash. None of this badge-kissing 'I love the club, the fans and the tea lady' garbage. At Boro they just turn up with their boots and a large bag with which to carry home the money. In a funny sort of way it's a more honest way of doing business.

I guarantee if you're not already doing so, just like my mate Metal Mick, you'll be eyeing up players who are as unlikely to join your club as Nicole is to put her hands down Micky's pants. You might, like Mick, even think your club can somehow persuade the player to go against their nature and give you a go. But he's wrong and so, most probably, are you.

13. FOOTBALL NUTTERS UNITE!

04/08/03

There are people who like football, there are people who love football and then there are the football nutters. We nutters are obsessed. If you're a nutter, you probably aren't even aware how much you are obsessed by football or how much you know about it. You listen to all the phone-ins, you strike up conversations at the bar with total strangers about the 4-5-1 system, you know who plays at obscure places like Layer Road or Turf Moor, you know who won the FA Cup in 1975 and can speak knowledgeably about the benefits of playing three central defenders with a holding midfielder. To you 'one in the hole' is a tactical option and not a manoeuvre a lady might ask you to perform.

If you have a deep knowledge or abiding interest in something such as Renaissance literature, you're regarded as an intellectual. If you profess a love for medieval history, you are regarded as cultured, so how come just because you know what year Cardiff got to the quarter-finals of the European Cup, you attract such ridicule from those who don't share your passion? It's all snobbery. Bollocks to them.

I recall a quiet afternoon in Las Vegas when I wandered into a large but empty bar area and got myself one of those three-foot high cocktails that comes in a blue plastic jug-type thing with two very long straws. It just tastes of fruit juice but boasts a few shots of rum and vodka, ideal to quench the thirst and give you a little buzz at three in the afternoon. At both ends of this lounge bar area are TV screens. The programme cuts back from the ads to a sport channel showing West Brom playing Newcastle. A small surge of excitement floods into my bloodstream and I go and pull up a seat near to the screen.

Within two minutes, a large chubby man sits down near me, his eyes glued to the screen. I can tell in one glance he's British. I don't know how you can tell but you can. It's like when you see Americans in the street in Britain, they just stand out somehow and it's not just the checked slacks. We exchange a brief knowing glance and give a small nod. Within five minutes another man has sat down with a defeated-looking woman in tow. The look of pleasure as he sinks into the seat clutching a pint of lager is all too familiar.

And there we were; three English blokes alone in the bar of a Las Vegas hotel casino fixated on a football match 6,000 miles away. That is what a football nutter does. We have a universal common bond. We should be proud of ourselves.

The sun is high in the sky. It is 88 degrees, the tarmac is melting and I'm wearing ice underpants to stay cool. It can mean only one thing.

It's the start of the new season. Thank God. Let's hear none of this rubbish about the football starting too soon, or the season being too long. If you're a football nutter like me, you never wanted the season to stop in the first place. Hell, I love football so much I even enjoy being bored by it.

But being a football obsessive isn't without its problems, as I'm sure you've found out.

The first thing to realise is that most people don't share your obsession. Sure, some people you work with will say they like football, they might even go to the match occasionally, but trust me, they're not mad about it like we are. They're not the sort of fans who will go and watch first-round Worthington Cup matches between two teams they don't support.

They won't want to talk to you about why the hell Harry Kewell is playing on the right. They don't care whether the UEFA Cup has a league stage or not.

They certainly will not know, as my mate Chris does, the shape of the goal nets at every ground from 1970 onwards. He was a big fan of those shallow, square nets they had at West Ham. He is also an expert on stanchions and everything to do with goal frames.

No, for the non-serious follower of football, the game is just light entertainment not to be taken seriously - like Ant and Dec, the Tory party or the Daily Mirror.

But at least these people know a little about our obsession. The biggest problem in a football nutter's life is dealing with those humans who know and care even less about football. To them we are an alien species.

For a start it means there's almost nothing to talk to them about. They don't understand that football is a universal language. You don't need to know anything about an indigenous culture to get along with the locals as long as they like their football. Go to any part of the world and say Georgie Best and watch their faces light up. This can even work in that largest of football deserts, America.

Football is always portrayed as a divisive sport which makes people want to eat each other raw and spit out the bones, but the truth is, more friendships are made through football than any other way.

But to non-football people, we are strange creatures. We are nerdy, uncool types, talking a funny language and caring way too much about meaningless things like late tackles, handballs and red cards. There's often a snobby, elitist attitude that goes with this, as though we're all cultural and emotional morons just because some of us have massive beer guts, tattoos and sing obscene songs in public.

Just because we think opera is an ugly noise sung by fat people, it doesn't make us dumb or unsophisticated - even though that's how the non-football media likes to portray us. Some of us have been to see modern ballet and interpretive dance. Some of us thought it was just anorexic self-indulgent crappola. Some of us have seen every Shakespeare play and were bored by almost all of them. Some of us have even got BA (Hons) degrees in English and History, admittedly despite not reading any of the books all the way through for three years and being high on mushrooms most of the time. So we're not all thick, despite what the Daily Mail or gin-soaked Sunday Telegraph readers might think.

Relationships for football nuts are very difficult. Try convincing a non-football-loving woman that staying in to watch Bolton v Blackburn on Sky on a Wednesday night is more fun than...well almost anything else she could want to do. And if you do go out and you just 'accidentally' end up in a pub with the game on a big screen, you'll be riding the sofa for the rest of the week, man.

Going out with a non-football lover means you have at some point to choose between the love of your life, football, and your current love which, when you look at it realistically, there's a good chance won't be around as long or matter to you as much as the football. It's a tough call.

You start to feel bad about your devotion to the game, so you end up trying to compromise, but sooner or later you're getting the "you love football more than you love me" lecture from her, but all your old footy mates are saying, "You're under the thumb son, you never come to see the reserve side play the local chemical factory XI anymore."

You get one of those achingly-painful twangs that go right from your gut straight to your heart for those good old, carefree days in the shadow of the steel mill, with the rain lashing in your face - the days before she came into your life and made you go to Ikea in return for regular sex and home-made cottage pie. You look inside yourself and you know that you've lost some of your soul. Was her idea to grow up and settle down what you really wanted? Didn't you just go along with it all because it was easier than saying no and because you didn't want to hurt anyone's feelings? The sadness is suddenly almost unbearable.

Okay, you can't choose who you fall in love with, but before it's too late you really should try and fall in love with a football-mad person because it'll make your life simpler and happier in the long run. This, as I'm sure you already know, is as difficult as trying to find a woman who loves prog rock or thinks bodily functions are always amusing. But keep trying, they are out there. Believe me.

But lads, if you think you've got it hard (no sniggering at the back, fourth form) it's ten times worse for the female football fan. Football women are shunned by the candy pink, girly majority who just want to talk about make-up, their 'addiction' to chocolate and something they've read in a magazine about George Clooney using vaginal deodorants on his dog.

These are the sort of women who say, "Ooooh, I'm addicted to my soaps", and care about EastEnders characters like it's real life. These are usually also the same women who think Michael Bolton's version of Dock of the Bay is superior to Otis Redding's. They may also own Lucy Atwell posters or cards - the ones with kids who have big radiation-style mutated heads accompanied with some sort of banal, sickly sentiment.

They will also own at least four copies of Unchained Melody, none of them by the Righteous Brothers, and have several records by Robson and Jerome. There's a very good chance they look like Emma Bunton. They have never heard of Frank Zappa. They drink Bacardi Breezers. They think Les Paul is the name of the local window cleaner and that Hunter Thompson is a moustachioed athlete from the 80's.

We football-bonkers men don't have to avoid these women because they avoid us like we are dog shit on legs. But if you're a woman who is football-daft and happy to tell any of the Barbie girls that you love the game but don't give a toss about the footballers' legs, arse or chest hair, this is tantamount to a declaration of lesbianism and is only compounded if you also declare a passionate disinterest in Victoria or David Beckham, don't watch Footballers' Wives and not only know the offside law, but can also spot a foul throw from 50 yards.

Men are expected to be mad about football and women are expected to cynically tolerate our obsession. But on the upside, a football-loving woman, should she wish to seek male attention, will never be short of a date. Indeed, men will want her with a longing that hurts their whole body.

We're football mad. Every new season fills us with excitement and anticipation. We look forward to the highs and lows in equal measure. We don't expect anyone else to understand our passion and we don't care that well-groomed middle-management executives think playing golf is better for your career or that the girlfriend's parents think you're a manic depressive hooligan because you admit to going to see lower-league football, on a bus, in the rain, on a Tuesday night.

During every summer I can recall since the age of nine, a part of me has always felt that my life was on hold, incomplete and hollow. It's an empty feeling that only football fills. And the weird thing is that I know hundreds of thousands of people all feel the same way.

So come on, bring it all on, bring it all on now. We're football nutters and we're proud.

14. I SWEAR. IT'S THE TRUTH.

11/08/03

I recall getting a lot of stick about this piece from parents who didn't want their kids to grow up mouthing obscenities, and they seemed to think that this was more likely to happen if we allowed football people to swear on the telly. Oddly enough, not having swearing on the telly hasn't stopped people swearing. Quite the reverse. What people should be doing is encouraging their kids to think, to be intelligent, to have something to say and be able to say it using swear words if they want. Fretting that they hear the odd 'bastard' or 'fucker' is just obsessing about the wrong thing.

All I want is some honesty and a bit of passion. Most footballers only know 73 words and without being able to use swear words this is reduced to around 28, which is why they're usually such boring bastards. It's not just that it's not allowed in football broadcasting, it's the fact that if a swear word slips out, the presenter has to apologise as though we're all sitting there, hair turned white in shock at the profanity. It's all rather childish.

I find it hard to believe anything more than a small minority of people would be in any way offended if a footballer was swearing on TV. We see them mouthing the words on the pitch, we all know what's going on, but it's as though the broadcasters have to pretend we're all coy schoolgirls who need protecting from the nasty words.

Since I wrote this, swearing on TV has become far more prevalent and reality shows - though a tedious art form per se - have presented the public as they are in everyday life. But despite these developments, football remains a swear-free zone. It also remains the home to much poorly-expressed, boring banter.

The lack of swearing has not encouraged more intelligent or philosophical debate, it's generally just quite thick men speaking in clichés. We can't dumb it down any more by introducing a swearing option. It'd be interesting to see how many people would tune into the SwearZone option to watch the game. I bet it'd be the majority.

This is still one of my big campaigning issues and I won't rest until it happens. Anyone who disagrees is a fucking cunt.

Remember when you were at school and you had to talk to the teachers? You couldn't talk to them normally. You had a different way of speaking to authority figures and probably still do.

You edit out all the swear words and references to moist body parts that might embarrass you and them.

You try and talk what my grandma would have called 'proper'. She thought the Queen spoke right proper. God help us if we all talked like a sour-faced, anally-retentive inbred anachronism, but it's true that using swear words or any level of vulgarity in elite company will almost certainly guarantee social disapproval.

The irony of course was that most of our teachers were probably so sick of us that they'd have loved to tell us to 'fuck off and die' every time their class of itchy, distracted pupils decided to try and light farts instead of working out the calorific value of a peanut.

So we were all in the position of not being able to say what we wanted to say in the way we wanted to say it.

In adult life, nothing much changes. Walk into your bank manager's office and say, "it's as fucking hot as a nympho's cunt out there", and your chances of the 20k unsecured loan are miniscule.

My parents told me that swearing was a sign of limited vocabulary - this was ironic because by the age of 12 I knew more words than they had learned in their entire lives. I was no Will Self but I knew many long-winded, verbose ways of expressing the most simplest of sentiments. This has stood me in good stead as a man of letters.

Swearing copiously can be a sign of a fulsome lexicon of expression and I don't see why we should think otherwise. Indeed, not swearing is sometimes a severe vocabulary restriction.

However, despite living in an age where every form of human depravity is only four clicks away on your computer, the one thing we cannot be allowed to hear is people talking about football on the TV or radio in the same way we talk about it in pubs or at the grounds.

The people who are reporting or commentating on football all swear in real life. I don't think Andy Gray sits at home watching TV saying, "Oh dear, that was a bit of a rough tackle."

So let's recap here;

We've got the fans all swearing at the match, in the pub and on the sofa. We've got the players all swearing all the time. We've got commentators who all swear in real life. Indeed, the only time they're not swearing or using colourful language is probably the two hours they're on telly.

Amount of swearing in real life: Loads.

Amount of swearing on telly football: Zero.

In fact, if someone says 'arse', as they did on 606 this weekend, there has to be an apology or suggestion of the more polite use of 'backside' instead.

This shyness of swear words is rooted in idiotic Victorian culture. This was a culture which was so uptight that it insisted on putting lace doilies around the legs of furniture because legs, not even inanimate wooden objects' legs, should be exposed. It lies in the notion that the content of what you're saying is less important than the words you use to express it. This is shite really.

So just who is stopping the true expression of the people being used? Who says you can't say fuck on telly unless you're Bob Geldof?

There's a Broadcasting Standards Commission who sit in judgment on what you or my delicate ears should or shouldn't hear. In a typically vacuous but pompous manner their website tells us they're 'Maintaining Values in Changing Times'. Well you're not maintaining my values, mate, and I object to you implying you are.

There are a couple of reverends on the committee, so that shows you just how out of touch they are. A cynic might be surprised that there isn't more paedophilia on TV, given the church's ability to attract so many that way inclined amongst their number.

Other members are a non-executive director of London Transport, a Visiting Fellow at the London School of Economics, a member of Oftel's Small Business Taskforce, the editor of the quarterly religious magazine Sea of Faith and the Vice Chair of Council of the University of Sussex. What a lovely cross-section of society. Do you think any of them know what's in your mind and soul? These are judgmental people who want to control our lives because they think they know how we should live.

If these people are not controlling our TV lives, then who is? It's a free country - well that's what we're told...but it isn't.

What we need in the coverage of football is an alternative commentary channel. They've already got FanZone (where the 'fans' are not allowed to swear) on Sky so why not have a sweary channel? Call it 'Proper Talk'. I'd even pay an additional subscription.

At first this sounds radical but that's only because we're so used to an anodyne version of the football world. But in reality, the non-swearing version of football that TV forces us to see is the weird and freaky thing. Wanting to hear 'natural' language in sports commentary doesn't make me uncouth, vulgar or childish, though I see nothing wrong with all of those elements in the human psyche. I just want reality, that's all. I just want to hear a manager say, "the referee was a fucking disgrace", rather than, "He might be disappointed with his performance."

I have never watched a football match without swearing or being vulgar. I've never been to any football match without hearing swearing and vulgarity. I've never played in a match without hearing swearing or vulgarity, so how come TV never, ever reflects this? Not once, not on one show, one time ever. It's time to change that.

15. "WHY IS IAN RUSH BETWEEN YOUR LEGS?"

27/08/03

I can't be alone in not liking football shirts or almost any football merchandise. I suppose for a generation of kids brought up on the garish, slippery nylon creations of the 80's & 90's it's just the way shirts are. They probably think nothing of them. I actually used to live next door to a bloke who owned a factory who made them in the 1980's, I think it was in some glamorous place in the north east like Tanfield Lea. He told me they were very cheap to make and I bet they still are but they're just part of a massive expansion of merchandise A.K.A. tat that clubs sell. Go to any club shop and it's like a day out at the £1 store. I'm not sure who buys all the key rings, polyester ties and plastic mugs but if they're going to sell stuff, why does it have to be such cheapo rubbish? Middlesbrough actually sell an uplighter emblazoned with the club crest for £15 along with plastic egg cups and wine gums.

It's all a long way from a wool scarf, a wooden rattle and a 100% cotton crew neck football shirt and of course, a lot of it is just knocked up en masse in factories off the M62 or increasingly in China for 5p and sold on markets in the old pit and mill towns of the north, which is where I suspect the lady in this piece got her knickers.

You can tell a lot of kids think the more merch you've got, the bigger fan you are, but surely a packet of sherbet lemons emblazoned with the club crest doesn't prove anything of the sort. And this is me trying in vain to point out the fact.

I can't remember her name now. She peeled the skin tight Ramones t-shirt up and over her head, revealing a large pair of pendulous breasts capped with bubble gum pink nipples. I was impressed and said so.

She unbuttoned her jeans and let them fall to the floor. My nostrils flared. My mouth was dry. My pupils dilated. I could scarcely believe what I was seeing. I thought I'd seen it all. I was a man of the world. But I wasn't prepared for this.

Staring at me from between her legs was the rather washed-out but unmistakable mustachioed face and proboscis of Ian Rush along with the LUFC badge. She was wearing Ian Rush knickers.

"You must be a big Liverpool fan," I said, unable to take my eyes off him.

"I don't think I could bear the idea of Rushie brushing up against my genitals. Mind you, he is red hot in the box." The potential for similar jokes was limitless I realised, much to my own smug satisfaction.

She looked puzzled, took the knickers off and inspected the crotch where Rushie peered out in that endearingly dopey, large nosed way he has.

"Who's Rushie?" she asked.

"He's the fella whose huge nose has been between your legs all day."

"Oh. I thought that was Freddie Mercury."

She must be blind I thought, which, given the appalling state my naked body, was something of a bonus.

"He never played for Liverpool though did he," I said hopping onto her bed ready for action.

"He might have done, I don't know anything about football," she laughed and sat on top of me.

"So if you don't know anything about football, why are you wearing Liverpool FC knickers?"

She shrugged and smiled, "I didn't know I was did I. I just put them on in the dark. My mam probably bought them for me."

"What did you think LUFC stood for then?"

71

She shrugged and laughed again, "I don't know. Lovely underwear for cunts maybe?"

I laughed. She was the best girl I'd met that day. I was going to ask her how she'd come to own the underwear but more pressing and frankly more exciting matters were at hand and it slipped my mind. An hour later we went our separate ways, never to meet again.

Anyway, I tell you this brief, meaningless mid 80's sexual encounter in order to illustrate something important about modern-day football.

Now while wearing football-themed underwear is always endearing, especially on a woman who likes the Ramones, it clearly doesn't prove undying allegiance to the club. In fact, all it probably does prove is they like buying cheap underwear off the market.

But so much about the game is about posture and posing and image these days. Clubs need income from merchandise so badly that they'll put the club badge on anything in a desperate attempt to pull in some income.

Hartlepool United even sells official blue wigs @ £2.70 a pop. Essential headwear on the north-east coast in summer I can confirm.

The implication behind all this is that if you're a true fan then you'll want or even need to buy all this to prove to the outside world how important the club is to you. But that's really not true is it.

Not wearing your club shirt, scarf or wig and not having the club Beanie Bear, key ring, set of eight coasters and branded vibrating egg gift set doesn't make you a less loyal or true supporter any more than that lass wearing Liverpool knickers made her a Liverpool supporter.

But to complicate things further there are fans who wear football gear out of some sense of fashion rather than club allegiance. However, football shirts are almost universally unpleasant things that soon make you feel like a boil in the bag chicken. They feel like pond slime and are made from radioactive asbestos fibres so indestructible they'll lie in a land fill for 500 years and still not decompose. In short, they're bloody awful creations and are no substitute for proper clothing.

Club merchandise used to only be available from the club shop which in Newcastle's case was even until the mid 80's, just a stall in the Green Market in the town centre. There was a shirt, a scarf and a rattle and maybe a plastic pennant on a bit of bamboo. That was your lot. Nowadays football merchandise is everywhere. It's stopped being special and exclusively part of our, the proper fans', collective football culture. It's now part of everyday life. It's up the crack of the ass of people who don't even know Paul Smith from Alan Smith and that's not right is it.

Though of course, I shall always be happy to see women in or out of their football underwear.

I sat there watching Dominic Matteo being interviewed after a Leeds match and I couldn't take my eyes off the motorway that had been mown through his fulsome eyebrowery. There is probably no less vain a player than Matteo. The big ugly Scouser is not a candidate for being a male model...not while there are monkeys that can be shaved anyway.

I'm actually not opposed to tarting yourself up. I am in no position to criticise expressions of vanity, having spent a couple of years in the heavy metal late 80's happily wearing a bit of eyeliner. But the craze for waxing eyebrows seems a step too far to me. And if you must, don't just rip off a third of each of the hirsute strips to leave yourself with an unnatural couple of oddly-positioned tufts. Be a bit subtle about it. Having hair is natural. You might have spotted this as a recurring theme.

When I wrote this it seemed symbolic of contemporary footballers, who had nothing better to do than go to beauty parlours and have eyebrow hair removed that they've worn throughout their lives with the minimum of distress.

How unlike the late 70's and 80's, when hairy-arsed hard men like Graeme Souness queued up to get their hair permed into a tight bubble and coupled it with a full Village People-style San Francisco gay moustache. That was when men were real men and used their wife's curlers.

"Wax my anus!"

It's not something you hear said every day (probably). But around Courtney Love's house it is apparently not unknown.

74

Mad Courtney may be unique in declaring her desire for a brown eye depilatory in a national magazine (see Q issue 200), but surely she isn't alone in this request. I'm willing to bet many of our beloved footballers are also paying for anal waxings.

And on what basis do I make this bold assertion? Eyebrow shaving of course!

It's rampant amongst our sporting and cultural icons. And if you're mad enough to wax or shave your eyebrows, you've already crossed the rubicon that will inevitably lead to a baldy bumhole.

Are you hung up about your eyebrows? Are they too hairy? Do they meet in the middle and make you look like a Neanderthal cave-dweller? Are you secretly creating two distinct eyebrows by removing the hair in the middle like it was an unsightly bush of pubic hair emerging from the side of a bikini?

A good example of this narcissistic fashion trend is Dominic Matteo, who appears to have shaved all but the outer half of each eyebrow. He now has the permanently startled expression of a man who is being ritually abused by Satanists with a cattle prod.

Look at the Gallagher brothers - not boys short of eyebrow hair, but now both with two definable eyebrows rather than the single big bushy one that nature gave them. Is this kind of vanity what we expect from hairy-assed rock 'n' rollers? Well, yes probably.

Of course, women have always done this. Remember Madonna's fulsome above-eye growths back in the mid-Eighties?

But until recently, it seemed men could escape without indulging in such painful but somehow pleasurable beauty regimes as eyebrow-plucking.

For decades men thought having a bath every week was the most any bloke should do in the health and beauty department. I remember a time when blokes considered the wearing of Brut or Hi Karate as being distinctly woofter-ish. Any odour other than that of eye-watering sweat mixed with coal dust and Brown Ale was eyed, or nosed, very suspiciously in the north of England.

But that's all changing now.

If you're spending time waxing excess hair from between your eyebrows, it shows three things about your life:

1) You've got far too much time on your hands.

2) You've got far too much money.

3) You won't stop at the eyebrows now, will you?

When I was growing up, the lack of facial or body hair was considered by many to be a sure sign of you not being quite manly enough. Indeed, anything short of a werewolf lupine-style face meant you were gay. It was obvious.

Somehow, body hair had got caught up with masculinity, despite the fact that we all had grandmas with moustaches. I had an auntie with a full beard. She shaved it every day and by five o'clock had a blue chin shadow.

On reflection, this may have been my Uncle Herbert in a frock.

But this was why we all tried to grow a 'tache at the first opportunity. Aged 15, I sported a Graham Hill-style upper-lip growth that looked more like navel fluff than a real moustache. I confidently strode into the American Tavern in Stockton on Tees - a pub that would serve you lager even if you were a baby in a pram wearing a false beard - and thought this pathetic growth established my over-18 credentials to any doubtful landlord.

It worked and I was in lager and lime heaven for the next three years.

Had I been born 25 years later, being hairless would not make me a poetry-reading, talcum powder-scented shirt-lifter, but instead it would make me a cool, fashion-conscious metrosexual.

Had I tried to argue this in 1975 I would have had the shit kicked out of me by real men wearing orange satin flared trousers, red platform shoes and lurid floral shirts with matching kipper ties.

Affluent footballers now have time and money enough to indulge their every vain whim. But if it's cool to shave your eyebrows, why not go the whole hog? Wax off all your body fur - give yourself the appearance of one of those hairless dogs and strip your tackle of all those bothersome pubic hairs too while you're at it.

I have to admit that I've actually done this. Actually, it's more accurate to say I've had this done to me. I had little option.

The scenario involved; a room in a Motel 6 just outside Bakersfield, California; a bottle of tequila; some heavy-set northern men; a woman with a razor and a can of shaving foam.

To be fair to her, whoever she was, she did a neat job - being careful not to cause a fatal loss of blood from a major artery. However, she did rub the freshly-shaved area with enough aftershave to make it feel like my entire lower portions were on fire. If you've never tried this, lads, I heartily recommend it - especially on cold winter mornings. It provides you with a very special, personal kind of central heating far superior to anything Ready Brek can do for you.

When it grows back it's sharp and rough enough to wear a hole in your underpants. Your balls feel like conkers and frankly, you can't stop scratching them. Nothing new there then, but at least you've now got a valid excuse.

Sandra Bullock once said in an interview that she shaved her pubes into a heart shape as a Valentines' Day present for some lucky man. Where Hollywood goes, our pampered footballers are sure to follow. How long will it be before we discover that a

Premiership player has had a Nike logo shaved out of his hairy back as part of a new sponsorship deal?

So when you hear commentators say 'that was a close shave there for the champions', you might think about taking him literally.

Remember when Rio missed his drugs test? He probably doesn't. It was the biggest football story of 2003 and prompted a thousand questions. Was he avoiding being tested so it wouldn't be revealed that he was actually loaded on crack and that's what makes his lips such a funny shape? Why was he shopping instead? Surely he wasn't such a Mimbo?

It was all a mystery. But in hindsight he was just an absent-minded, dozy bugger who would also forget to defend occasionally, probably because he's thinking about how he can 'pimp his a ride' do up his 'crib' or some other such gangsta-lite MTV style nonsense.

I just thought the whole affair an exercise in pointless bureaucracy and phoney moralistic posing. Why are footballers being drug-tested anyway? Is it to make sure they aren't taking performance-enhancing drugs?

Well, I don't understand what the concept of performance-enhancing drugs really means, so I thought I'd try and challenge the notions behind it. This didn't stop people writing in and saying I was corrupting their children and did I really want everyone out the brains on drugs etc. To which my reply was, 'they probably already are.'

There's some sort of moral outrage about drug taking, even though the majority of us are loaded on something most weeks. In sport it's called cheating apparently. Zidane took creatine, which is banned in France but not in Italy. So is that illegal or not?

If you take a drug like creatine which allows your body to recover from injury quicker, how is that any different from putting antiseptic cream on a cut? How is it different from a sticking plaster on a wound? How is taking something which helps you develop muscle mass more quickly really much different from lifting weights and eating high protein foods to achieve the same thing.

Conceptually it's the same. And if the football authorities are taking on their shoulders the work of the police in finding illegal drugs in the players' bodies, where will it end? Will they be investigating if they account properly for their tax or if they know anyone who has ever speeded in their car?

Of course not. The word 'drugs' changes everything and brings out the nanny police. It's all a bit pathetic really. Players get sacked for having a bit of grass in their blood while going out on the drink and getting into fights is all part of a night out with the lads and is essential for team bonding. It's so obviously hypocritical rubbish.

I personally enjoy altered states and have done so all my adult life. These days I use wine, beer and cider but I still consider getting high an essential part of being a rounded human being. Why should footballers be any different? Mind you, if a player is stoned on grass he'll not be in the first team for long now will he, so why all the fuss...don't dull their buzz man!

It's been a crazy week; a week of sex and drugs and football. Players seem to be behaving like Motley Crue on tour in the 80's. Only without the tights. However, while drugs and rock 'n' roll are rightly inseparable, sport is for some reason the only expression of creativity and individualism where the performers are condemned for using them.

Bear with me on this one. I'm going to say something no-one else will publicly say: I'd rather footballers did take drugs.

The use of drugs is condemned for several reasons and not just because they're illegal - in fact, their illegality is hardly ever really the issue in sport.

Instead, it's the supposed performance-enhancing aspects of drugs which are being condemned. Drug users are cheats right? But no-one ever says this about writers, poets, painters or musicians do they?

Without performance-enhancing drugs The Beatles wouldn't have written all their good stuff. There'd have been no Jimi Hendrix, no Bob Dylan, no Miles Davis, and no John Coltrane. Or Oasis or The Libertines for younger readers..

But players are role models aren't they? If they take drugs, everyone else will. No. Humans have spent the entirety of their existence on earth getting high on one intoxicant or another. As a species we like it. We need to do it. It's part of what makes us what we are as creatures. It's natural.

The unspoken truth is that almost everyone who has ever created anything of value, anything that has moved or stirred your soul, was either on drugs at the time or used them to inspire or placate their worried minds.

So why is it different for football? What drugs exactly are we testing players for? Can you get busted for having nicotine in your blood? It's probably the most addictive drug available after crack cocaine and is only legal due to a historical accident. Who or what is everyone being protected from?

We all know Rio passed his drugs test, though this may have been a surprise to Man U fans who have seen some of his sluggish performances. But say he didn't. Say he had traces of marijuana in his blood. Why would that be bad? Let's remove the illegality factor - would it be so bad if Rio had toked a few spliffs to relax after a game rather than going out on the lash with the boys? Sitting at home listening to Peter Tosh records, eating pickled onion Monster Munch and wondering if you're talking out loud or in your head will get you into a lot less trouble than going to some expensive nightclub with the lads or spending the night having a threesome in a lay-by with a bird who may or may not be 16.

It may have inspired him to be a better player, it may have opened his mind to greater levels of possibilities, creativity and vision on the pitch. Don't forget Bob Marley was a pretty good footballer!

Say he tested positive for cocaine. What does coke do to you? It makes you talk a load of shite for hours (so no change there then) and it gives you unshakeable confidence - something useful in a competitive sport. Managers try for years to instil self-belief but you get it with one toot of Peruvian marching powder. It can also inflate your ego to planet-size, give you the permanent horn and make you paranoid; all things that are already essential to being a top Premiership player. Okay, it enlarges your heart, raises your blood pressure and destroys your nasal septum, but no pain, no gain.

How about a dose of speed? A team racing on amphetamines would be hard to stop. Talk about players having good engines, it'd make the likes of Michael Owen faster than pure white light.

Okay, performing to a high standard on LSD or mushrooms is going to be difficult, largely because it's hard to find the goal when it's turned into a quicksilver mirror and begun limbo dancing with six skeletons and the ghost of your long-dead uncle Alf.

But the careful recreational use of powerful hallucinogenics could provide footballers with the same open-minded, alternate view of reality that you need to really create something brilliant. You don't produce something as startling as Hendrix's Are You Experienced? by taking vitamin pills and soya shakes. Turning off their minds, relaxing and floating downstream could be part of weekly training.

Now, I'm not recommending players jack up heroin in the penalty box - the last thing we need is more dozy goalkeepers nodding off in the middle of a penalty shoot-out. Nor do I want to see match day turn into some sort of Grateful Dead concert.

Players turning up E'ed off their face would probably be a tad counter-productive.

But all the anti-drug mania behind the FA's manic drug-testing policy is totally overwrought and misplaced.

Yes Rio broke the FA rules - but why do these rules exist in the first place? The way I see it, if you're stoned out of your box you're not going to get in the first team anyway - though of course more than one Arsenal player in the late 80's played while pissed and still won the league. But it's an unchallengeable fact that drugs enhance creativity in many people and God knows, we need some more creative footballers in this country. Drink clearly turns some of them into testosterone-fuelled wild dogs but I don't see the FA insisting on tests to prove they've been on alcopops.

If drugs tests exist to prevent cheating, shouldn't they also ban paracetamol? Getting rid of a headache before a big match is hugely performance-enhancing. Using fiery jack on your sore groin is performance-enhancing in more ways than one.

Hell, eating the right food before a game is performance-enhancing but I don't hear anyone wanting to ban carbohydrates. Where do you draw the line? Should a sugar rush be outlawed?

I guess what I'm saying is, I just don't understand. There's an assumption behind all these rules but exactly what that is, I really can't work out. It's probably something as sweepingly inaccurate and frankly irrelevant as 'drugs are bad for you kids'. But then again, so is eating lard. So is driving a car. So is buying a litre of vodka and necking it in five minutes. So is living in Iraq. None of these things are illegal but all of them can affect your health.

Three thousand people a year are killed by cars in Britain; shouldn't the FA be testing players to see if they've been driving? From a health risk point of view it would make more sense.

As with much about modern life, that which seems to be straight, sensible and normal is actually irrational and does not stand up to scrutiny. Everyone on all sides has got themselves into a lather about something which shouldn't even be an issue. The Grange Hill kids have a lot to answer for. Just say no – to drug testing.

18. DRESSING INAPPROPRIATELY
10/12/03

There was a time when the very idea of wearing gloves or bloody tights while you were playing football would have not only attracted ridicule, it would have made you less than a full man. It was, to put it in the vernacular, fucking poofy.

Apart from a brief flirtation with bizarre, loose-fitting long johns-style leggings by Leicester City's Keith Weller in the 70's, players were expected to run around enough to keep warm without gloves, hat or coat. I'm not sure when this all changed, though I suspect it was in the late 90's when gloves started being worn - initially by overseas players who had come from warmer climes and found the bitter north-east winds that blow in off the North Sea a little less pleasant than the mistral blowing in off the Sahara.

Now it's almost the norm but I still despise it. It still seems totally inappropriate. I refuse to believe you need to wear gloves or tights to keep warm when you're playing football. I may however be an old man shouting angrily in the wilderness on this one. There are more important things in life to get annoyed about than gloves it's true, but it's symbolic of something wider about the game that I find infuriating.

After this was initially published I received an e-mail from someone in Burbank who claimed to have been there when we played this gig dressed as druggy, hippy Christmas characters. The bloke who'd booked us told his boss he knew we'd turn up in such odd regalia and said it was all part of our act and just a bit of fun. He not only got away with this lie but was congratulated for original thinking! Now he's someone quite high up in one of the movie studios in Burbank apparently. The strip club with the showers is long gone though, I'm assured.

As anyone who knows me will tell you, I am no style guru. In fact, many would go as far as saying I'm pathologically scruffy.

Running an online business means spending almost all your time in front of a computer, and that gives messy buggers like me an excuse to dress like a tramp. You have no sartorial standards to maintain, no peers or work mates to mock you. Indeed, it's one of the best things about the job.

Dressing appropriately for the occasion is a talent I've never had. No matter how hard I try I always look messy or just plain wrong, so now at my advanced age I've given up, and I'm still keeping my vow - taken at the age of 15 - never to own a suit.

Even when the dress code is fancy dress, I still rarely get it right.

In 1990 we were due to play a gig around Xmas-time in downtown LA at a club that was right next door to the most bizarre strip joint I've ever seen. This place was in fact a series of shower units where the ladies would perform. There was no stripping involved, just nekkid showering. So it was at least clean and smelled of soap. Mind you, watching women get washed is surprisingly dull after about five minutes.

Anyway, we'd been booked to play a fancy dress party for a company's Xmas bash. So naturally we dressed up in festival apparel.

We rented several costumes - a psychedelic elf, a stoner snowman (which naturally came with a cartoon-sized joint and eyes that rotated), a large brown hairy animal with an illuminated red nose that we think was a reindeer but looked more like a rabbit with antlers, a drinker's nose and unpleasant crusty stains. And lastly, a dreadlocked Santa. I was the dreadlocked Santa, complete with a massive wig of white dreads, a strap-on beard with mini-dreads, and a red, gold and green Santa suit.

Rather than change into the costumes at the gig, we changed at the motel, and took much delight in wandering around like this all day. Hunter, who was the psychedelic elf, especially enjoyed the multi-coloured swirly tights and long pointy slippers. You have not lived until you've seen a six-foot two-inch, 16-stone Teessider in psychedelic tights, believe me. It's like all your nightmares brought to life.

We'd set up the gear earlier and even done a soundcheck, so we arrived about ten minutes before we were due to hit the stage. As we went in we could tell something was wrong. No-one else was in fancy dress. In fact, everyone was dressed in suits and bow ties. It was a respectable law firm Xmas lunch. Evidently, when Lenny had booked the gig, he thought the guy had said, "it's a fancy dress night", but in fact he'd actually said something about everyone being 'dressed right'. Lenny, doubtless being a bit pissed on lager, had put two and two together and got 87.

Anyway, we had to get on with it, we had nowt else to wear. It probably worked in our favour because our appearance took their minds off the below-par set. We all had good excuses for being rubbish - the bloody Santa sleeves really got in the way of my guitar, Tony's antlers kept falling in front of his eyes, Lenny was sweating so much inside the snowman suit he was leaving a river of sweat on the stage. The dreadlock wig was so heavy that my neck was aching and the strap-on facial hair so huge and itchy it felt like I was wearing a beard of bees.

Anyway, we did our thing, got paid and left. Sitting in a nearby bar, still in full costume, we swore never to do it again. But just at that moment a woman from the gig came over to chat to the drummer. Some women specialise in loving drummers; I think they reckon he'll have a good rhythm in bed. So she asked Hunter what a psychedelic elf keeps in his tights. Naturally, he was only too keen to show her his Yuletide log.

87

I got to thinking about this wearing of inappropriate clothing when I saw just how many players now wear gloves. Gloves on a football pitch to me are the most inappropriate of dress items. If you're so lazy that your hands are getting cold, then you should be running around a bit more. That's the bloody truth isn't it? It used to be ridiculed, but now it's accepted as normal. But not in my world. I suspect the gloves are not worn for warmth anyway; they're worn so players don't ruin their new manicured nails and make their moisturised hands feel rough.

If we let players get away with glove-wearing, next they'll want to wear bobble hats and scarves. Then it'll be leg warmers over the socks. It's the thin edge of the wedge. Soon they'll be calling off matches because it's too cold or too wet or because horrid people are shouting in the crowd. They've already managed to get away with wearing those bollock-squeezing lyca tights under their shorts even when it's 70 degrees.

It's both namby and pamby and we should ridicule players for it. Football is becoming more like a middle-class dinner party every day and glove-wearing is just another symptom of it (not that you wear woolly gloves at a middle-class dinner party, but you get my drift).

There's a whole book to be written about these 36 hours, or at least a novella.

I remember the first time I went to California - one night I was standing on the tenth-floor balcony of a hotel on Ocean Way in Santa Monica looking out towards Malibu as the golden July sun sank into the liquid mercury sea. I saw how beautiful it looked, how brilliant it felt, how well people lived and I actually felt very bitter that by accident of birth and economics - and because I had unambitious, dull parents - this kind of life had not been available to me before now. I was very bitter indeed.

Thankfully, I hadn't yet been to this multi-million dollar house in Pacific Palisades, because it would only have made me even more angry at having grown up in a cramped house in the middle of an open-air chemical factory in Teesside.

This was the first time I'd ever been in the presence of seriously rich people. It's very different to just going round someone's house who's on a good wage. Back in 1990 this house was worth five million dollars, so now it's probably nearer 25. It had over 35 rooms - nine bedrooms, 11 bathrooms and one lad from Teesside feeling a little out of his depth.

Now clearly, a lot of money can't make you happy if you're a miserable bugger, but luxury is a fantastic thing when you taste it for the first time, and I became convinced that if I ever had this kind of money, this is how I'd live; a big fuck off pool in its own wooded grounds, a fully-stocked bar with its own jukebox in a massive house with panoramic ocean views decorated with rock 'n' roll memorabilia and art. If enough of you buy this book, this is where the profits are going. Do drop by for a beer.

I never saw the point of being modest about your wealth. You may as well splash it around, get a bit wide and have a good time. Someone once told me that this is a typical northern 'cash for flash' attitude but it makes sense to me.

As for putting coke on your old fella, I seem to remember reading that Errol Flynn used to do this all the time - all the better to service Hollywood starlets. Just when you think you've invented some new form of debauchery, you can be pretty sure that someone else did it 50 years ago at least, hedonism being a natural urge in the human animal.

I don't really celebrate Xmas but evidently a lot of people do. And fair play to them. They seem to enjoy it. I gave up ages ago because I couldn't understand what I was supposed to be celebrating or why. I'm not really of a religious persuasion, and it doesn't really make sense to celebrate the arrival of Santa Claus, even though he does dress in Middlesbrough colours and would probably be a better striker than anyone else at the club.

And I've never needed an excuse for a couple of weeks of self-indulgent bingeing on food or alcohol, so it all seems irrelevant really, especially as there are no little Johnnys running round the place to get upset and inform the social services about my Scrooge-like approach.

So I don't send cards or buy anyone presents, not at Xmas anyway. Obviously, this means I have no friends and everyone hates me, but it's worth it not to have to write Xmas cards to your hated relations and pretend to be delighted with a soap-on-a-rope from your Auntie Ratface.

There was a year back in 1983 when, due to a severe and persistent use of magic mushrooms, we celebrated the Winter Solstice instead on December 21 by decorating a tree stump with tinsel and playing Jethro Tull records. We had no money at all because the dole hadn't come through so our celebratory meal was a single but very large swede that we'd stolen from a nearby field. It was an odd year, 1983.

Xmas is like a hypnosis which descends on the country. It excuses all sorts of cruel and unusual behaviour, ranging from the photocopying of arses to the wearing of sequin-encrusted underwear on your head. People who've hated each other all year end up having sex on the boss's desk at the Xmas office party and people who have been in love all year decide they actually hate each other because one of them bought the other something from Poundstretcher for Xmas: "Is this how much you love me?"

I was once bought an Arsenal strip by my parents for Xmas in the early 70's. I have never felt so depressed or furious. How could they have been so wrong? They returned it and brought home a Blackpool shirt instead. Yes, Blackpool - they thought it was Hull City's old gold but it was actually Blackpool's tangerine. After that, I never shook the thought that I was being raised by idiots.

Last year I told you about my mate who received the ultimate present from his Suzi Quatro look-a-like girlfriend - a blow job while watching Middlesbrough. I still secretly believe this is the best thing to have ever happened to anyone in the history of the world but you may think otherwise when you read this year's festive football tale.

It is a tale that involves the use of illegal narcotics and naked folk...oh and a football too. So draw the curtains, take your hands out of your pants and pay close attention as I take you back 13 years to southern California.

Xmas Day out there is a strange experience. For a start it's over 70 degrees, and being on a beach at Xmas is just plain odd for a boy from a windswept outpost in the north east of England. I mean, you wouldn't spend Xmas on the beach at Seaton Carew would you?

Palm trees are wrapped in silver foil and everyone wishes you 'happy holidays', presumably for fear of assuming you might not be a Christian.

So by 10am on Xmas Day 1990 we were hanging around Venice Beach. The sun was burning off the marine layer of cloud and the weather was set fair for a warm day in the 70's. We were listening to a guy wailing out Xmas melodies on a very loud, very luridly-painted guitar through a portable battery-powered amp.

He wrestled Jingle Bells out of feedback with judicious use of the whammy bar. It was fantastic and most definitely not the sort of thing you'd see on a street corner in Middlesbrough on Xmas morning.

Me and the Beer Pigs lads were sitting round eating refried bean tacos and drinking Michelob, while the good people of the world were visiting friends and family, opening presents and roasting turkeys. We were not. Did we care? Nah, we loved it. We were having a ball. We had over a thousand dollars in cash on us.

Lenny had accidentally fallen in love with a stunning girl called Rachel from Pacific Palisades and, better still, she was a rich girl, so we loved her as well. Her family lived in a multi-million dollar home with sea views over the Pacific and we had an open invitation to attend their Xmas Day party. We'd even got washed and put fairly clean clothes on for the occasion.

We turned up in the late afternoon to be greeted by Rachel. It was a huge house; all solid wood floors, big colourful sofas and elaborately-patterned Middle Eastern rugs. Deep-fried tofu with chilli dips was being served as a snack by a catering company who were all dressed all in black and wearing metallic gold animal face masks. There was a pool house which looked more like a rainforest, so crammed full was it of tropical vegetation. A music system, which I never actually found, pumped 70's rock music throughout the whole house. Luxury is easy to get used to - it took us about one minute.

There was a superb bar set in a games room, not much smaller than a pub, which we instinctively gravitated towards. Things went the way of most parties - respectable chat for a couple of hours then, as darkness fell and the drink took hold, things got a bit wilder.

Tasteful French art deco silver plates with lines of Peruvian marching powder were passed around by the waiters as though it was After Eight mints.

I don't remember now how it started but about 12 of us decided to play a tournament of strip Fusball. Fusball, as you probably know, is table football. Where they got the Fus from I don't know. Every time you lost a game you had to take something off. This meant that you could only lose three or four times, if you were wearing socks, before you were naked. I'm terrible at table football and was wearing no underwear - I haven't got the wrists for it (Fusball that is, not underwear) so it wasn't long before I was naked as a razor, as was everyone else by the end of the tournament. Even the winners.

This probably sounds acutely embarrassing now, but life was so strange and wild that it just wasn't. We seemed to have lapsed into this freewheeling, million-dollar hippie lifestyle very easily for four working-class northern lads. We had nothing to lose and only a good time to gain.

Naturally, when you've got a room full of mostly naked people under the age of 30 all playing table football or darts, some hanky and indeed panky started to develop. A woman with a tattoo of a dragon on her thigh took Hunter by the hand and gave him the most unusual of Xmas presents.

After a bit of foreplay she rubbed some finest Colombian nose candy in his old man - right down what your doctor would call your piss hole. Now this has a remarkable effect - it gives you an erection for at least 12 hours. It just doesn't go down no matter what you do or how often you do it and, believe me, Hunter did everything he could to make it go flaccid.

At some point I fell asleep under a large table in the kitchen. When I woke up I discovered someone had rested my head on a large aubergine, like it was a vegetable pillow. I was still naked and now somewhat chilly. I went in search of my clothes but couldn't find them anywhere. I grabbed an Indian blanket from a sofa, wrapped it round me and went in search of the others. Tony was swimming naked except for his cowboy boots with a new lady friend. He hadn't slept all night and was as wired as a fusebox.

Lenny was in Rachel's bedroom doing unspeakable things with one of those big church candles, there were bodies everywhere half asleep on floors and sofas, the smell of cannabis and coffee filled the air. I felt like I was in a dream. I was still utterly stoned.

I wandered up to the top floor of the house, marvelling at the opulence of the place. A huge stained-glass window at the top of the landing depicted Jimi Hendrix playing a Stratocaster as The Beatles, Mama Cass and lots of other 60's rock stars looked up at him.

Suddenly Hunter emerged from a bathroom.

"Aye aye big man," I said. "You okay?"

He said nothing but shook his head, then pointed at his suspiciously bulging jeans crotch.

"What's the matter?"

"It'll not go down man. I feel fuckin' faint. There's not enough blood left in me body. I've been having cold showers trying to make it go away." He suddenly hit himself in the crotch in frustration.

"Well I tell you one thing Hunter. A permanent erection is a hell of a Christmas present to get from a lass."

"Aye it's true like - better than a bottle of Old Spice anyway."

"Yeah, but much more difficult to wrap."

Later that day we had been invited to play in a Brits v Yanks football match on the beach. Hunter was still in a state of

94

arousal. He was pale and drained. He said it now actually hurt and was turning a funny colour - well, a funnier colour than usual.

He didn't feel up to running so we stuck him in goal. During the first half a big strapping local lad burst through our still-stoned defence and volleyed the ball goalwards. It struck Hunter full square between the legs. It was one of those nasty ones where everyone instinctively gives a low groan of empathy. He collapsed to the sand. We ran up and found him making a funny gurgling noise. I rolled him over. He was laughing. His engorgement had finally receded. A swift blow to the bollocks had done the trick.

Once again, football had come to the rescue. Ever was it thus, eh.

I can't imagine what it must be like to support a football team that wins things all the time. I'm convinced it's worse than supporting a club like the Boro because when we beat a side like Arsenal or we have a modicum of achievement, it feels so brilliant precisely because it is so rare an event. Whereas the big teams fans expect to win and so they can never really experience the joy of it quite as intensely as we do.

I think that's largely true of much in life. You need light and shade. Balance out the chocolate cake with a boiled potato. Or something. You know what I mean. After you've been cranking out electric riffs for a few hours, it's nice to do an acoustic set.

This piece is set in Jedburgh, which is a slightly odd town because in the winter it has a pleasurably melancholic, plain, dour windswept border town feel about it but in the summer it's full over-60's coach tours looking for tea and toilets and maybe a bag of chips if they're feeling adventurous. They all pile into the Edinburgh Woollen Mill shop with an eagerness that would lead you to believe they have never even seen wool before let alone donned a cardigan. Most of the knitwear is probably made in China now and the wool probably comes from New Zealand so there's nothing intrinsically Scottish about it any more but that doesn't seem to matter to the knitwear hungry old 'uns.

In this piece I confess my affection for ginger; the hair, not the root – though that's brilliant as well. It may be a rare thing but I find the combination of copper hair and white, almost translucent skin fascinating on a naked woman (less so on Mick Hucknall) and a pair of them together was a kind of ginger heaven.

I am not a gloater by nature. I shall not be strutting around; shouting the odds, either literally or metaphorically, after the Boro inflicted the first domestic defeat of the season over Arsenal on Tuesday. But for the rest of the season it will remain a small, warming sensation inside me, like a baked potato in the underpants.

A small victory in a hard world is worth a lot. For once in your life you feel like you're ahead. For once, fleetingly, you feel magnificent. Although you know it may never be this good again, just the knowledge that the odds have, however briefly swung your way, is a brilliant feeling.

Last night as I sat on the sofa, beer and peanut butter sandwiches in hand, grinning at Boro's win like a man who had sat on his wife's vibrating egg, my mind wandered back to a night of similar, elusive, unexpected and fleeting glory in Jedburgh many, many years ago. What do you mean you don't know where Jedburgh is? Jedburgh is the last town you go through before entering Scotland going north on the A68. It's got an Edinburgh Woollen Mill and everything. It's a fine Border town, even if the biting cold wind that whips off the Cheviots can freeze your scrotum to your thigh even in mid July.

Me and the lads in the band had taken the trip north to play at a party that was being held by a friend of a friend of a cleaner who worked in a pub in Seaton Delavel. We knew all the best people.

It took place in a kind of mini baronial palace on the edge of town. It was a big gothic-looking place. The sort of place you might rescue of woman from a locked tower by climbing up her unfeasibly long hair. We half expected to be met by blokes in chain mail with swords but instead we were greeted by a load of Scotsman in kilts and those smart little bum freezer jackets.

After the usual jokes about sporrans and dirks we put the gear up in the ballroom and set about sampling the local poisons.

This was the sort of party where inhibitions were cast aside right from the get go. There was none of the usual prowling around each other by the lads and lasses present. It was full steam ahead necking of the drink, boogying of woogying and hands down pants mode pretty much from when we hit the stage at 10pm.

This was in our early days when we still had a lot of energy and thought we might actually become famous or something. That night we were bloody great. It had to happen once. I even managed to remember all the chords to our curious metal version of the Beatles 'Dr Robert' for the first time, something which I don't think I could do anymore without the book.

In my mind it was a crowd of 500 but it was probably 70 at most. But some fiercesome boogie was performed by all and sundry.

We finished around 1am by doing a 25-minute version of Roadhouse Blues. I once worked out that I have already spent nearly seven days of my life just playing Roadhouse Blues. Sometimes I wake up in a morning and think I'm still playing it. I think it's become part of my DNA now.

I was last off stage after milking this fleeting drunken admiration for all it was worth. I stepped down into the arms of a woman with the most flaming of red hair. Now, as anyone who knows me knows, I like a bit of the old red hair. It looked like her whole head was on fire; either that or she had badly rusted metal hair, which seemed unlikely.

Who she was, what her name was or where she came from I can't remember indeed, I probably never even knew. But the resulting physical encounter in one of the bedrooms was especially memorable. And like waiting for Boro to beat Arsenal, you wait and wait and wait for it to happen but you can't believe it when it actually does. You can't believe it when she whispers those words in your ear, "would you mind if my friend joins us," ah yes, and you turn to see that the also ginger friend is, if anything, even tastier. For that moment you suddenly feel invincible. Even as it happens you know this is one of those rare glory days. They pass you by, in the wink of a young girl's eye, you know.

It was like I was a prime steak dinner for two red setters. I was eaten up and licked clean.

A while later Hunter came looking for me. I was lying asleep still naked on the bed, the women long gone. He grabbed my bollocks to wake me up, he's polite like that. I told him what had happened.

"But you're such an ugly get," he said disbelievingly. "Enjoy it while you can lad, 'cos I bet that never happens to you ever again in your life."

Well he was right of course. But for a few hours I basked in the glow of ego that only being a sex god to two drunken ginger women can give you. Who would have thought Jedburgh was so rock 'n' roll?

And in the same way, soon enough this weeks win will be a distant memory and when we get beat 4-1 at home by the full strength Arsenal side, reality will strike us only too hard but for the moment, let us bask in the hard-earned, much-desired glory of beating the league leaders in their own back yard. Every dog has its day, even if it is with a couple of Red Setters.

I bet everyone has got at least one story to tell of unrequited love. This is mine and it was very nearly requited - if requited is an actual word.

I dragged this story out of the vault before the FA Cup semi-finals in the year that Millwall got to Cardiff without playing a Premiership side, thus proving that cup football isn't always about the best teams winning, it's more about the luck of the draw. It's only in cup football that we're left with any degree of unpredictability in the domestic game now that the league can apparently only be won by one of two or three sides. So rather than being devalued, which is the common view, it should actually be more revered.

Middlesbrough, like most towns, has an Italian community, and Edie was a beautiful part of that community. She seemed impossibly glamorous to me in comparison to the pasty-faced lasses I grew up alongside. I'm told she works in Milan these days as an important banker. And you thought everyone from Teesside ended up in jail didn't you?

I've been remembering a girl called Edie. She came to heart and mind because of this weekend's FA Cup semi-finals.

Edie was from Tuscany. She had thick, dark chocolate hair, mushy pea green eyes, Sangiovese red lips and appeared to be hiding two large butternut squashes under her shirt. In short, she was as near to this young boy's dream woman as it was possible to get. I once nearly, very nearly, had sex with her. The fact that I didn't has been the cause of lifelong pain and regret to me. To be so close to glory but so far away is a very special and peculiar torment.

She'd given me the eyes at a pub in Stockton - I think it was the Berni Inn. I thought it must be fate because in 1978 no-one who was a self-respecting rocker drank in the Berni. I'd probably been dragged in there by a friend who was on the sniff. It was widely regarded as a smoothies pub - full of men in crushed velvet jackets and neatly-ironed Oxford bags who liked to fight after eight pints of Harp and lime, and women with Purdie cuts who liked Abba. To cope with the cultural alienation, I used to put Thin Lizzy's hit 'Don't Believe a Word' on the jukebox, drink Snakebites and try to be aloof.

So I'd got talking to her and it turned out she was a cut above your average Teesside lass, even though, being from an Italian family, she did smell intensely and richly of garlic. In 1978 garlic was as foreign to Teessiders as moon rock. This was a time before Pizza Hut, Deep Pan Pizza, Pizza Express or indeed pizza-face. This was a time when we still thought black pudding was exotic and that Tudor's finger-staining steak 'n'onion crisps were as good as actual real steak. We thought a battered sausage was the height of culinary sophistication. The only foreign food we had eaten in our lives was a Vesta Chow Mein.

But I didn't care about the garlic aroma. Let's face it lads, we'd ignore anything if we think there's a chance of mutual downage of underwear. Anyway, I considered myself to be a broadminded sophisticated lad, albeit one whose arse was hanging out of his threadbare jeans.

I thought I knew a bit about Italian culture having long been a fan of progressive rockers PFM, who sang in Italian (except on Chocolate Kings - an album I highly recommend to all proggers). I knew Gianni Rivera was the best Italian footballer bar none, I could tell the difference between oregano and parsley in my mam's herb garden and I'd once got drunk on wine. So I thought I was culturally well-equipped to handle going out with an Italian from Middlesbrough.

Imagine someone whose voice is a cross between Bob Mortimer and Claudio Ranieri. It was very sexy.

We got on great. We went out a few times (though The Deer Hunter was probably a bad choice for a date movie), then she asked me round her house one afternoon when her mama was out. This was in one of the leafy, posh parts of Middlesbrough (yes, they do exist). One thing led to another, as it inevitably does in a linear universe, and we had retired to her bedroom to do what the younger generation would now call 'the nasty'. We knew it better as plain old-fashioned humping. Clothes were removed, everything was perfect.

There was much fiddling, rubbing and poking, as is traditional on such occasions, and I was just about to get in the saddle when there was the quite unmistakable sound of footsteps on the stairs.

Carry On film tradition requires the bloke to leave via a window and a drainpipe clutching underpants and shoes. However, this being real life, that didn't happen. Instead, almost as soon as we'd heard the footsteps, her mother opened the door. The first thing she must have seen was my bare and blemished arse, as I was still frozen between her one and only daughter's splayed legs, condom on, ready for action. For a fleeting second I thought if I just stayed very still she might not spot me. It is to such insanities that you cling in moments of desperation.

Inevitably, she exploded in a roar of shock and awe.

But I was an argumentative teenager, an ornery sod when I wanted to be. Which probably explains why I said, "Howay, don't overact, it's all perfectly natural."

This didn't go down well. There was much screaming in Italian.

As I gathered my clothes together I hoped fervently that the family didn't have any Mafioso connections. There was even more high-pitched screaming and general outrage between mother and daughter as I hastily pulled on my pants, still wearing aforementioned condom (well, it seemed just too vulgar to pull it off in front of her) half throat-cuttingly embarrassed, half amused to death by the situation. I was ushered, now fully clothed, to the door and told in no uncertain terms to never darken their door or sheets again. I'd gone from glory to heartache in about two minutes.

I saw her again a couple of weeks later and we had a laugh about it all, but there was no way we could see each other without her family exploding. So we drifted apart and that was the end of our affair. For months afterwards the disappointment of being so near glory was physically painful and even now I look back on it with a stab of pain in my heart for what might have been - this may just be a build-up of cholesterol in my arteries though.

If you like, I had reached the semi-final but failed to get to the glory of the final. I'd done all the hard work. There's nothing worse than losing at that stage. Even if you get to the final and perform badly, at least you got there.

And this is an apposite lesson for the up-and-coming FA Cup semi-finals. A semi-final leaves you with nothing. You don't appear in the record books even as a runner-up. You're nothing. You might as well have lost in the third round and concentrated on the the league. All that temptation of glory was just a diversion that messed with your mind. It is the worst of all situations. Much like going to a Berni Inn in that respect.

2004 was an epic season for Boro fans. We fucking won something, son! It was shocking and bloody marvellous and I think even neutral fans enjoyed our success in the League Cup.

And, though the final against Bolton was monumental, that of course happened in Cardiff. For me, the big game was the semi-final leg at the Riverside against Arsenal; a side that regularly spanked us by four goals.

It was a big day from the start. It was a day of reunions and a day for celebrating the past and hoping for better things in the future. For one evening it felt like Middlesbrough was all one big family who all knew each other, all felt the same and all celebrated together. We partied in the streets and the pubs and the sheer bloody joy of actually getting to the final of a major trophy was so overwhelming that it felt like something really important had happened.

The only parallel experience I have had was the night in 1997 when Labour won their landslide victory, finally shedding the country of the loathsome Tories after 18 years.

Then we did it all again on the way to the UEFA Cup final in two home games which frankly stretched credulity, reality and sanity.

I have only just sobered up and put my trousers back on after Tuesday night's spine-tingling and utterly glorious victory for the Toxic Teessiders.

It was the finest night I remember at the Boro, better even than all those promotions from Division One, finer than the semi-finals in the 90's.

Such nights are the very lifeblood of the game outside of football's superpowers and I think they should be celebrated by all fans of the non-footballing elite. They're a throwback to a time when football was more democratic, more varied and less predictable, when glamour didn't mean money, power and ladyboy haircuts. And in the week that Bob Stokoe - a true working-class hero of the game - died, it was more than appropriate that Middlesbrough, possibly the least fashionable club in the Premiership, or indeed the whole of Western Europe, should have laid low a side that's in a different league in every way.

Bob Stokoe took 250-1 Second Division outsiders Sunderland to FA Cup glory in 1973. Their 1-0 win over Leeds was a quintessential 70's moment - all sideburners, unkempt hair, guts and mud-caked glory. Even for us on Teesside it was somehow a proud and scarcely believable moment that no-one would forget for the rest of their lives. Cheers Bob.

Tuesday's win at the Riverside brought back those days to me. It was utterly magnificent. More magnificent even than the second guitar break in the Atlanta Rhythm Section's version of the song 'Spooky' and you know how tasty that is...don't you?

I arrived on Teesside to be met at the station by Lenny and Tony who had flown back from California specially. We had all taken superstitious precautions in an attempt to appease the Arsenal-biased gods. I was wearing my Wishbone Ash 'Live Dates' t-shirt - it's 28 years old now and mostly decayed through excessive exposure to my especially-corrosive sweat. It's also now skintight, cuts the blood off to my armpits and is about four inches short of my waistline. In short, it looks more like a sports bra. Not that I've ever worn a sports bra. Actually, that's not true, but there lies another tale. But I'd worn it in '76 when we won the much-coveted Anglo-Scottish Cup so I decided to draw on its clearly powerful properties once again.

Lenny had his lucky school tie which he wore to every match in the 73-74 Big Jack promotion year. Tony said he was wearing Boro knickers, claiming that though he'd never worn them to a football match, he did regularly score in them, and this surely was a good sign.

Over three pre-match pints we all assumed we were turning up to witness another four-goal defeat. We didn't think Arsene Wenger would put out a ropey old side again and when we learned he had, it was greeted with both relief and some annoyance. There was a touch of taking the piss about it. It was as though they were saying 'we don't need our first XI to beat Middlesbrough'. Well it turns out you do, Arsene. Sorry about that. I know your focus is on bigger and grander projects. You didn't have to turn up at all if it was all a bit too stressful on your delicate players, mate.

There was certainly no need to wake Mr Keown up from the retirement home; you know how the modern world frightens him, especially young bald Italians who run fast towards him. That being said, apart from being too lazy to track back for our first goal, Patrick Vieira was superb in a frankly poor midfield. Nice of Jose Reyes to pop his cherry for us at the Riverside too with an own goal, though I thought local lad Stuart Parnaby had scored the winner and was nearly in tears at the poetry of it all.

As we left the ground we were all agreed that the only downside of this momentous victory was the increased chances of Bernie Slaven baring his arse in Binn's windows again. The Yin to the Yang of any Boro success.

I don't think anyone was sober in Middlesbrough. It was like VE day, people were kissing complete strangers and doing strange dances, though actually that happens in Middlesbrough on most nights at chucking-out time. I saw a man dancing with an Afghan hound, he had it up on its hind legs holding its front paws and did a brief waltz. On reflection, it may have been an especially hairy woman, but nonetheless it was a night for extraordinary happenings.

There were drunken re-enactments of Keown's rugby tackle on Maccarone which looked more like a clip from 'You've

Been Framed' than something you'd see on a football pitch. A grown man kissed the television, with tongues and everything, when the results came on the local news. Tony lowered his trousers to reveal his girly Boro panties at a taxi rank and got his arse slapped by Ormsby Alice - even the coppers laughed at that. Everything seemed beautiful suddenly. Even the Cleveland Centre briefly stopped looking like a 60's planner's bad trip.

If Arsenal had won, their fans could not have felt anywhere as joyful as we did. When you're bloated on victories and success, you just don't have the hunger. For us this was success wrenched from season after season of mediocrity, of being bored witless by the football at the Riverside. One fan fell asleep, pissed out of his head, when we played Arsenal in August, and has since been banned from the ground - not for being asleep but for being drunk. Clearly, the management of MFC hadn't realised that intoxication and sleep have been the only two things that made supporting the Boro these past few years tolerable.

If I had one wish, it would be that modern football could deliver this kind of unpredictable steaming excitement regularly instead of being a cakewalk for the same three teams. It's nights like this that gives football its true glamour. It's the diamond in the coal. It's the grit that makes the pearl.

When all is one and one is all, to be a rock and not to roll.

23. PLASTIC PEOPLE OH BABY NOW YOU'RE SUCH A DRAG
18/03/04

The best football is like the best rock 'n' roll; fearless, wild and thrilling. But as simple as this might sound, a lot of people haven't a bloody clue what I mean when I talk about rock 'n' roll football. This was an attempt to explain it all. I will confess I am in love with the whole romantic notion of being in a band and playing chords E, Am and D to a few pissed punters, and add into that my love for all things Californian and you get pieces like this one.

Over the years I've had a lot of e-mails from people in bands who know exactly what I'm talking about when I talk about the code of the road and the unity of being in a band; it's a unity forged in inebriation that stays strong through good times and through those other times when you could happily kill each other. It must be similar to being in a football team, only without the stretch Hummers and women called Pinot Grigio of course. And you tend not to spend so much time naked in a big bath with all your mates too often either. Well we didn't anyway.

Personally, I've never understood how anyone can live a life doing a 9-5 job. I'm glad someone is there to do all the stuff that needs to be done but I just couldn't do it. I couldn't live like that and I couldn't have someone telling me what to do all the time. I am an ornery bugger though.

Hanging out, not being in a hurry and having no appointments is how I like to live my life. I've never been bothered about kids, a career, keeping up with the neighbours or wearing the right clothes, so I was a natural at a life of rock 'n' roll-based dissolution.

I remember when it was first published an e-mail came in to F365 which simply said, "What the hell was all that about?" Maybe I should write some York study notes.....

"Are you mellow inside? Can you make it through the night? It's the code of the road. Pull, no matter the load."

For those of you not familiar with the extensive back catalogue of Nils Lofgren, this is the chorus from one of his best compositions. It's a ripping little tune and one we used to play regularly in the band. It seemed to concisely express the essence of touring and being on the road. Only "Good golly Miss Molly, she sure likes the bone," has the same ring of universal truth.

There's a unique mixture of glory and heartache when you're travelling round in a van with a band. It's sometimes romantic and it's sometimes brilliant. When you're on the road, there's a different Highway Code. You do feel like a cowboy riding into town on your steel horse...especially when you're touring America. Admittedly, it's very hard to feel like a cowboy when you're sitting in a service station on the M69, but certainly much easier when you pull into a diner in the middle of the Mojave Desert.

One of the best things about the whole thing is that while others are on their way to work, caught up in the 9-5, you're lying on your back in a motel room, possibly with a lady on top of you doing all the work. The good people of the world are going about their daily business but all you wanna do is have some fun. There's no-one to tell you otherwise.

Your day doesn't start till 8pm, so you've got plenty of time to lie around and be philosophical about life, and if this involves hanging out in beachside diners and bars which play The Black Crowes at high volume, then so much the better. When it's good, it's hard not to feel smug. You've got nothing to do, it's up to you, you've nothing to say, but it's okay.

Weeks come and go like the ebbing of the Pacific Ocean. The day destroys the night, the night divides the day. Night arrives with her purple legion and the freaks come out to play.

But then there comes a time when it's the last thing you want. You get sick of the rootless nature of it all, being around the same people all the time. You tire of seeing pretty people play, hungry for power to light their neon way and give them things to do. Then there's the endless intoxication. Newcastle Brown can sure knock you down. Sometimes, you just want to be still and be sober and not have the smell of a stranger on your fingers. The rooms smell like hotel illness and all you feel is down while the town gets high.

Nights when not even another version of 'Bad To The Bone' will give you your spark. Nights when playing a messy version of Al Kooper's classic 'I Just Can't Keep From Crying Sometimes' is the only thing that keeps you from going a little south of sanity. But you still can't remember how to play Ry Cooder's 'The Very Thing That Makes You Rich Makes Me Poor' despite the fact that it seems to be the most profound statement of the human condition.

That's when you know it's time to go home. Take the next exit out of town and leave your angels, your devils, the thorns in your pride. Time to stop hanging out with vultures and empty saviours and misers who make love with their wealth.

Now if it's like that for someone on the very lowest rung of rock 'n' roll's ladder, I wonder if it's the same for Premiership footballers? As any of my long-suffering readers will know I've always thought there was a fundamental connection between football and rock 'n' roll. Is the start of a season like the start of each tour; full of optimism and hope? Everything seems possible. But slowly the decay begins after a humiliating defeat. It's a long slide from glory to mediocrity. It's a long journey from hope to despair but hey, the time passes quickly. Then you suddenly find that small victories become big things and the big things become impossibilities.

So is there still a fundamental connection between football and rock 'n' roll? Some of the players clearly live a life of part-time dissolution and are no strangers to the Red House over yonder. And the pack mentality is clearly still strong, even if they've got some way to go to match a typical week in the life of Motley Crue circa 1986.

And even if Footballers' Wives is a vivid, gaudy, amyl nitrate-laced invention, it still has some ring of truth. Okay, not the death by fucking, the hermaphrodite babies or the women called Cabernet Sauvignon (though they do sound like the essential ingredients for a Janes Addiction song). No, I mean the whole vibe; the plastic fantastic world, the worship of money above soul. The hard-eyed women with fake blonde hair and high cheekbones who somehow look like transvestites.

The world of cock tattoos is as at home in football's highest echelons as it is in rock 'n' roll. And of course football, like rock 'n' roll, has its groupies. Even in Barnsley. I remember reading the German bloke who kept goal for them in the Premiership's account of how routinely women would come up to him even when he was with his wife and ask him for sex. This is Barnsley. And I can't even remember the bloke's name he was that famous.

So yeah maybe rock 'n' roll and football are sometimes still close relations, but there is a crucial difference and things are changing. Footballers rarely get any better with practise after about age 23. If you can't cross a ball by then, you won't be much better at it in five years' time. This isn't because you can't get better by practising; it's just that footballers don't practise enough. A couple of hours training a day are nothing. Sometimes their vision and reading of the game improves but their skill rarely does. I couldn't name you one player who can cross a ball successfully nine times out of ten...why not?

Some players like Jesper Gronkjaer who are actually specifically employed to do this seem to have treated their position as a professional footballer with something amounting to contempt, so inconsistent and plainly unskilled are they at the art they've been employed to deploy. How can you so repeatedly hit a cross so long that it goes out for a throw-in? Footballers have nothing else to learn except how to play football. They've few other calls on their time apart from occasionally pissing into a jar - and some of them can't even be arsed to do that. So why don't they sweat blood to get better? Why don't they work on being two-footed?

There's nothing more embarrassing than seeing someone like Ryan Giggs desperately trying to get the ball on his left foot because the right one swings like a dead ham. Why do players routinely kick the ball lamely into the wall at free-kicks? Why can't they learn to not do that? It's the same scenario every time. Did Beckham get good at free-kicks by accident? No he just practised for hours. Most others can't do it because it involves dedication, skill and hard work - all three of which you can apparently get by without in football.

If you're in a crap band, which can't cut it live, you won't earn jackshit, mister. Frankly, there's nothing like a few months on the road to get your chops together (and I ain't talking about boy bands here - standing in a row with a smart suit and careful haircut doing a line each from a song is not being in a band no matter how 'wild' Westlife claim to be on the road).

And of course the worst thing about this is that footballers are paid at least half a million quid a year, even if you're a Leicester City player, to be this ordinary. Rock 'n' roll, like football, is the only profession where you can be ludicrously paid for a job which entails no more than 16 hours a week. The difference is, there are still so many in football who insist that they are still overworked and tired despite the fact that they do almost nothing, almost all of the time. It's a pathetic whine.

At least your average guitarist has the good grace to admit that he spends his time off-stage lying around, getting blown by women called Mercy, hoovering drugs up his nose and generally living H on the H.

Football used to have some spirit back in the days when it was a mean old jezebel. Now the players are more concerned with style, appearance, designer labels and money, it's quickly losing its edgy, raw, emotional rock 'n' roll vibe.

It's getting superseded at all levels by corporate culture. But maybe that's what the people want today. After all, Dido's album is number one...

24. KIDNAPPING WOMEN FROM TEWKESBURY
08/04/04

We live in weird times, although things go along pretty much as they have done for centuries. There are wars about religion and money, people still get born, live and die and try to make the best of it along the way. Nothing much changes but now it all happens on TV and in the papers.

And that's the weird thing. The cult of celebrity is so voracious and hypnotises so many people that ordinary life gets reported as though it's shocking or somehow fascinating. Maybe if you've grown up with this culture it all just seems normal, but to me, it seems like a form of insanity.

I guess it's all part of the huge expansion of all media in the last ten years. Thousands of pages and hours of programming has to be filled with something and so eventually, after the genuinely interesting stuff has all been used up, you get down to reporting footballers shopping in Harvey Nichols or discussing what handbag Wayne Rooney's girlfriend has just bought.

I vividly recall Spike Milligan saying about ten years ago that eventually, when all the other ideas have run out, someone will do a programme called 'Guess The Celebrity Arsehole'. Dozens of has-beens and never-likely-to-bes would put their arses up to the camera and you'd have to guess whose it is. It could be called 'Through The Arsehole'. It sounded like madcap comedy at the time but now I can seriously see it happening. Soon.

Do you feel like a freak? Do you feel marginalised? Are weird thoughts going through your head? Does the world around you seem to be slightly unreal? Does everything everyone else is doing seem slightly mad to you? Do you, every day, stare at people and wonder 'why are you so feckin' stupid?'?

Well here's the shocking news. You're not alone. Welcome to the mainstream and you're fine, you're sane. It's just the media that have messed our heads up. I have some experience of this...

It's a warm sunny August evening back in 1980 and we're pulling out of Tewksbury after a day gallivanting round pubs annoying landlords by putting Rush's 'Temples Of Syrinx' on the jukebox. I'm with a fat lad called Humpty and his band Metal Machine as a roadie and we're on our way to Shrewsbury for another noisy humiliation in front of a small number of people. There's six of us in a 1972 twin-wheeled transit van along with amps, musical instruments and bags of wires that no-one ever used but seemed to go everywhere with us anyway. It's a tight squeeze but Humpty pulls up to pick up two hitchhikers on the outskirts of town.

This was back in the days when you could hitchhike relatively safely without everyone thinking you were an illegal immigrant, a terrorist or a paedophile on the run. It was two sisters - in their late teens, crimped-haired (very popular at the time) and jeans so tight that they must have been restricting blood flow to their legs. They were not without good looks if you liked heavy metal ladies who smelled of Pernod and frangipani oil...which luckily we did. Mind you, we also liked women who smelled of brown ale, chips and coal tar soap. We couldn't afford to be choosy.

God knows why they got in the back of a van full of patchouli-stinking grebos but, like I said, these were more innocent, trusting times.

However, we did have a case of Heineken, some of Zippy the bass player's mam's diet pills (loaded with low-grade amphetamine) and a Tupperware box of Humpty's mam's scones which, though not strictly edible, were hard enough to be very useful for killing things that were edible, such as pigeons. We introduced ourselves to the girls with our trademark cheery, beery northern bonhomie. They appeared fearless, possibly because they were half-cut on Pernod and they could swear like a docker.

Now I know what you're already thinking, that this is another tale of sweaty, grubby sexual congress, perversion or indiscretion involving inanimate objects, vegetables and possibly a greased pig...well, you'd be wrong this time. This was back in 1980 don't forget, it was a more innocent time before we learned how to coax underwear off complete strangers in less than ten minutes.

So there we sat all very polite if a bit squashed, sharing lager with these two sisters. They were nice enough, quite posh really. They came with us to Shrewsbury, where we said our goodbyes.

We thought no more of them until after that evening's gig when two coppers came into the pub and asked if we'd been the blue twin-wheeled transit that had been spotted giving a lift to two women outside of Tewkesbury. It turned out that the sisters had run away from home and were the daughters of a prominent JP.

We had to go and answer a lot of questions at, as is traditional, the station. They split us all up and questioned us individually about the girls. For a while I think they thought we'd kidnapped them. Being a bunch of odiferous long-haired geezers who looked like they were - and indeed given half the chance would be - up to no good, we probably fitted the bill.

Anyway, we convinced them that this wasn't the case and that we were just being kind-hearted lads, albeit with the ulterior motive of getting in their knickers if we did but know how such a thing might be done. After midnight, they let us go back to the field we were camping in - this being a time of extreme poverty.

In the morning, we went into town for essentials - Rizlas, cheap-but-strong Armadillo sherry and Mars bars. While getting the confectionery from a newsagent I spotted the local newspaper - you know the kind of thing, the ones where it has massive headlines about a local dog that has got the longest tail in the county or some such irrelevance.

There on the front page was a headline which read 'Rock Band Questioned By Police' and the story told of how a 'well-known touring rock band' had been questioned the previous day about the two missing daughters of well-known local JP Lord Dogbreath of Winalot or whatever his name was. We were called 'long-haired heavy metal hell-raisers'! Only two of us had long hair and we couldn't have raised hell even if we'd tried.

But it read well and sounded good and played up to a familiar stereotype. How they'd managed to make anyone believe that a hell-raising rock band would be touring Shropshire is anyone's guess but it's a small world in a small world. We laughed about it at the time but this was an early lesson to me in not believing everything you read. It has only got worse since 1980.

In fact, it amazes me at all that anyone bothers to buy newspapers anymore, littered as they are with lies, distortions, implications and opinion dressed up as fact. Of course, the football pages are no less guilty of this than the news pages - where everything about Britain is always in crisis.

You'd think we lived in a perpetual state of crippling anarchy if you believed the papers and the TV. Currently in crisis, according to various newspapers in the last week alone, are the NHS, teaching, further education, student loans, railways, roads, all public services, pensions, council tax, immigration, arse sizes and, of course, football.

The country is awash with terrorists and the nation is stuffed to the gills with drugs, alcohol, pizza and junk food. Children are all out-of-control illiterate morons who smoke fags and sniff cocaine off the pregnant-again swollen bellies of legions of single mothers called Tracey from Liverpool.

Of course in the real world we live in every day, almost none of this is anywhere near as bad as it's sold to us by the sensationalist headline-obsessed, pumped-up media. In fact, Britain has never been more stable and prosperous, which, as anyone who grew up in the 60's and 70's with no central heating, an outside bog and income tax of 83%, will tell you. A record amount of kids' books were sold last year, there's more people working than ever before and we're living longer than ever despite being two pant sizes bigger than we were in the skinny-ass 70's. Oh and almost everything is cheaper in real terms than it was 20 years ago as was brought home to me when I found a receipt of £1500 for a Pentium 133 computer in 1996.

The media is so bloated and self-obsessed that the truth has become marginalised. Worse than this, the sheer weight of the media obsession with celebrity is turning a whole section of society who read Heat, Nuts or Twat, or whatever trashy bollocks you care to name, into braindead zombies.

An alien would think that all of us - every one of us - cared about David Beckham and his wife and what they are or are not doing, because it's reported at such length and in such detail. But here's the feckin' truth - most of us don't give a shiny shite. They could be shaving baby goats and wearing them as a hat for all I care. I really, really don't care and how many people do you know who really do care? Are there any at all?

It's not as if Beckham bought Aleister Crowley's old gaff Boleskin Manor on the shores of Loch Ness, tattooed 'do what thou wilt shall be the whole of the law' onto his forehead and began leading black masses in order to call up demon spirits, is it?

This and most other footballer stories are all exactly the same: Footballer got drunk, footballer had sex with woman - this is mundane, ordinary stuff but it's pumped up into a frothing orgy of indulgence.

But in the parallel universe of Media Land this is all big stuff. And journos are literally incontinent with excitement about something that is utterly irrelevant and uninteresting. It happens all the time. The more trivial and inconsequential the better.

If a small problem is always called a crisis, if the mundane is portrayed as shocking and if saying, "I like the sunshine, me", is said to mean, "I want a transfer to Real Madrid", then it makes a mockery of any form of communication.

Worse still it leaves you with no words to describe a genuine crisis or problem and so it renders the press useless as anything more informative than six pints pub gossip. So here's an idea; instead of reporting speculation and invention and opinion masquerading as fact, just report the facts. And why don't we stop buying newspapers until they do just report the facts? Not what they think the facts will be, could be or might be if something else equally unlikely and irrelevant happens, but what they really, really are. In other words, report what has happened and nothing more. Within a week the whole way journalism operates would have to change. Leave all the mindless gossip and pontification to us, when we're drinking beer or supping tea and eating toast.

We often forget that one of the best things about a brutal capitalist economy is that we, the people, really have the power if we just choose to exercise it. If everyone stopped buying the Star or the Sun or the Mail, we could have them shut down. The same goes for McDonalds, Coca-Cola or Hello magazine. So remember, we have the power - do you really need that copy of the Star or the Sun? Remember you're paying Brian Woolnough's wages - can you live with that knowledge?

We get the reality we allow to be created. We can change it if we can only quit lying on the sofa masturbating, sober up and stop eating pizza long enough to be bothered. But can we be arsed?

As any of my keener readers know, I like to go on long and intoxicating trips around America and this piece was written during a three-and-a-half day journey across the country on Amtrak from Sacramento to Chicago. It was one of those journeys that you know is going to be legendary in your life even as it unfolds. You know it's something you will never forget.

Two of us were cramped up in a small sleeper cabin periodically being berated by this massive black guy who seemed to run the train along the lines of a front-line battle unit in Vietnam. We all had to dutifully file into the dining car in the right, prescribed order or we'd get shouted at. The toilets backed up after two days and by the time we pulled into Chicago almost nothing was working. We'd broken down for 12 hours out east of Reno in the heart of the desert (sounds like a Johnny Cash song doesn't it?) and there was nothing we could do and nowhere we could go and it was 110 degrees outside.

We pulled into a small town out on the plains of Missouri and people all came to the train with boxes of fruit and other goodies to sell like it was 1850 and they were itinerant traders plying their wares.

We met people from all over the country; hippies from 'Frisco; very religious but meek people from Wisconsin and gay students from LA. We sat and yakked with them all. It was all so far from the stereotype of America we get in Europe. I loath the vilification of the States by the liberal left in the West. I resolutely refuse to fall out of love with the country just because from time to time they elect a president or a government I don't like much.

The America I love is the America of Willie Nelson, Miles Davis, Buddy Guy and the Grateful Dead and Dylan and Lynyrd Skynyrd. The America of Hunter Thompson and P.J. O'Rourke and Kerouac, of Easy Rider, Manhattan and The Sunshine Boys. The America of Jerry Seinfeld, George Carlin and Jack Lemmon. The America that is forever riding out on the western plain that defends freedom and lets you be who you can be but doesn't hide behind gated communities. I still buy the deal. It's all still out there somewhere.

I am always enthused by most Americans' lust for life, their refreshing lack of cynicism and their innate belief that anything is possible and that you have the right to dream. They're usually very polite and on this trip, most of them were keen to present themselves and their country in a positive light, often even keener to say, "we're not like the stupid Americans you've heard about". But it wasn't necessary. I've been around long enough to know that stupidity has no national or geo-political boundaries. Now if only they could get into football a bit more.

At the time the 2004 European Championship was going on and England were falling at the quarter-final stage again. Unlike any other journey I had made out there the invention of the laptop and a mobile internet connection meant I could stay up to date with what was happening. When I caught some action in a bar, it led to many interesting discussions and a lot of good, high old times......

I'm a cowboy. On a steel horse I ride. Actually, make that 'in' a steel horse I ride.

Through the Midwest of America I'm rolling on down the line. Through the anonymous burning hot summer days and the dark steamy nights on an 80-hour Amtrak sleeper train trip from

Sacramento to Chicago and I'm on a slow but methodical bender, listening to Tangerine Dream during the night and Van Halen during the day as we wind through the heartlands of America.

You can't sleep - there's too much to see and yet there's nothing to see. As Nevada gives way to Utah and Utah fades into Colorado which in turn becomes Nebraska, the land stretches out infinite and bleak and fascinating, in a way that somehow brings to mind watching Darlington play football.

We're going through two time zones, or is it three, and what the hell is a time zone anyway? How does time get changed, man? So I'm pretty messed up. This may be due to the vast quantity of Bud Lite I've consumed, which if you've never drank it, is not dissimilar to drinking one part water, one part lager and one part dog piss. You have to drink at least eight pints of the stuff before you notice the slightest effect and the indigenous people think we're insane to be able to drink so much of it. But hell, it's 100 degrees in the shade out there and no-one on board can make tea to save their lives so what are we supposed to do to keep hydrated? Drink iced tea? Bah! I think not my colonial cousins.

To pass the time we're playing 'spot the largest pair of buttocks' as we pass through towns. This is what I am calling the inaugural Titus Bramble Award.

The leader so far is a woman in Sacramento who was wearing white leggings and what looked like a crumpled green tarpaulin as knickers underneath. Her buttocks were in total, and this is no word of a drunken lie, at least four foot across. More weird still was the fact that each buttock was rock hard, not sagging but each was pitted like one of Jupiter's moons with cellulite. This country is Freaksville make no mistake, and it's hard not to love it really for all its quark, strangeness and charm.

I've just spent a few days in the mountains of northern California and saw real-life mountain people who frankly do not appear to have fully evolved yet as humans, so much so that they make Wayne Rooney look like Robert Redford.

We've got nothing like Bubba in Britain. Here's one typical example: A male of the species, apparently hairless, mid-forties, a big fat face like an 18-month-old baby, weighs at least 20 stone. Walks down the street wearing a huge pair of denim shorts that stretch from his knees to his armpits and are held up with rope braces hooked through the belt loops. I'm not making this up. He's bald, shirtless but has big black boots on and pristine white socks. It's 100 degrees in the shade but he's not sweating.

I'm so shocked that I can't take my eyes off him. It's like a car crash as he walks up Old Highway 53 in Clearlake with his wife/mother/ape thing who is 4' 10", wears glasses so thick they make her eyes the size of a boxer's fist and appears to have got caught up in some old curtains. I guess it was a dress once back in '65 maybe. She's staring around her wildly and thrashing her arms about as though fending off a flying fish attack.

And I thought growing up on Teesside was weird.

Clearlake could not be named more inaccurately as its lake is not only not clear, it is bright green with algae in the summer making it look like a giant bowl of pea soup.

The great thing about being in a country where most people have no idea about football is the funny and often unanswerable questions you get asked about the game. I've been keeping notes on these because I'm such a sad git and here's just a selection so far from this tour of duty.

They're all questions we'd like answered I think...

Q: (Asked during Portugal game) Why can't David James catch the ball when it comes in the air from the side?

Q: What exactly does the England manager do?

Q: (Asked after a typical Neviller sprint down the wing) He runs weird. Did he get a bad injury to make him run like that?

Q: So there's no way for England to win if the scores are even?

Q: I thought Beckham was in a guy in a boy band?

Q: (Posed after a Michael Owen miss) Should a goal-getter be that small?

Q: (This one asked by a woman in the Nike store in Vegas) Are Manchester United the same as England?

Q: (Asked after P. Neville came on) Why has a worse player come on the pitch? Is that a rule?

And finally my favourite. Not actually a question but a statement of fact made by someone I can only call Big Girl in a pub in Monterey during a re-run of the Man United v Man City game:

"Most of these soccer players don't look like real men."

No, Big Girl, no they don't.

26. SEX AND THE SINGLE MANAGER
03/08/04

Ah yes, Sven and his magic Swedish nadger. When the history books are written about his reign, there'll not be much about the quite successful if a bit dull football. It will be mostly comprised of steamy tales of between-legs antics. There was always an anti-foreigner agenda for some in the media, especially in the right-wing press like the evil Daily Mail, but it became almost like a 13th Century witch-hunt for the evildoers when this story about Sven, his secretary and his employers all came out in the spring of 2004.

Sven had been having sex with women! My God! Didn't the Vikings do this to our fair ladies over 1,000 years ago? The stupidity reached its peak this particular week when the Mail reported the 'cesspit' at Soho Square and tried to vilify the man just for having it away with a secretary. I mean, it'd never happen in the offices of a national newspaper would it?

I really, really detest this conservative, uptight aspect of British life that some of the press pander to and ferment and I was foaming at the mouth a bit when I wrote this one. How dare the silly old farts at papers like the Daily Mail try and define and dictate how we should behave in the name of selling a few papers to people called Patricia and Nigel from bloody Sunningdale?

Of course, it was just normal life. A bit of shagging, a few white lies and that's it. No-one let off a nuclear bomb, everyone was consenting and used their own organs in the traditional manner. There is a thick seam of moral outrage always waiting to be vomited up to the surface in Britain. Whether the stories are about politicians, movie stars or football managers, it's perpetuated by people who are just not getting enough sex themselves and don't see why all these people should be having such a good time if they can get neither rumpy nor pumpy.

So they try and claim the moral high ground about non-issues like this. Sven, to his credit, looked bewildered to be treated by the press in this way because unlike most of his critics he has a brain. I can imagine him thinking, "what kind of medieval country is this?"

Personally I wish he'd just got his cock out at a press conference and said, "come on then – who wants it next?"

This column is all about sex.

Not the shiny, unreal airbrushed sex you see on the telly or in jazz mags.

I'm talking about sex between older people. 'Older' for the purposes of this discussion is anyone over 40. I know this is not really that old but in terms of the contemporary media, it certainly is.

If you're reading this and you're 19 years old, this will, I know, seem like an unfeasibly long way away. But time and gravity quickly takes its toll and soon your bollocks will be swinging round your knees and it'll take you all night to do what you used to do all night. So pay heed.

Speaking as a slightly wrinkly old 'un meself, I get the impression that popular culture dictates we really shouldn't be doing either the rumpy or the pumpy at our advanced age. We have lines on our faces, our muscles are sagging and strenuous effort of any kind leaves us short of breath. However, not being young is not actually a crime. Not yet.

The demographics show that we baby boomers are living the life of riley, generally blowing the kids' inheritance and behaving in a thoroughly irresponsible manner. But despite this undoubted reality it seems that sexual prurience is behind the newspaper campaigns to get Eriksson, and pretty much everyone else who's over 40 and having sex, the sack.

It's as though in this bizarro world, sex is just wrong or bad or immoral and that a bloke in his 50's being 'outed' as having it is the moral equivalent of buggering puppies in front of the children.

Old blokes like Sven having 'relations' (which are always 'steamy' - perversely I like the idea of Sven having it away so vigorously that his whole body is actually steaming) with their younger secretaries is portrayed in the press as morally repugnant and offensive. On Radio 5, the prattling idiots kept asking female staff what was so attractive about Sven, like women usually only screw Brad Pitt look-a-likes.

But I've got news from the front line; we over 40's are getting our end away far more than you young lads would ever believe and what's more, much to the Daily Mail's distress, we're having a great time doing it, despite the culture of the thin and the young being ever-dominant.

Older blokes have all the advantages. Due to being a bit numb downstairs, we don't, as the Pointer Sisters would have it, 'come and go in a heated rush'. We've got loads more money than 20-year-olds to live high on the hog. We can appear youthful to older birds and experienced and wise to younger women. We've done a lot more stuff in life and are just generally more liberated. We don't really care that much about anything because we know that death's sweet release is only a few decades away.

You might think it's undignified to see us on the town headbanging to Metallica or playing air guitar to the White Stripes but I have to tell you, we're having a superb time and your mockery means nothing to us. We've seen and heard it all before. We will still go out and drink pints of lager and buy UFO records and we will still insist on shagging to Sly and the Family Stone records and the Daily Mail just can't stop us.

I don't read tabloid papers. I get scared that they'll melt my brain into a blob of mush. And anyway, I'm too busy listening to the Faces to read about the latest Eastenders goings-on or anything that involves fat lottery winners from Wakefield. So I have to rely on my well-endowed and gorgeous if dissolute colleagues to document the worst excesses for me.

The Daily Mail is usually the worst offender. Jeff Powell et al like to play at being our moral guardians, protecting us from foreigners and various other evil botters. "No decent person can deny now that Eriksson should promptly follow Palios in being sluiced away as the Soho Square cesspit is disinfected," pukes Powell in a stinking belch of moral outrage.

Remember only two things have happened here; some sex and an inaccurate press release. No-one has died. Everyone was consenting. Sadly for the Mail no asylum seekers or single mothers were involved.

In typical Daily Mail style, it's the inclusion of 'no decent person' that is crucial. It's a way of justifying bigotry when the facts are bland and inoffensive. Elsewhere in the Mail Sven is referred to as 'a skirt-chasing Swede with yellowing buck-teeth, silly rimless glasses and a receding haircut'.

In other words, he looks quite like a lot of 50-odd blokes. He's ordinary. And is there anything more disgusting than ordinary blokes getting their leg over?

While there might be an argument to be had about how good Sven is as England manager, I have yet to meet or even read anyone in the real world who thinks that shagging secretaries is at the high end of the human scale of depravity and degradation. It's normal life going on as normal. Yet, the Mail and others are apoplectic about it and the reason they're apoplectic is because there is a section of British society always teetering on the edge of an outraged orgasm, ready to be appalled by almost anything; everything from the decline of the quality of Marks & Spencer's skirts to working-class women in pubs drinking vodka and kissing with tongues. You know, all the important stuff.

Football is the single biggest cultural event in British life. We're daft beyond reason about it and even people who aren't are affected by it in their everyday lives. So football stories become barometers of the nation's morals. It is as though the very state of the nation is brought down low by Sven's fondness for playing the little fella in the hole.

But in reality it isn't. And away from the Planet Mail it doesn't matter at all. And as ever, we have the power to change all this simply by not buying tabloid newspapers. Within weeks the Mail and their ilk would be gone from our lives. A nice thought, isn't it? So do it.

I'm sure all this hysteria is symptomatic of a deep-seated psychosis. Important stuff is happening that needs addressing - terrorism, war, belly-swollen poverty, the return of the mullet and the domination of tea bags over loose tea (a particular concern to this tea junkie). At best all this sweet FA business is just inflated trivia but at worst it represents just how far some of Britain has to go before it is at ease with itself about the nature of real life on 2004.

It was around this time that we saw the rise of the phenomenon of Citizen Neville. The previous year Red Nev had proposed players go on strike in protest at Rio's suspension after missing his drugs test. In 2004 they refused to talk to the press because The Sun had been terribly childish in their criticisms of David James after an England game. So in a rare gesture of solidarity, they all refused to talk to the press after their next match.

The reaction of outrage from the TV and papers was a pathetic whimper and they totally misread public reaction. Most fans don't give a flying one about what a player has to say after a game. They're largely inarticulate and offer little insight. The media thought we'd be outraged that we couldn't hear from our heroes, but we were really just relieved. If we cared at all.

Thinking of this, of course, led me to a gig we played in Dormanstown with an early line-up of the band before Hairy Tony joined and we became The Beer Pigs, though he was hanging around at the time. We were called Big Riff and played rubbish versions of AC/DC and Quo songs. We were really dreadful and if you saw us, I apologise for the noise.

If you've never been to Dormanstown, I'm assured it's a much nicer place than it was in 1980, but that wouldn't be difficult. It was possibly the roughest town in Europe. We were lucky to get out alive. And all for £20 and a few free pints.

If you've ever had pint glasses thrown at you while you're on a stage trying to play an especially tricky minor 9th suspended jazz chord, it's an experience you'll never forget. Someone is trying to maim you just because they don't like your music. I mean, it's okay not to like the music, but Jesus, do you really want to hurt someone so much just for playing it?

Fortunately these days, you can really only get plastic-ed off in clubs - but it was not always so.

Let us peer back through the swirling mists of time to the freezing cold winter of 1980. A winter so cold that in Newcastle it got down to minus-23 one night, which is especially chilly if you've got a four-foot gaping hole in your kitchen wall as we did at the time for reasons that now escape me. Perhaps the mice had eaten the wall - they'd eaten everything else and had even started to set up a temporary holiday home in the fat-laden grill pan.

We'd struggled down to Teesside in a knackered twin-wheeled transit van with one windscreen wiper, a fuel tank that fell off if you filled it more than half full and no heating. That's what you got for £250 back then.

Ian Hunter once said that it's a mighty long way down rock 'n' roll from the Liverpool docks to the Hollywood bowl, which may well be true, but he forgot to mention it's even further to a club in Dormanstown, Middlesbrough.

Dormanstown in 1980 was the roughest place on God's earth. Beirut had nothing on this. Hunter, our drummer and a local lad, once memorably said that "evil was invented in Dormanstown", and knowing Hunter he probably helped with the recipe.

We set up, cranked everything up to ten and set about battering the 'audience' into submission with our twin guitars of doom. Something odd happened almost right away. People got up and started headbanging. At first I thought this may have just been the locals overdosing on their medication and that it was some sort of collective epileptic seizure. But no, as we ground out third-rate covers of Foghat songs (what do you mean you've never heard of Foghat?) the boozed-up denim and leather locals got their not inconsiderable rocks off and partook in extended heads-down no-nonsense boogie.

131

It must have been the sight of 50 people getting their groove that infuriated one bloke at the back. I was just introducing the next song when I saw a dark shape falling out of the sky. About half a nanosecond before it hit me, I realised what it was and instinctively jumped back just in time to avoid it breaking on my head. Instead it shattered on my arm and made an impressive impromptu bloody version of a Jackson Pollock on my forearm. Fortunately it missed any major arteries but it did make me look like I was a cutter.

As any Englishman would, I told the glass flinger to 'fuck off', but as we kicked into the next number, I noticed I was bleeding on the stage and as rock 'n' roll as this was, I thought it was probably a bad sign. Not as bad a sign as the second glass that hit me on the shoulder and cracked into three sharp shards, mind.

The next few minutes are a bit of a blur - perhaps due to the blood loss - but we reconstructed events later. After being hit by the second glass, Hunter, all 6' 2" of him, left his drums, jumped off the stage and ran to get the glass-thrower, with me and Lenny three steps behind him. Our bass player at the time was a bloke called Ginger and he stayed behind to "watch the gear, lads", which was the best move he made in his short musical career.

Hunter, being big, as mad as a goat, as hard as iron and fiercely protective of his mates, caught the bloke as he was running out of the club, dragged him by the hair down the steps, jammed his head under the front wheel of our van parked out front and told Lenny to get in the cab and start it up, which Lenny duly did.

Naturally the offender was somewhat perturbed by this turn of events and was screaming, "don't kill me". As the engine turned and Lenny revved it, the police arrived. Needless to say we didn't kill the bloke. Everyone was arrested and later released. Glass-throwing and fighting was what passed for social interaction in Dormanstown. I went to hospital and got stitched up, no-one pressed charges and we didn't play there again.

This was far from the only time in the following decade and a half that we encountered hostility to our music, but it was the only time that I was glassed. People would throw all manner of things at us from half-eaten sandwiches and cans of piss (they really hurt) to Polaroids of themselves doing bodily functions and on one surreal occasion a book called 'Looking After Your Poodle'. But it was the only time I was glassed.

This bloody incident came to my mind after last night's game and the players' shunning of the media.

Rejection and criticism is something everyone who ever puts their head above the parapet has to get a thick skin about - but there's only so much you can take before you snap and I'm guessing that's what happened to England's players.

Why would you want to talk to people who have been metaphorically glassing you? You might say 'they earn 40 grand a week, they should be able to cope with a few names', but the amount of money you earn doesn't make any difference. At some point you have to let people know that you can't be pushed around forever. And who among us was not delighted by the hurt little boy look on Richard Keys' face. You'd think someone had stolen his toffees. Marvellous. Then to listen to Talksport telling us that the players would 'never beat the media', it was pretty clear just how massive their collective ego has become.

It is of course an incestuous relationship between media and players. They both make money out of each other, but the bottom line is that we will still go and see football even if there are no sports pages in the papers or if it's not on the telly. Ultimately the game is bigger than the press and in that sense Talksport should really be telling us 'you'll never beat the players', because long after Talksport has been consigned to the radio graveyard, football will still be being performed to hundreds of thousands of fans every week.

I'm as critical as anyone of the prima donna pampered lavender-scented modern footballer and it almost pains me to have to defend them, but when you see the massed ranks of the media making substantial livings off their talent while taking the piss out of them remorselessly and unjustifiably, I know which side I'm on.

28. TURN OFF YOUR MIND, RELAX AND FLOAT DOWNSTREAM
29/09/04

This was inspired by watching Wayne Rooney score a hat-trick on his European debut at Old Trafford against Fenerbahce.

It was an almost mythic occasion; the dawning of an immense talent on a bigger stage. And unlike so many other footballers who are sold to us as a genius, you can't over-hype Rooney. He is that good. He has the spark of the infinite in him. He looks like the thick-set son of old school labouring stock, solid, working-class and plain. You can't dress him up in a posh haircut and suit and make him something he isn't. He is what he is and will remain so. His genius is in his boots and as such is refreshingly simple and honest in an era full of spin, marketing and hyperbole.

That game really blew my mind, man. I get spacey, trippy flashbacks from time to time even though I've not taken any acid for years. It reminds me of the illusions of everyday realities and stops me taking things too seriously. I used to enjoy tripping at football matches because it made everything seem so utterly ludicrous and yet totally exhilarating, but I was never able to play on stage while I was out of my brains. In fact, I had trouble playing when I was pissed, which was a bit of a problem due to me being a bit pissed a lot of the time. Tony was able to play bass and sing backing vocals even with a bottle of Jack in him, I couldn't even keep a beat.

I never understood how the Grateful Dead could take to the stage tripping out of their skulls and even play in key. As soon as the guitar started melting and the air smelled of colours I'd be away with the silver sparkling fairies to chat with the Godhead.

I wonder what Rooney would be like on acid? I bet he'd look like a hobbit.

I'm in a £14-a-week flat in Walker, Newcastle on Tyne. It's the bitter winter of 1981 and the mushrooms are kicking in, the psilocybin racing through my bloodstream and up through my cerebral cortex.

Reality was altering utterly. I had stopped living in a linear reality and had instead taken a step sideways into an entirely different but identically-formed reality. In this reality I realised death was just something that your body goes through and wasn't to be feared. I realised that all material things are illusory and that our attachment to the physical world is the source of all our pain.

I was doing time in the universal mind and I was feeling alright. Music was colour, words were shapes. Everything was invested with more profundity and depth than it was possible to express without waving my arms in the air a lot and saying, "err...it's like...err...like...err...you know...far out".

Aldous Huxley suddenly made sense as I stared at the folds in my jeans. I had the feeling that I knew all that there was to know, up to and including why our bollocks just dangle there and are so vulnerable to a kicking. Everything was everything else, from the smallest microbe to the eons of dark matter in the universe and that we knew this when we were born and had spent our entire lives closing down our minds, running away from the true nature of things because it was all too much for us to take. I looked at the cat, she already knew this and seemed to be asking me why it had taken me so long to realise all this. I apologised to her.

The nature of everything was clear. Some things were precise expressions of the infinite - Frank Zappa's solo on Rat Tomago on the Sheik Yerbouti album, the space Miles Davis leaves between notes on Blue In Green on the Kind Of Blue album or simply the song Northern Sky by Nick Drake.

Now when your mind has been blown, nothing ever looks or feels the same again. You do not return to the point of departure and the doors in your mind that were blown off the hinges are never repaired.

This means that you get flashes of trippy intensity blowing into your regular reality all the time. It can be provoked by almost anything. The smell of toasted teacakes, a rainbow smear of oil in a puddle or the tone of Jeff Beck's guitar all do it for me sometimes and to be honest it can be jolly inconvenient. I got spaced out by the smell of cinnamon in Starbucks while in Chicago and just stood there staring for an indeterminate length of time.

So I was watching Manchester United playing Fenerbahce, not expecting to have my mind blown. I pitied poor David Bellion's enthusiastic attempts to be a top footballer. I was thinking how good Gabriel Heinze looks at left back...then Rooney scored his first goal. A great strike but it was his second goal that did it. As he received the ball I knew what was going to happen.

It all seemed so inevitable - it's the way he lets the ball do all the work, the way he dummies to shoot only momentarily before striking it, it all happened in slow motion and it all seemed utterly perfect and in harmony. It's as though Rooney is a shaman. He looks like a creature of middle earth with funny little ears and a globular head. His skin seems strange as though he's not fully human. Every time he receives the ball it doesn't feel like an ordinary player has got it, it feels different; it feels a bit weird really. It really blows me away. The only other player who has blown my mind like this was Johan Cruyff, who was a magician as much as he was a footballer.

Strangely though I think we're seeing the very best of Rooney now. I'm not sure he'll ever be as good in the future as he is right now. It's like all the footballing genius is flowing through him uninterrupted by self-doubt or analysis.

His doors of football perception are now wide open but, as we get older, we close those doors a little bit at a time and it gets harder to be as you really are. You start thinking too much about everything and you ossify into one state of being rather than being a free spirit. Plus; you feel guilty about shagging grannies and generally being a slave to your libido.

So the moral of this tale is that you don't need to be out of your mind on hallucinogenic drugs to enjoy watching the Roonmeister, but sometimes he makes you feel like you are. "Turn off your mind, relax and float downstream, it is not dying our John," as my old granny used to say.

You might have noticed I like to ponder things. This is usually due to being a few glasses into a night out but in this case it was flying out to the west coast that led me to muse on the nature of things. This was at the start of a trip that also included living in a log cabin in the Sierra Nevada mountains, trying to ski in Badger Pass (there were no badgers), being freaked out in the plane graveyard that is the Mojave, and eventually led to Vegas then down to La Jolla, a tropical three-day thunderstorm, and Laguna Beach.

As soon as the plane touches down on Californian soil I say hello to California Johnny. He lives out there waiting for my return to the Californian life that's been on hold since I last left. He's quite different from me. He's laid back, he's far more arty and nothing much troubles him. Sometimes I think the real me is the California me, sometimes I think it's the Teesside lad.

Okay, I'm messed up, I admit it, but I often wonder if I'm the only person who is like this when they leave British shores. I have this theory that we're all tied down by our inherited history and class in Britain either literally, financially or mentally and you only really see it for what it is when you leave the country and go somewhere that judges you by what you say and do now instead.

The football which is such a regular part of my everyday UK life has far less relevance over there. And although I still keep in touch, the basic day-to-day culture of the game just drifts away. I'm not sure if it's a good thing. It certainly frees up bits of my brain to think about other stuff. People have said that being overly-focused on football has made me stupid. Fuckers. But they may be right. Nonetheless, I still think I'll end my days of this life on west coast soil, probably listening to Neil Young while drinking Merlot.

So since I had to write a column just after arriving, that's what this one is all about.

How much do you need your pain?

So here I am in sunny Monterey, California. It's mid-December and it's over 70 degrees in the sun. The skies are blue, the drinks are cold and food is tasty, tasty, tasty. It's hard to feel anything other than very good, despite being jet-lagged out of my mind.

Taking a step out of the football loop, especially in the depths of winter, is quite odd. I can stay in touch with the scores and the match reports. If I can find a hotel or bar with Fox World Sports playing then I can even see Premiership games. All the facts are still available to me at any time of the day thanks to t'internet, but the one thing that you can't get is the feeling of being in the football loop, the feeling of the ongoing dynamic of the season that comes hand in hand with the daily - no, hourly - following of football in the UK.

And sitting in the sun feeling, frankly, pretty damn good, I realised something. I had lost my pain. I don't mean my rheumatic knee, or that unpleasant itching downstairs, I mean culturally.

I think that's why I keep coming back to California. All the grit that makes my pearls back in the UK is irrelevant here. No-one can classify me by my accent, other than as someone not American. Being northern here makes no difference to anyone. Teesside could be a village in Upper Volta for all most Californians would know; though I did meet a woman yesterday in a wholefood restaurant in Pacific Grove who once dated a lad from Preston, poor lass. She bore the scars well.

Supporting Middlesbrough is as meaningless as someone supporting the Mighty Ducks in the UK. I have a perverse pride supporting the Boro - it's all wrapped up with being the underdog, the unfashionable and the unglamorous. Not flashy or gimmicky or fly-by-night. I wear it like a badge of honour at home but the importance or meaning here is zero. I'm freed of it and everything else here. The monkey who I happily feed to keep on my back has run off and got pissed on tequila sunrises. Fair play to it.

Everything that makes you who you are before you come to California can be shed and you can in effect, if you wish, become a new person.

Reinvention is a way of life. You're not bound by your past. The future is more important than what has already gone. Where you're headed matters far more than where you've been. In short it's the very antithesis of living in the UK. It is liberating if you like to feel rootless. I do.

A fundamental part of following football is the ongoing mood swings caused by the success and failure of your club and the success and failure of other clubs. Once you lose the daily dynamic, it all just slips away, so the question I want to ask is 'how much do you need your pain?'

We most often know ourselves not by what we are but by what we are not. It's much easier to say who or what you are not than define who or what you are. Football helps us understand this further.

If I said I was more Wayne Rooney than Thierry Henry you'd have a pretty good idea what I meant and who I was. If you meet someone whose football hero is Michel Platini, then you'd have a clue to who they were compared to someone whose hero was Terry Butcher. You'd instantly know whether you were likely to get on.

We often use football to channel our anger and discontent at aspects of society or even individuals. Some footballers come to represent all you hate about a person or people in real life. I'm pretty sure that the hostility towards and mocking of Lee Hendrie is less to do with Lee himself and more to do with how he seems to be the very essence of chavness that infects our towns and cities. It's like he is a cultural representative.

Now imagine you didn't have football to channel all this anger or malcontent - what would happen to it? Taking a few weeks away from the angst and bitterness of it all is a bit of a relief but I can't imagine being free of it forever, though maybe I would be a happier, calmer man.

Maybe football doesn't channel our anger, maybe it just makes us angry. Really angry. Maybe it angries up our blood and makes us hate things and people that otherwise we'd be happy to get along with, or on the other hand maybe it just helps us understand the world better and helps diffuse the discontent and fury that might otherwise find more socially-unacceptable forms of expression.

I can't decide but rest assured I am prepared to lie here in the sun and drink Mexican beer until I discover the truth.

Las Vegas is one of my favourite places on earth. It's better even than Bridlington.

A lot of people think it's a just a gaudy gilded palace of sin. Which of course it is, that's exactly why I like it. It is fundamentally a very honest, straightforward place. It exists to exploit your weaknesses and to give you a good time while it does so. That's a good deal to me.

It sits like a vivid hallucination in the most impossibly beautiful, bleak and yet richly-coloured Mojave Desert, both sleazy and romantic all at the same time. I almost bought an apartment on the Strip in the new MGM building and only the fact that I had a £100,000 tax bill to pay off in 12 months stopped me.

I first went out there in 1993 and it was half the size it is now. Back then the MGM was the big new hotel. It holds 18,000 people, which is like a small town. Its pool even had its own beach. Since then I've been back a few times and spent Xmas and New Year there in 2004/5 at the Bellagio hotel, which is where they filmed the remake of Ocean's 11.

The Bellagio hotel is still the best hotel I've ever stayed in, even if you do have to stand in line with some of the fattest people on earth for 45 minutes to get into the breakfast buffet. Mind you, it's worth it. There's even a guy there wokking up Chinese mushrooms and fried rice. But you will see some seriously-bloated people filling their bodies with vast quantities of eggs, potatoes and thick slices of bacon. I'm sure the earth would spin faster if they didn't exist. They're weighing us all down.

Because I was doing quite well and not paying any tax - hence the big bill later - I could afford to stay at the Bellagio in a room which faced the dancing water. The bathroom in itself was bigger than any room I'd ever stayed in. It had the largest, most deliciously comfortable bed I have ever had the pleasure to lay my weary body down upon.

When I'm in Vegas I am almost never sober but I'm almost never really drunk. I just maintain a level of inebriation throughout the day and night. I sleep 'til around midday and just generally live the life of a lush. There are great bands, comedians and art to see and if you can't have a good time then you're really just not trying hard enough. There are many tales to tell and told they will be in the fullness of time.

This was a classic back-of-a-napkin thing that I wrote while very far from sober in the classy darkened Caramel bar in the Bellagio. They played some brilliant music that night or in fact it may have been the day. But you can't tell of course because there are no windows and you totally lose track of time and also your own soul. It's brilliant.

So there I was, sitting in the Caramel bar in the Bellagio Hotel, Las Vegas on Christmas Day. I'm higher than God and I'm wondering if Britney Spears is going to come down and shake her, no doubt artificially enhanced, thang - she keeps a suite at the Bellagio apparently and is often to be seen around the place on what you and I would know as 'the piss'. There was a bit of a row the other week because a waiter refused to cut up a $180 steak for her dog. Well you've got to have some standards, haven't you?

So we're sitting there but Britney is a no-show today, which is a pity because I would have liked to get her views on the future of English football. I'd also liked to have seen her try to dance to Pink Floyd's doom-laden 'Welcome to the Machine', which was playing at high volume - an interesting choice for a party night.

So without Britney to entertain us, we turned our conversation, as is inevitable sooner or later, to football. Being as far from sober as Vegas is from reality, we decided to do that most middle-management of things. We decided to 'brainstorm', a no-holds-barred session of thinking of things that would make things better or more fun for football in 2005.

Ruled out from the start were things which clearly weren't going to happen such as teams running out to the psychedelic hippy guitar noise of Quicksilver Messenger Service, the reintroduction of terraces, pole dancers in the centre circle or players being stripped naked and put in stocks after especially bad performances. We also avoided anything too complicated like the politics of club funding, due to the fact that it's all too hard to work out and we're a bit thick.

And in honour of great treaties of the past we declared that this agenda would henceforth be known as The Vegas Imperatives. So after much heated debate and much distraction (barmaids in leather corsets), this is wot we thunk up like:

1) A wage cap for clubs. No more than 50% of the club's income to be paid to players. You can pay 49% to one and 1% to the rest if you wish but this would stop most stupid managers and chairmen paying people like Seth Johnson the GDP of Switzerland.

2) A maximum of five non-UK players at any club. Not because we hate foreigners but because we're sick of seeing mediocre players from all over the world playing for our clubs when we have mediocre home-grown talent of our own. And everyone likes seeing a local lad do well, it's part of the romance of the game. A cap of five wouldn't stop the best players coming, but it might make clubs think twice about signing the Winston Bogardes of this world.

3) Remove the transfer window. Whatever the reasons it was introduced, it has robbed us of one of the best parts of the game - speculation about who we're going to sign. Which for some clubs' supporters had been more exciting than the actual

football. The January window has led to the football equivalent of binge drinking, and as we all know, that transcends almost inevitably into unfortunate liaisons with people we wouldn't normally go near. And projectile vomiting.

4) Turn off the video display advertising around pitches. It's bloody distracting for fans and it must be for players as well. I purposefully avoid any brands I've seen advertised just to prove to myself that I've not been hypnotised by the global capitalist conspiracy.

5) No ex-player can manage a Premiership club before spending at least three years at a lower-league club. Being a good player doesn't make you a good manager, does it Bryan? Get some proper experience, prove yourself and stop trying to cop big wedges of cash off your reputation.

6) Radically reform or remove Match of the Day. It's pathetic and lame and we're forced to pay for it by law, so we should have a say, shouldn't we? Now officially more unpopular than ITV's grindcore rubbish. That bad.

7) The following phrases to be banned by all media journalists or commentators - 'Italian Job', 'Flying Dutchman', 'Double Dutch' and 'Gallic temperament/spirit'. Think up something else, you morons. And while we're at it, spitting is not 'the worst thing a player can do' okay? Putting your thumb up an opposition player's bum is far worse. As Aki Riihilahti will tell you. It happened to him.

8) Players must pass an IQ test before being allowed to be interviewed or be 'in the studio'. We don't want more monosyllabic, cliché-drenched utterances from these people. Why does anyone think it will be anything other than embarrassing for all concerned?

9) Shirt-pulling is illegal so why does it go unpunished almost all the time? Also, why do keepers get the benefit of the doubt when they fall over and drop the ball - 50% of the time it's because he's a klutz, not because he was fouled.

10) Abolish all the stupid league names. Let's have it 'one' to 'four' then we all know where we are. Coca-Cola League One? Stop taking the piss.

11) Players' nicknames should not just mean putting a 'Y' or 'O' on the end. We want more invention and creativity please.

12) Ban gold boots - who the fuck do you think you are? It's football, not glam rock, you ponce.

13) All contracts are to be just a year long - contracts are a sham anyway, so let's not pretend a five-year contract is a 'major commitment to the club'. It doesn't 'keep him at the club for five years'. We all know he will be off like shit off a shovel as soon as there's more money in it for him. There's almost no loyalty anywhere in football and you're kidding yourself if you think otherwise.

14) No seeding in Champions League, European Championship or World Cup draws. It's just a legal way to fix the competitions. It should be random and if the four best teams get drawn in the same group then so what? That's the whole point of cup competitions.

15) Make it five up and five down instead of three. Let's spread the money around by giving more teams a shot at the big money, while also stopping clubs getting away with a terrible season.

16) Lastly, fans who say when they've lost their manager that they want Martin O'Neill are to be dragged through the streets by wild horses for being so predictable and unimaginative. O'Neill doesn't want to manage you whoever you are. He's just waiting for the Man United job. Get over it.

There you go then. This is my agenda. There are other things we'd like to see happen of course. This is just a few basics. You will have your own I'm sure. But remember, it's our game is football. It's not anyone else's. It belongs to the fans, not anyone else, no matter what we're told. If we don't go, or pay to watch it on TV, the game dies. It's that simple. So it's about time someone in authority took notice of us, isn't it?

31. WHERE THERE'S BLAME THERE'S A CLAIM
18/01/05

Sometimes I find it hard to believe the times we live in. There are people who sit in a state of permanent vigilance, ever prepared to be offended by almost anything. And as soon as they are offended they will call up the police or some other institution to make their offence known. Next they'll want some money as compensation for the distress.

When Wayne Rooney scored against Liverpool he stood there in front of the Kop with his hands behind his ears, and they are good-sized ears, mocking their silence. Now, I take all this as part of the craic of football. I wish players took the piss out of fans more. When Jose Mourinho shushed Liverpool fans with his index finger, fans that had been pelting him with abuse flew into an outrageous strop. Look, he's inciting us to riot! How dare he?! It's so very lame and immature. Some fans seem to believe that they have the right to heap insult on a player but as soon as he responds, they behave like the little kid who's had his sweets stolen.

Shut up and grow up, I say.

Ah, to be back in the green and pleasant lands of the north of England under leaden skies with sleet beating against my window and a roaring log fire in the grate.

I have not been totally sober for about a month while on holiday. It's been great. I have enjoyed a fine range of adult beverages all across the states of California and Nevada and I wouldn't dream of blaming my distended, bloated belly, increased blood pressure and numb liver on anyone or anything but me and my passion for the falling-down waters.

However, it would seem that in today's victim culture, I should really be writing to the brewing giants to complain that their finest beverages are making me fat, giving me headaches, damaging my internal organs and making me very thirsty in the morning. Worse still, they're bringing my life into disrepute because their products are causing me to behave in a lewd and riotous manner in public. How dare they do this to me? I'm a victim of the brewing industry's lust for profit - feel my pain - and give me some money as compensation.

But several people really are suing McDonalds and other fast food joints for making them fat. It's really happening. Other prosecutions have been brought for the coffee being too hot.

A woman in Irvine, California filed a lawsuit against a restaurant claiming 'negligence and intentional infliction of emotional distress' when she found an unopened, unused condom in her soup. She said she spent the next 15 minutes in a restroom vomiting and has since seen a psychiatrist and taken medication for depression and anxiety. Can you believe these people?

A woman in jail in Georgia is suing the jail because it's infested with spiders.

Even a woman who appeared on the trashy 'Who Wants To Marry A Millionaire' show, where women competed to marry a bloke with lots of dosh, tried to sue a San Francisco rock station when a DJ called her a 'skank' on air, claiming she was 'offended and humiliated'.

The case was thrown out because no-one could really define what a 'skank' was and also because the woman had voluntarily subjected herself to 'inevitable scrutiny and potential ridicule by the public and the media anyway'. She didn't get it.

Two blokes even had an action brought against Penthouse magazine because the promised naked pictures of Anna Kournikova turned out not be of Anna but of some other woman photographed at distance naked on a beach somewhere. They were 'distressed' by this discovery (presumably it had upset their wanking satisfaction). Worse still they won. Penthouse settled out of court.

These are all crazy but are all true. There appears to be a class of people who wait with baited breath to be offended, injured or psychologically upset by almost anything at any time. These are the same people who watch something full of sex or violence on TV that offends them deeply for two full hours and then write and complain about it in detail to the TV watchdogs.

We're all victims in life. If we're lucky we fart around pretending to be significant for 70 years, then we die after a life hopefully of laughter, love and orgasms but also pain, humiliation and shrunken genitalia. Nature makes victims of us all. It takes the piss but there's sod all we can do about it. We've just got to get on with it and try and have as good a time as possible.

But the victim culture seems to have spread to all parts of society. It's as though some people think we don't have any responsibility for what we do at all. It's always your parents, your teachers, your boss, your neighbour's Irish wolfhound or your wicked Uncle Ernie who's to blame for your sins. Most of us probably think this is all a bit stupid but the culture has become totally established, even in football.

Take this weekend's latest Rooney incident. Standing in front of the Kop with your hands behind your own substantial ears should not in any circumstances cause Liverpool fans to commit an act of riot or violence. It might annoy you a bit, you might want to call him a tosspot, but it's not an incitement to social unrest or phone throwing. No-one's ears should be able to do that.

Even so the FA had to 'take a look' at it and even though they rightly said there was no charge to answer, why was it even thought for a second there might be? Because of the blame culture.

I've heard phone-ins where fans complain about a player's behaviour towards the crowd, saying he swore and made gestures. Some even report players to the cops.

I can't believe the hypocrisy. As fans we pay money to shout abuse at players, or some of us do anyway, and if a player wants to give it some back, why would you be offended? You calling him a useless wanker and him telling you to fuck off is not something to get upset about, let alone report to the police. There are real crimes happening out there.

Even if El-Hadji Diouf spat at me, I wouldn't report him to the cops or stewards. Life is too short to get outraged by something so minor.

A player could unfurl a banner which read 'I consider all Middlesbrough people and players to be utter and total bastards' after scoring against us and I wouldn't care, it wouldn't incite me to riot. Nor would I think it had brought the game into disrepute. It'd be odd, sure. It'd be surreal, but I like that. It wouldn't be morally or spiritually corrupting to football or society though would it? Nah.

I would even argue that elbowing someone in the face doesn't bring the game into disrepute. How can it? Doing it doesn't make it acceptable within the laws of the game or make anyone else do it in any walk of life. It doesn't make the game any less enjoyable, any less or more exciting. It doesn't make me want to elbow anyone in the face. The next time I see it I won't be looking for a fight after the game, I won't be telling kids it's okay to elbow people and frankly I don't know anyone who will. So what the hell is all the fuss about? Only the bloke who gets elbowed has got anything to moan and get angry about. Send off a player for doing it by all means, but let's not get into a moral frenzy or waste time with an 'investigation'.

Similarly, when you hear fans who get into fights outside matches claim, as an excuse, that opposition fans were taunting them - as though the decision to smash a chair over someone's heads wasn't their own - it all rings a bit hollow. Being insulted by strangers is no excuse for violence unless you already want to be violent.

"He called me a twat, your honour, and suggested I was a champion of self-abuse and my wife was sexually profligate, so I felt compelled to argue to the contrary with the aid of a crow bar."

"Oh well, in that case, I don't blame you for beating him to a pulp then. Case dismissed."

But the FA is paranoid about players inciting crowds - do they think we're all Pavlov's dogs? I suppose that's why they think players are role models and that we will slavishly copy everything they do. But that's largely anecdotal rubbish.

If footballers have so much influence, how come I don't see many kids with Robbie Savage hair? Does it not apply to him? Do kids go to bed dreaming of looking and living like Joey Barton? Did David Seaman make kids want to grow ponytails and keep horses? Just because a kid likes a footballer, it doesn't mean they want to live or be like them, even if they'd like to play like them. I mean, I like The Libertines but I'm not going to get a crack habit.

And when outraged parents say of players caught brawling, spitting, throwing pizza or taking drugs, "Well if they see their heroes doing it, they'll think it's okay to do it too", the answer to that is simple - you tell them it's not okay. That's your job. It's certainly not the FA's job to try and do it for you. If a dumb-ass footballer has more influence on your kid than you do, then surely there's something wrong at home. That's just common sense, isn't it? I've never had parents who looked out for me much or who cared what I was up to, but it still seems only sensible to me that they actually should have.

I spent my youth getting wasted on anything I could get my hands on, not because all my heroes did it, though they did - and by the way almost every single work of art, music and literature you like was created in whole or in part by people who were real fuckin' high - but because I had no adult influence in my life to suggest that I might err, well, die and that I might not want to be so wasted all the time if I was happier about myself and life in general. I loved Zeppelin but they didn't tell me what to do. Maybe I wasn't listening to the backwards-masked messages in the outplay grooves closely enough.

I'd love to see a situation where the football community and its authorities didn't blame itself and its customers for the ills of society, didn't keep trying to grass each other up, didn't make mountains out of molehills. I'd like to see the witch hunt for drugs stopped and all the lame disrepute claims ignored and all the silly 'inciting the crowd' allegations forgotten. Can't we just be a bit grown-up about all this? Please? Not a week seems to go by without an avalanche of phoney outrage and accusations.

But sadly, in the current culture of blame and victimisation, that doesn't seem likely. It seems like everything is everyone else's fault...except perhaps, our own.

I'm not a bad lad. I'm nice to animals and I'll buy you drinks all night long. I'm not, as some have said, a 70's-style football thug who wants a return to the days of en masse fan violence inside and outside the ground. No thanks. But I do like the game to be played with a bit of old school masculine aggression. But this is frowned upon now. Many people are quick to condemn it as immoral and reprehensible. It really gets my goat and my goat Colin does not like to be disturbed.

Every season there is a week or two of moral outrage about something in football. And so it was in February 2005 when Arsenal played Manchester United at Highbury and it all got a bit heated with Roy Keane getting into Patrick Vieira's face.

So this is another of my pieces of bile about how the game of football and the culture that surrounds it has been stolen from us. Somehow, somewhere, it got nabbed from the fans by a bunch of people with an entirely different and alien agenda who want to turn it into a polite sport for the middle class to occasionally enjoy, and it is usually these people who come forward after an aggressive game to pontificate on the dreadful state of all things football. It usually leads to comparison with that gouge-fest of a game for gentlemen called rugby and other such garbage.

In the real world you couldn't find a true football lover who didn't rub their hands with glee that night - it was thrilling, visceral football - but afterwards there were the usual threats of prosecution for Rooney and others for bringing the game into disrepute, mostly for the high crimes of swearing a lot and displaying some genuine aggression.

154

The people who administrate football at the FA are hapless amateurs who are not only over-promoted, but also self-deluded. They think they're being all modern and family-orientated and inclusive by stamping down on swearing and aggression. Who told them to do this? I don't know. They took it upon themselves to try and placate and please people who don't really care about football in the first place

Then Rooney was counted as swearing 341 times in a minute (or something) and this was used as proof that he is a dreadfully uncouth and loutish person who is a terrible example to children. All of which I find really fucking offensive so I went off on one and got all hot under the armpits about it...

Are we not men? We are devo. Eh? Ask your dad.

No, but seriously, are we not men?

What is all this nancy-boy talk about the bad behaviour at the Arsenal game? Don't you live in the real world? Haven't you seen really bad behaviour? Because if you have you'll know - Roy and Paddy having a few verbals does not make the list.

All the lavender-scented self-appointed guardians of our great game have been busy telling us how petulant the players were and how much bad language there was, and wasn't that foul-mouthed Wayne Rooney a disgrace etc etc. Well I for one just want to say, shut the feck up you whiners. I actively enjoy swearing and bad language. This does not and I'll repeat this again, it does not make me a moron of limited vocabulary. Quite the contrary, it expands the lexicon of expressions I use substantially.

I love football because it is passionate, aggressive at times, cocky, flash and a bit mouthy. It's not lawn bowls for God's sake. It's not a BBC4 discussion on the nature of existentialism.

For the record I would like to speak for all of us football fans who don't get our panties in a wad over swearing, pushing and shouting footballers. I thought the shenanigans in the tunnel were entirely appropriate and I absolutely loved it. Surely millions will have rubbed their hands in glee and thought, it's going to be good tonight. I did. A big game like this is brilliant drama and, just like in rock 'n' roll, if you take away the edge you take away the soul.

It made the whole event more exciting and I suspect it did exactly same for many other people but somehow, we're not allowed to say it's exciting; we've got to condemn it. If we don't condemn it then we're thugs, idiots, irresponsible or plain stupid. Who are these moralistic monkeys on our backs? Leave our game alone.

We've got to listen to Gary Lineker telling us his kids will have been watching and would copy them and isn't that awful. Well, if Lineker's kids are so hypnotised by what they see on telly, maybe he should give up small-screen work and supervise them a bit closer. It's all bollocks. I heard not a single swear word on telly growing up but I still knew half-a-dozen words for the female front bottom and I used them all. And I bet Gary's kids will too. It's alright. Stop worrying so much about nothing.

As a kid I and everyone I knew had a filthy mouth. We spewed obscenities all the time. It was okay. We turned out fine. I lived in industrial Teesside; we used industrial language all the time. It didn't deprave or debase me.

Football isn't an anaesthetic to calm us down. It isn't the ballet. It's not political discussion. It's working-class art. Swearing is part of the art. If you can't enjoy the swearing, you are missing out. You don't understand the nature of the people who play the game. Being polite is not mandatory.

If you don't enjoy seeing the bitter vitriol of an Alan Smith volley of invective, then you don't enjoy language at all. The way Rooney snarls and swears is magnificent and an art in itself. Don't take it so seriously, you're not obliged to copy him. If your kids come out with the same language it's because it feels good and because it's expressive.

Don't the critics understand that this behaviour is a crucial part of football because it allows us to vent our own anger and frustration at the world? It helps channel life's tensions and injustices. In other words, they act like petulant nutters so we don't have to.

If you thought the players' attitudes and behaviour was out of order, maybe football isn't your game. Maybe you don't like your heart to beat fast, for adrenalin to course through your veins, but some of us live for it and in an increasingly timid, bland, anodyne culture, God knows we need it.

Arsenal had just surrendered meekly in the Champions League yet again and it seemed like they'd never be successful in Europe even with a side that was so good domestically. It seemed like they didn't lack the talent but rather the temperament to succeed, and I wanted to find a way to express their situation, which is when I remembered George.

People think that I made up the whole love pump thing, but it is true, you can get them fitted. It's not quite as much fun as the whole contraption working on its own but it is more reliable after six pints of lager, so it's swings and roundabouts really. Viagra was just hitting the market around this time so I don't know if that would have done the job for him as well but he seemed to have got quite attached to Mr Love Pump and he was popular with the ladies, though this may have been something to do with being a very rich man and living in a swish million-dollar home in the heart of one of the coolest areas of LA.

If you've nothing much to do, there's a whole book to be done of analogies between physical conditions and football teams if anyone can get drunk enough to write it. So that's my next book sorted then...

What is more important? Talent or temperament?

Good players can choke. Average players can rise to an occasion.

This is a story about a man I met in California this summer. He's a great bloke. He's not really called George. I thought his story was symbolic.

George was shocked to get the news. He always thought it'd be the drink and drugs that killed him. He was only 49, it didn't seem fair. He considered himself to be in his prime. He was making great money doing A & R for a major record company, lived in a big house off Laurel Canyon in Los Angeles, got as much pussy as his not inconsiderable libido could handle and drove around town in a metallic gold Mercedes convertible. He was the man, but soon apparently he was going to be the dead man. What a bitch.

The doctor had given him a 30/70 chance of surviving his prostate cancer. He didn't like the odds; George had never been any good at gambling. So he had the operation and the chemo and lost his hair and three stone in weight and waited. He briefly considered praying for his life but couldn't bring himself to stoop so low as to get religion. After all, he reasoned, if there was a God, he'd clearly got it in for him by giving him the cancer in the first place, so what would be the point?

He went to see his physician.

"There's good news and bad news," he said.

"Gimme the good news," said George, hoping that it would be good enough to ease the pain of the bad news.

"Well the good news is that you are not going to die."

"That's fuckin' good news," said George, relieved.

"The bad news is that you can't have kids."

'That's the bad news?', thought George. He didn't want to have kids anyway.

"Hey doc, that's okay with me. I'm happy to be shootin' blanks."

"Ah, no you misunderstand me. I mean you will not be able to physically procreate."

George frowned, trying to work out what the guy was saying.

"You mean I won't be able to get wood?" he said, never one to use euphemisms.

"Exactly. It's quite common after an operation on your prostate."

This was bad news. Really freakin' bad. Jesus H, how was he gonna live without his endorphin rush? Even cocaine wasn't as good as sex.

"...but I may be able to help you," said the doctor, pulling out a leaflet from his draw. "You can get one of these fitted."

George looked at the brochure. It was full of diagrams. It looked complicated but apparently involved putting a small metal rod in his dick.

"What's this shit?" he said.

"It's a penis pump. We can get it fitted in you, so that every time you need an erection, you flip a valve and attach a can of compressed air and, well, you inflate yourself. You can then perform as normal. It's very successful. Once you're done, you flip the valve and let the air out."

George stared incredulously at him: "You're kidding me man. No-one blows their dick up like a balloon. You can't do that!"

"I can assure you it's very possible and works very well," said the doctor. "You just have a small metal valve in a fold of skin under your scrotum."

George went away and pondered at length about whether he wanted a mechanical cock installed. It was the only option he had if he wanted sex again, but how the hell did you explain it to women? "Just a minute while I inflate my cock babe." It wasn't exactly romantic. He could see women running away screaming as he produced his can of compressed air. It was weird even for LA.

He went home, watched porno and tried to beat nature. But he couldn't. He was as soft as a marshmallow. He had to face up to the truth, as tough as it was.

What the hell, he thought. He had nothing to lose and he had always liked to be different and take chances. So he had the device fitted.

And it turned out to be the best thing that ever happened to him. While some ladies found it a bit weird, most thought it an excellent contraption. He could be as hard as he wanted for as long as he wanted at any time he wanted. It was 100% guaranteed. The only time he had any problems was when a woman, being a bit too vigorous, popped the cap off his valve and deflated him halfway through - there was a hissing sound followed by a rapid deflation.

The very thing that he thought would kill him had in fact turned out to be a blessing in disguise after he faced up to the realities.

And I thought of George when I was watching Arsenal's limp performance in losing to Bayern. Like George they've got to face up to realities and, like George, they need to be able to perform when the big occasion demands, and not just when you're playing Crystal Palace.

The truly flaccid nature of their performance in Germany should tell them something.

They need help. Wenger clearly has not got the answers to their European problems. He can't make them perform adequately. If he could, he would.

So they need the football equivalent of a penis pump - something to get them up for the big occasion, something to make them hard and ready to perform. Until they do, they're always going to be the ones getting fucked.

I still think this is a brilliant idea. I had to have one eventually didn't I, and this is it. It's a great way to make football more competitive and more exciting and it would give clubs a chance to share in the game's wealth. I'd happily take a drop in the skill on display for more exciting games. There's little enjoyment in seeing a side of multi-millionaires waltzing around a newly-promoted small club and beating them 5-0. It's a bit soulless.

It will never happen though because the 18 clubs in the G14 (don't ask why there's 18 in the G14, your brain will melt and leave a stain on your good shirt) would have their dominance threatened and would never go along with it.

That doesn't mean it's not the right thing to do though. I went on Danny Kelly's radio show to talk about this. He loved the idea but we ended up talking about the Groundhogs and Stackridge instead, so that was my radio career as a football pundit pretty much scuppered for going off topic about something that is of no interest to anyone but sad old 70's rock obsessives.

Don't you just hate international weeks? No regular football for a fortnight and a couple of often tedious internationals to endure with all the usual bland, meaningless cack falling from the mouths of Sven, Beckham, Owen and the rest. It breaks the natural rhythms of football life. Glorious normality is on hold while the internationals happen.

However, it does give me chance to dream of a different football world, a world not dominated by the big three, a world where football would actually be competitive and every season ten or more teams would have a chance of winning the league.

All we need for this to happen is to banish Manchester United, Arsenal and Chelsea to a European Super League of 22 teams. There'd be three teams from England, Spain and Italy, two from France, Germany, Holland/Belgium, Portugal and Eastern Europe and three from a 'minor countries' group consisting of Scotland, Austria, Switzerland and other small nations.

I think this would be brilliant. Let's remind ourselves of a few facts here. Most of us don't support any of the big three. Most of us can't compete financially or in any other way with them. Most of us are sick of season after season being a cakewalk for one of them. Most of us would welcome a chance for our team to win the Premiership or even finish second or third and get a UEFA Cup spot. Without the big three at the moment Everton, Liverpool and Bolton would be fighting it out to be champions. It'd be nip and tuck all the way to the last game.

And the reward for winning the Premiership would be promotion to the European Super League. The lowest team from every country would be relegated out of the league, thus allowing a turnover of sides to benefit from the Euro League money. This would also increase competitiveness and decrease complacency within the Euro League - finish third behind your country's other two teams and you'd be out.

Euro Super League clubs wouldn't be able to play in domestic cup competitions either - there could be a Euro Cup for them to play for.

You might think this is crazy but if something isn't radically altered, football as a proper competition will be over in the top leagues. Not just here but right across Europe. The same teams dominate season after season. The same clubs have won the FA Cup almost every season for the past ten years.

The fact that fourth place is now flagged up in all quarters as a major prize for the likes of Everton or Liverpool shows just how deeply insane the game has become now. Fourth place!

Fourth place was always nowhere, now it's seen as bigger than the FA Cup. That's just plain wrong.

If we got rid of the Champions League and put in a Euro Super League, we could get back to a competitive domestic league where most sides could beat most other sides on any given day.

It's the only way forward and it would improve the finances of clubs substantially. The winners of the Premiership would have at least a season in the Primo Euro League and would garner all the cash rewards. But given that the Premiership would be more competitive, there'd be a chance that more clubs would actually win the league and thus more money would be more widely spread.

When one of the big three is relegated at the end of the first season, they would have a financial advantage, but this would be offset by a Premiership wage cap which would mean a lot of the high-earning big stars would leave. This would make a level playing field, forcing clubs to be more realistic in what they pay and avoid the risk of Leeds-style tits-uppage.

The Euro League would be big and glamorous and cosmopolitan and exotic. The domestic leagues would be gritty and exciting and there would at last be a chance of winning something. Yes, there would be less quality in some of the football played, but crucially it would be more exciting. And exciting football beats exhibitions of skill in my book.

With relegation from the Super League being based on your position in relation to your other country's clubs, every season there would be a turnover of up to eight teams, which would keep the league fresh and interesting.

The whole idea behind this scheme is to keep football interesting and exciting and to prevent the money being concentrated forever into two or three teams. Fans would have something less predictable and meaningless to watch.

You might think this is crazy but things can't go on like this. Something's got to change. Remember it's our game, we're the ones who it's played for. Do you really want another ten years of the same three teams competing for the title? It's not a thrilling thought is it? It's my way or the highway.

I could go on all day every day about how the self-appointed and largely-unaccountable guardians and administrators of football have messed around with fans' enjoyment of the game in the name of giving players more rest and time off to, err, well, go shopping I think. In 2005 there was no league football over the Easter break, which really pissed me off. With the obligatory week off prior to the weekend's international games, most players had two weeks off. Then later in the season everyone complains about fixture pile-ups.

I don't even want to see players getting the week off before an international game. It has not improved England's success. It hasn't made us play better football and it isn't what the fans want. So why does it still happen again? It's just become a knee-jerk habit and no-one even thinks about it any more. Except me. So I indulged in a bit of shouting and pointing and once again it made no difference to anyone - but that doesn't mean I'm not right.

Footballers do almost nothing almost every day. It's a total doss. It's a part-time job. We should stop pampering them so much and make them work for a living. Never mind reducing the amount of games in a season, let's increase it. If, as most players do, you play 40 games in a season, that's less than 60 hours of football in ten months. That's six hours a month, or about one hour every five days. If you're Frank Lampard and you play 60 games, that's about an average of an hour every three-and-a-half days. It's not that much is it?

But if you tell someone they're tired, then they will get tired. Give them an excuse and they'll take it. Rather than protect players' fitness and keep them injury-free, they are now injured more often for longer. Football is an insane Alice in Wonderland world of upside-down values and ideas but no-one seems to notice or care really as one hysterical, ridiculous notion after another becomes established as the norm.

If you had any doubt at all that the authorities who run football in Britain have zero idea about the nature of the game and the fans that put millions of quid in their pockets, then the Easter weekend should have opened your eyes.

Bank holidays are a peculiar institution in Britain. North Yorkshire is magically turned into one giant caravan park as couples from far-flung places like Dewsbury and Todmorden come to spend three days peering miserably out at the icy rain sleeting in from across the North Sea. It's as though it's some kind of penance or aversion therapy. Perhaps they're only happy when they're sad.

On Good Friday afternoon the A1, A19, A64 and A170 are littered with the debris of caravans that have fallen apart after laying dormant since August Bank Holiday. Every mile there are red-faced men changing bald, shredded caravan tyres as their disgruntled wives and children look on, hands on hips, wishing they'd just stayed at home.

Swarms of high-performance racing bikes, piloted by people with metal plates in their heads, veer around the country roads at high speed. A bloke was stopped outside Thirsk for doing 175mph on his bike. Perhaps he mistook the A170 signs for a speed limit. North Yorkshire has the most biker deaths in Britain apparently - the scattering of body parts onto the moors and fells is all part of the Easter Bank Holiday resurrection shuffle.

This is why I never leave the house on a bank holiday; except to see football, of course. But that was a pleasure denied to me this year by FIFA, UEFA, or was it the FA? I don't know which faceless institution decided that we should be treated to a thrilling weekend of international football instead. I recall wondering that as I took a nap during the highlights of the Wales game.

Well excuse me, but football ultimately belongs to the people who watch it - and before you think this is a romantic fantasy, tell me how long football would last if we didn't turn up or watch it on telly. Not long. So it's ours, right?!

And I want my bank holiday football back. I need it back. Time was we'd have a full programme on the Friday, the Saturday and the Monday, but that was when men were men and the ladies liked it that way. Our current crop of little darlings would be limp with exhaustion after such exertions. They'd have no energy left to get a new haircut or wander around Porsche showrooms saying 'do you know who I am?'

If players could do it 30 years ago when they were patently less athletic, often had substantial man breasts, ate plates of steak and chips before a game, kicked a lead-heavy wet ball across pitches that had not seen grass since November and were often 78% sand, then they can do it now when the finest physical and emotional pampering is available.

This Easter we were not even allowed one day of Premiership football, never mind a long weekend jam-packed with games, which is exciting and vital precisely because it is gruelling and intense and could be pivotal in the outcome of a season.

But in today's blander, safer culture this is seen as 'A Bad Thing'. In an era where the money keeps the money, those with the money seem to have the power to gear everything to suit them. Well I don't care if it suits the clubs or the players or anyone else to rest at Easter, the fact is that I want to see football and I think we, the fans, matter far more than clubs or authorities. We've got time off work and we want to see our teams. This isn't the time for internationals.

Internationals are light, low-fat snacks to be eaten between the satisfying hot dinners of club football. Play the internationals on a Wednesday, have your league match on a weekend - it used to work just fine.

The FA don't seem to understand how we live in Britain. We graft longer and harder than any other European country and on public holidays we want to get wide and let our hair down. Am I the only football nutter who has been left with an empty, hollow feeling about having no top-flight domestic football for two weeks?

It feels like a part of my cultural heritage has been taken away from me and I really, really, really feckin' resent it.

Next it'll be the Xmas games for the axe. Then it'll be a winter break; then a break for tatty-picking week; a few days off for Valentine's Day; a weekend break for Chinese New Year. Then it'll be games called off for bad light or rain.

Being a professional footballer is already essentially a part-time job. It's not eight hours a day in a factory or a call centre, is it? But apparently, there's still not enough time in the day to say, practise kicking with your weaker foot or learn how to cross a ball without hitting the first man more than 50% of the time, even though being able to do this would make you much better at your job and even though the majority of top-rank players are unable to kick with both feet or cross a ball consistently accurately.

No, instead of actual hard work, all they do is a couple of hours' training for three mornings a week, three hours' worth of games maximum and the rest of the time is spent with blonde women sitting on your face or buying 24-carat gold cock rings. This is what the clubs call 'resting' between games. We would more accurately call it 'larging it big style.'

Fair play to them, who wouldn't want some of it - but don't let's pretend it's harder work than it really is. I know I'm making light of the extreme physical exertion required to play football at pace for 90 minutes and the fact that I'm a breathless old blob meself doesn't help but nonetheless, I can't help but feel that the balance has shifted way too far in favour of players and clubs and too far away from what the fans want.

Take a player like David James. Called up to the England squad, but never going to play, he's effectively having two weeks off on full pay. I mean, it's a piece of pish isn't it? Players who didn't play the two international games are having two weeks off with their feet up. This is never mentioned when everyone complains about being 'fatigued'.

They don't need all this hallowed time off around international games and more importantly, I certainly don't think we should be scheduling the internationals to replace the Easter programme. The roots of the game matter. So a word to the wise: Stop messing us around and pay some respect to the people upon whom you have gorged and made yourselves rich. What we want matters more than what you, the clubs or the players want. Do it again and I shall force you all to spend Easter in a one-berth caravan in Filey. Don't say you haven't been warned.

I know I'm in a minority in feeling the whole concept of the BBC is wrong, but I'm not alone either. The notion that by law you have to pay the government to own a television and they pass the money on to the state broadcaster seems to me to be the worst kind of nanny state-ism.

The BBC's supporters justify its presence on the basis that the market wouldn't deliver such quality. It would be wall-to-wall rubbish game shows and reality programmes featuring the mentally subnormal or emotionally bereft and the BBC is a bulwark against this, except it isn't because the BBC is stuffed with rubbish game shows and reality shows. Ooops. Admittedly they haven't gone as far as My Celebrity Tudor Wedding, but it's only a matter of time.

In essence the BBC's supporters are saying you can't trust people to make or watch good telly unless you force them to pay for it. This is utter rubbish on many levels, not least of which is the fact that so much of the BBC's output just isn't that good and certainly isn't special, but also because in a digital age, the whole notion is simply anachronistic.

I'm not sure why they can't just let us abandon the licence fee and build a pay-per-channel option into our digital packages. Let's see how many people pay for their mediocrity then. They don't do this because they suspect their revenue would drop massively when people are not threatened with jail to cough up their £3billion of cash every year.

Another spurious argument - you can tell I've got up on old Dobbin here because I've started using words like spurious - is that without the licence fee, British TV would end up being like American TV. As if this is the ultimate proof of the dangers of the market economy. However, almost all the best drama and comedy of the last ten years has come from American TV - often the pay-per-view HBO but also on the major networks. So that argument simply doesn't hold any credibility at all.

The BBC's duty is to inform, educate and entertain. That's their mission statement - don't you just hate management speak? But that is such a broad remit that it includes everything on earth that has, is or ever will happen. Nothing at all in any human or animal activity can be excluded from the concepts of information, education and entertainment. What else could its duty include?

However, the football fans' outrage at someone so clearly hopeless as Graeme Le Saux being groomed as a pundit by the BBC was a step too far, and though no-one ever admitted it, I think the pressure was brought to bear on the BBC, who realised they'd royally screwed up and elbowed him out of the World Cup, much to his chagrin. So he left. Hurrah! Result!

Since we're all forced to pay them for owning a TV, you can't just use the 'turn it off if you don't like it' argument with the BBC. We all have a share in the bloody institution and we're forced to pay even if we don't watch it. So they should expect more scrutiny and protest. There'll be a time in the future when people look back incredulously at this age of the licence fee, much like we look back on burning people with six toes as witches...which I think they still do in some rural parts of Norfolk.

I'll be honest with you, I really don't like the concept of the BBC. Yes, admittedly, there are some good programmes on occasionally but they're usually made by independent companies.

The BBC is middle-class, liberal and thinks it's better than us. The BBC I hate is the one that does the news and the sport so ineptly, so regularly, and which last night dipped to a new nadir in its presentation of the England match.

I just don't want to hear John Motson giving that stupid schoolboy snigger after almost every single utterance. It sounds like he's doing the commentary purely for his own small-minded amusement.

His and Lawrenson's treatment of Azerbaijan was shameful. I'm not sensitive about anyone having a pop or taking the piss out of any footballer but you'd think from their attitude that the opposition were footballing morons. It was sickening. Their treatment of the goalkeeper was nasty and just plain wrong. You keep the ball out of the net whatever way you can - I don't need to hear Lawrenson's camp Prestonian tones defining his worth.

I've never thought Gary Lineker was any good as a host. Never. He used to be bumbling and inept but after ten years of being lavishly paid with our money, he is now professional, but still appalling to watch. Not just bland but smug. Not just boring but actually stupid. He offers nothing. He is out of tune with the football fans in this country but crucially in tune with the BBC executives, who think he's a working-class boy made good who they can pat on the head.

Alan Hansen could and can be excellent but he's dragged down by the lazy, smug, don't-give-a-toss attitude that pervades the BBC and, let's face it, when you don't have to be profitable, where's the incentive to actually be any good?

The pundits that sit alongside Hansen are woeful. Alan Shearer can't get beyond saying 'to be fair' in every second sentence and grins like a stupid boy who's been caught farting in class. Gareth Southgate looks like a head boy. Peter Schmeichel is bewildering. Peter Reid is quite possibly pissed

173

and a less articulate man you'd be hard to find. Then there's Graeme Le Saux....Jesus wept.

I know I lot of you must feel the same because BBC football coverage is shocking. They make basic technical errors like showing replays when the ball's back in play, thus missing vital action. The sound goes in and out, though that's sometimes a blessing as we get respite from the pundits and commentators talking garbage in clichés, tired old expressions and unoriginal thought.

But the very worst thing is that we have to pay for it. Yes, we have to. There's no debate or argument - if you turn off you still have to pay. Don't give me that crap about how awful telly is all over the world and especially America where they don't have a licence. I don't care.

The BBC is stuffed to the gills with crapulence and over-indulged non-entities spouting shite. It's full of news reporters more concerned with their reputation and CVs than disseminating the truth. They're hopelessly biased towards many liberal middle-class issues - wholly unobjective in their news coverage but replete with pomposity that they are the last repository of the truth. And I have to pay them to tell me this. Have they no shame?

I'm not sure why pissing in sinks or anywhere else for that matter has played such a memorable role in my life. It seems to be a recurring metaphor. So this is the first of two pissing in sinks stories.

A lot of people, mostly women, write to me wanting to meet Tony but he's not short of company and he conducts his still hedonistic lifestyle from his apartment in southern California

Now in his mid 40's and as hairy as ever, even if it's all turned grey, he seems to live on fresh air like tumbleweed. He's not changed at all since the first time I met him in 1979. While the rest of us worry about life, the universe and everything, he is chemically unable to worry about anything. He just grins his way through the years listening to Motorhead and Hawkwind, playing his simple but thunderous bass and inviting women back to his room.

He lives for his music, women and alcohol in that order and they're three good priorities in life I think. Beats the hell out of working in a building society and saving up to buy kitchen units from Ikea I reckon. Typically I said that in an email to Tony recently and he replied and I know he was laughing when he wrote it, "....why do you care what other people are doing with their lives? Let them get on with it if they want it like that." That's typical Hairy T. He invented live and let live.

So if you ever see a man with a big mane of grey hair walking along Venice Beach with broken teeth and ice blue eyes and a big shit-eating grin on his face, that'll be Tony. He has an easy charm that seems to enrapture women who are after a good time. A two-night stand is a major commitment to him and there are a million stories to tell about his prowess. I used him in this column to illustrate how football's authorities treat rioting Italian fans differently to British supporters, simply because they do it all the time.

I walked into my room to find Hairy Tony pissing in my sink. The basin was a bit too high for him so he was standing on his toes and arching the piss up and into the basin. His aim was good but he was still splashing all over my toothbrush.

"You dirty bastard," I said, not unreasonably.

"It's just natural," he laughed his rasping broken-toothed laugh.

This was Hairy Tony's argument against any criticism of his bodily functions wherever, however and upon whomever he performed them.

"Look at this - does this look normal to you?"

He shook off the last drops and turned to show me his whanger. It looked like a pork sausage that had been chewed on by a butcher's dog.

"Does it normally look so horrible?" I enquired, not being a medically trained man.

"It is a funny colour like. It's Suzanne's fault. She was sucking on it like it was a raspberry mivvy last night, then I went over to Mary's and she was at it again!"

Suzanne was Tony's curvaceous, far-too-good-looking-for-him girlfriend of the time - this being the summer of 1988. But typically for Tony, he wasn't content with one fantastic-looking bird, at the time he had at least two others on the go and several more what he called 'part-timers'. These women were scattered everywhere from Newcastle to Bristol.

The weird thing about this behaviour was that the women involved all really knew what Tony was like. He was, and indeed still is, a rogue; a bad lad but with a heart of gold. Can't keep his pants on but he doesn't really mean anyone any harm.

The more he spread his seed around, the more action he got - which was quite an achievement for an unshaven, straw-haired, Worzel Gummidge look-a-like bass player. His infidelity wasn't really taken seriously by anyone.

And yet Lenny, my self-styled cerebral guitarist cohort, once got caught up to his thighs by his girlfriend with another lady and, in front of us all, was accused of being the most evil man on the planet. It was the first and only time he'd cheated on her. However, the words, "but Tony does it all the time", didn't help his cause. "But that's just what he's like," she said as though stating the obvious. He was excused any moral judgement.

The lesson of this story is that if you do something a lot, no-one takes it seriously anymore. This may be especially true in football.

Can you imagine what would have happened if, when playing Bayern at Stamford Bridge, a few hundred Chelsea fans decided to throw flares on the pitch and inflict first-degree burns on Oliver Kahn?

I'll tell you what would happen: British teams would be expelled from European football for years.

But in all certainty this won't happen to Italian clubs.

Given that Chelsea at one point were being threatened with expulsion from the competition for complaining about the opposition's manager hassling the ref, you would think that this week's events in Milan would prompt some UEFA reaction greater than a couple of games behind closed doors. But it won't happen.

Increasingly, it seems that football's governing bodies make policy up on the hoof and apply it inconsistently depending on who commits what it defines as crimes.

I don't think I'm paranoid or overtly nationalistic. I deplore nutters at games who want to fight, burn or intimidate people wherever they come from. England has its fair share of crazies who use the game as an excuse for a ruck, but we're far from alone in that. Can you ever imagine a match being abandoned in

England in a hail of burning flares? Our press and media would declare it the end of civilization and would actively welcome an extended ban on English clubs in European competitions as punishment.

This doesn't seem to happen in Italy. A club gets a couple of games behind closed doors for coining a ref in the head. Burn a keeper? Ah, it's just the usual hotheads. Don't worry about it.

It seems as if because it happens all the time in Italy, it is somehow not as bad as if it happened in England, where assaulting players with burning fireworks is thought of as rather ungentlemanly. In Spain we've seen blatant racism on the terraces, but has anything been done about it really? Meanwhile, we create front and back-page headlines about the very occasional monkey chant.

In Britain we can be quick to self-flagellate ourselves for our sins, possibly because others are quick to do so too, but after the terrible scenes in Milan we should really get more perspective about our football culture. We're certainly no Hairy Tony.

38. ONE LONG BACCHANALIA OF MATERIALISM
07/06/05

I like to think I've lived a bit. Maybe I've lived higher on a bigger hog than most folk, even if I haven't exactly been Keith Richards. But the majority of my partying was done on a tight budget. You couldn't say that of any professional footballer now - the days when a player went to the match on the bus belong to a different age, almost to a different planet.

Footballers are now so distanced from the people who, one way or another, pay their lavish wages. In fact, a lot of them seem to live in an alternative universe to regular working people and it's making it hard for clubs in unglamorous or unfashionable parts of the country to attract players, just because their lifestyle expectations can't be met in the more obscure cities and market towns of the country. You just can't get a body wax in Barnsley except at a car wash.

I should also add that bacchanalia is one of my favourite words and it receives a gratuitous outing here.

It's often been said that women are a civilising influence on men. Clearly, whoever has been peddling this myth hasn't been on the piss in Newcastle's Bigg Market at midnight on a Friday when Tyneside's finest banshees are wailing, out of their minds on the drink. Indeed, the first time I ever saw a woman taking a whazz was in Newcastle, just behind the Duke of Wellington pub. At the age of 16 I was so transfixed by this sight that I almost got my head kicked in by her boyfriend, who was standing guard while she dropped knicks and squatted: "She's just havin' a fuckin' piss son, now fuck off."

I thought this made Newcastle all the more thrilling. As a Teesside lad, Newcastle was a big glamorous place - the place I went to buy Be Bop Deluxe albums from Virgin Records back when it was a small shop down a side street.

We were less well-travelled in those days. Most working-class people didn't have a car. London was a distant impossible-to-reach city. Leeds was the Deep South. Even a trip to Darlington seemed like an adventure even though it was only about nine miles from my house. So even at the age of 18 when I went to Newcastle Poly to fart around and take a lot of drugs and read the occasional book for three years before being awarded a degree, Newcastle still seemed like a big city and fantastically exciting compared to anything I could experience in Stockton or Middlesbrough.

There was a kebab shop for a start. Amazing as it may seem to you now, kebabs were not the commonplace source of post-pub ecoli poisoning they are today, not in my neck of the woods anyway. The moment I bit into my first kebab after a skinful of drink was a moment I shall never forget, not least because it passed through my digestion system in less than 45 minutes.

Then there was the casual street vomiting. I had been drinking in pubs for three years by the time I turned up at college. Despite looking like a baby, I still got served. I grew Gary Nev-style facial hair in an attempt to look older but I just looked like a baby with a false moustache. No-one cared. But in all my years drinking up and down the high street of Stockton, I had never seen gangs of blokes walking from pub to pub, vomiting up great streams of ale as they did so, quite casually, to make room for another few pints. Yet this was quite commonplace in the Bigg Market.

In recent years this seems to have declined in popularity as a leisure activity of the drinking classes, possibly because beer is much stronger and you don't need to drink such a vast ocean of it to get mortal. Back in '79 the strongest lager you could usually get was Carling Black Label. I once drank eight pints of Heineken - which was the 3.4% stuff back then - and was still virtually sober. That's wrong when you're 16 years old.

And then of course there was the proliferation of Geordie women, who I found as accommodating and gorgeous as their Teesside sisters, but there was a lot more of them, crucially including a sub-sect of women who liked heavy rock. This was marvellous. You could meet them in the City Tavern, the Haymarket, the Farmers Rest or Percy Arms. They all liked Whitesnake and Thin Lizzy and they had tight jeans and crimped hair and bought their clothes from Fynd in the Handysides Arcade. They often smelled of patchouli and always smelled of Pernod. They were, and indeed still are, brilliant. I was in love. With all of them. Virtually.

But times change. This grubby northern oik has been all over the world - competed in pickled chilli-eating contests in La Jolla, seen bears in the mountains of the Sierra Nevada and almost fallen out of a ski lift half-way up the Jungfrau. Life is very different to how I thought it might turn out. But it's not just me, everyone is the same. Most of us have been there and done it.

We're complacent about our innate cosmopolitan nature. We eat Mexican food, wear Italian clothes and listen to Norwegian death metal bands. It takes much more to impress us these days and I'm sure if you're 18 this is all the more true. While I grew up thinking pizza was exotic foreign food, to you, it's simply the basic stuff of life. I grew up thinking Indian cuisine was as alien to the digestive system as nuclear waste, but to you it's typical British nosh.

And of course, the richer you are, the more this is true. I've been lucky enough to blag my way into the finest hotels, restaurants and underwear from west London to Las Vegas. It's all good. But it impresses me less and less. Once you've taken mescaline in the Mojave Desert and watched UFOs flying overhead on their way to and from Area 51 or have been blown in the toilet of a Boeing 767, 39,000 feet up, you feel like you've seen much of what life has to offer. And this is just little me, a guitar-obsessed geek with bad hair from an unfashionable chemical dump in the north-east of England.

Imagine how jaded life must seem to rich footballers. We hear a lot of about the money they get paid, but let's just pause and think what it would really mean to earn a quarter of a million quid every month. Everything is within your means. Money has no value because you can buy anything. It's like it's free really. What do you care if something costs £1000 or £10,000 - it's like pissing water away.

It's a peculiar freedom that's bestowed upon these often-intellectually-challenged young men. You can do anything you want so what do you do? You buy a massive house on a new executive development, a stupid big car and an even more stupid blonde girlfriend who will allow you to behave like a twat to her as long as you buy her expensive jewellery and give her enough money to buy Harvey Nichols.

Now here's the problem for football clubs. It gets harder and harder to attract players to places like Middlesbrough, Blackburn or Portsmouth because the best, most well-paid players are jaded souls who increasingly see their lives as one long bacchanalia of materialism and they just don't see their expensive tastes being indulged in the old northern mill towns or rundown ports of England.

For shallow, international jet-setting players, there is little glamour in playing in the north of England unless no-one else will have you or the money is too big to turn down. And there lies the problem. Clubs like the Boro have to wedge players up massively just to get them to consider playing for us. Christ, even Newcastle had to offer well above 40k a week plus seven million quid for Chelsea reserve Scott Parker. It is madness and it's the part of contemporary football culture that I despise the most.

I still cling to the belief that it's frankly the biggest fucking honour of your life to play for Middlesbrough and if you don't appreciate that you can head south again Jack, even though I know that almost no-one born outside of the town would ever think that was true anymore. I find that sad. Mind you, I have travelled from a time when Newcastle was glamorous, so what the hell do I know?

Once in a while, I drag my very high horse out of its stable, (he's called Sidney) and climb into the saddle for a bit of a rant about things which angry up my blood. This particular issue has always bothered me. But it's not just the National Anthem; it's everything else that has to happen before kick-off. It gets worse every season as yet more mascots, small children, corporate sponsors and any other smegger who can be milked for a few quid is now allowed to be in the tunnel, on the pitch or dancing naked on the crossbar before the start of an international game.

Radically, I just want players to run out and start playing football, but these days after they've sung both, increasingly-long versions of the countries' anthems, juggled the small children that now must accompany every side onto the pitch for some reason - is this the football equivalent of the 'baby on board' car sticker? - by the time they've tossed a coin, had sex with the man who is dancing in the fake fur chicken suit, shook hands with every opposition player and all the officials and stroked the grass, over 20 minutes have elapsed and everyone has lost the will to live.

And then to add insult to injury England don't even have a specifically English national anthem, they just have Britain's despicably dour dirge, the sentiment behind which I can't empathise with in the slightest and which actually embarrasses me. All of this means I'm mad as hell before the game has even kicked off. So that's what all this wind and piss is about.

See, I've just got angry about it all over again. Bastards! At least I managed to shoehorn in a reference to one of my favourite musicians and song-writers, Roy

Harper. He nearly died after kissing a sheep you know. Well who wouldn't?

I have never sung our national anthem. If I did sing it, I would be lying. I'm not appealing to any deity to save anyone whose role in life is to wear vivid matching clothing, a sour sneer and a rectus expression of disgust. She ain't no human being. She rains over us.

God Save The Queen is Britain's national anthem, but why is it England's? When Scotland play, they sing Flower Of Scotland and Wales sing Land Of My Fathers, but England still sing God Save the Queen. Should we not be singing some other song as well? And who decides these things?

Somehow God Save The Queen has become England's anthem and also the UK's when we're competing as a unified entity. Where's the sense in that? If we have to have an anthem, England should have a separate one like the Welsh and Scots (what do Northern Ireland sing?). I propose it should be One Of Those Days In England by Roy Harper. Here's one verse, tell me it is not one million times better and more inspirational...

"One of those days in England, and birds in every garden in the land, one of those days in England when the passion never ends, a slowly moving season by the fire of my friends."

There's lots of other stuff about Albion (that's olde England not West Bromwich) and Sunday's joint cooking in my tree. It's perfect. Get the Bullinamingvase album, hear for yourself and get into one of this country's finest writers and musicians.

Our geo-political make-up is a bit of a botch job really. Try explaining it to an American. Yes, England is a country but no, England isn't the UK but yes, the UK is a country as well, but it's a country made up of err, well, four countries. No, they're not states. No, none of the countries are independent like proper countries but they are sort of, a bit. But not totally. They all speak English, even the ones who aren't English. They all have different national anthems but not when they compete as Britain, when they have England's anthem. Yes, Britain is a country too, it's the same as the UK but Northern Ireland, well that's a province, I think. We call it a country and often define it separately from Great Britain but sometimes don't and it's not part of Ireland, only of course it is, sort of. Oh bugger it, let's go get beer.

However, even if we accept the need for anthems, which I don't, the anti-Royalist sympathy which is shared by a large minority of the public is not allowed to express its pride in its country. Instead, the only option for the English/British is to have to thank the Queen and hope she reigns o'er us for a long time and presumably quells the rebellious Scots too - which is the now unsung sixth verse. I'm sure the Scots love that. It's uninspiring drivel and I'd argue means almost nothing to most of us under the age of 60, which by the way doesn't mean we have no pride in our country or are unpatriotic; Quite the reverse.

On a more basic principle I don't understand what purpose it serves having football teams sing their national anthems anyway.

Firstly, everyone boos each other's anyway, so playing them just incites bad feeling. Secondly, most players just pay lip service to them or just stay grim-faced and silent. And as England's manager, should Sven sing it? Or should he sing it in Swedish, or sing Sweden's anthem? I don't understand. It all makes no sense. Thirdly, what the hell is the point of an anthem anyway? Is it supposed to stir the troops before the battle? But this is sport. Not war. And anyway, how is singing your allegiance to a half-German family who had to change their name to Windsor to sound more English, and all their horse-faced inbred balding offspring, going to do that exactly for the England players? And frankly, if you need to sing a song before getting fired up to play for England then you shouldn't be there in the first place.

Although so few fans know more than the first two lines of Flower Of Scotland that they have to put the words on the scoreboard, at least it sings about the country itself and not about some irrelevant monarch, which is probably why they all belt it out with such gusto, even if most are just making vowel noises to the approximate tune because they don't know the words.

Likewise, the Welsh anthem celebrates the actual place. Land of my Fathers - macho place Wales, no time for women in their anthem. 'A land of poets and minstrels, famed men' - yes indeed, men like Shakin' Stevens and dope-smoking guitar-noodling hippies Man (best song Bananas - 'I like to eat bananas 'cos they got no bones, I like marijuana cos it gets me stoned' - they don't write them like that any more). They're not singing to a monarch are they? Not even to mythical queens like Rhiannon. No, it's about the bloody country, which is a bigger and more profound concept than singing about your king or queen. They're temporary - though the Windsors are not temporary enough for me.

It's insulting to us the citizens (sorry, make that subjects - we're not good enough to be citizens yet apparently). It makes no bloody sense. Just because it's always been done is no reason at all to continue with the facile and meaningless charade.

While some countries' anthems doubtless have more merit in sentiment and tune than the English/British one, the Chilean song comes to mind as especially forceful and anthemic, saying as it does that Chile 'be either the tomb of the free/Or a refuge from oppression', which is a raised fist stadium rock Bon Jovi-style anthem if ever I heard one, I'd still rather the teams ran out, shook hands and got on with the football. The start to every international seems to take 20 minutes these days by the time they've brought on the mascots, had the long and tortuous anthems, all shook hands, put their hands down the ref's shorts and exchanged pennants. What the hell are pennants anyway?

187

Who designs them, under whose instruction and who makes them? Is this medieval jousting or something?

And best of all we'd be spared all the old farts lecturing us about how thuggish all the booing of the anthems is in the first place. So in short, a better world for all.

Now sing after me, "It's one of those days in England with the country going broke and Sunday's joint is cooking in my tree..."

We all take travelling long distances for granted now. We think nothing of jumping on a plane to New York or Vegas or Copenhagen. But when I was a kid in the 1960's the furthest I got from home in the first nine years of my life was Scarborough, which is just about 40 miles from Hull. In 1970 we travelled from Stockton-on-Tees to Torquay. It seemed like we were going to a different country, so far away was it. I'm not kidding, Torquay had palm trees and everyone talked in a strange accent. That was the definition of foreign to me. It was the furthest from home my mam had ever gone and she was in her late 30's at the time and it'd have been the same for my dad if he hadn't had to fight Rommel in the desert with the 7th Army.

Even by the early 80's working-class kids who had no money still hadn't done much travelling. I think the first time I went to London was in 1973 to see the Tutankhamen exhibition with the school. Eight years later I returned to see Neil Young. And that was it. So going to London still felt like a foreign country when we first hit the smoke with the band. I have to say we never really enjoyed it much and even now, after spending a lot of time down there for one reason or another, I'm always glad to get out of London. It always seems to be a dirty and cold-hearted place where no-one will look you in the eye because they're scared you might stab them or insert a brick into their bottoms. People in London, by and large look a bit miserable most of the time.

Plus in the late 80's I remember fans of London clubs singing "what's it like to lose your job?" at us Boro fans in the middle of Thatcher's big depression. How very witty. Later in the early 90's when house prices crashed and economy was shredded by more Tory incompetence a few of us tried chanting "what's it like to have negative equity?" but it never really took off, probably because it was too smart arse by far.

I was last down there to see Govt Mule, one of my favourite bands and it was one of the best gigs I'd ever seen. But as soon as it was over, I wanted to get away back north. Maybe I'm just a reactionary retard though!

Every week I get lots of emails from you all saying something like, "Why don't you stop being serious about football and tell us more stories about taking drugs, shagging birds and playing guitars and then make it something to do with football." I'm paraphrasing but that is the gist of it. My reply is usually that I don't want to bore all the other readers who could frankly care less about me and mates vomiting over naked Valley Girls while in the throes of passion and how that's like how Chelsea have treated the Premiership.

But then again....

Carrie wasn't possessed by the devil, nor did she have the power of tele-kinesis, but she was blonde-haired and blue-eyed and she loved nothing more than a skinny-assed hairy youth. This is where I quite literally came in.

We didn't play down south much back in the 80's. This wasn't because the south didn't want to hear our over-driven noisy UFO-influenced metal but because the south was full of, well southerners and as such we instinctively avoided it. We didn't get southerners. They were odd. They voted Tory. They had money. They liked Haircut 100. They had started drinking beer out of bottles, which previously only winos and lads in Newcastle who could take the cap off a bottle of Broon with their teeth had done. They drank more lager than beer, which back then was a sign of being gay by the way. Never mind yer shandy drinkers; lager drinkers were only one stop away from being ballet dancers who ran hairdressing salons called Blow 'n' Go...unless you put cider in it of course, making a Snakebite, which was every biker's mother milk and single-handedly explained the popularity of the New Wave of British Heavy Metal. NWOBHM.

Some had even started putting wedges of lime in the neck off bottles of Mexican lager. It was all a sign of nancy southern rubbish to us. Fruit and beer. Together! What was wrong with Roses' Lime Cordial? You'll be asking us to eat pineapple with gammon next. That's sweet and savoury on the same plate tha' knows. That's two different meals. And as Sheffield's finest John Shuttleworth has told us in song, you can't go back to savoury from sweet.

Yes. We were proper men, albeit ones in very tight pants who smelled of patchouli and wore eye-liner. Aye we were bigoted and narrow-minded like our fathers before us, but culture was less homogenised back then and we were always too poor to go anywhere so what did we know? We thought we knew everything but we knew nowt.

This was back in the early 80's before everyone in the north moved south to work for the health service for minimum wage and live in a house with 16 other people in order to afford a mortgage on a wheelbarrow covered in a tarp in a hole in the ground in some desperate hell hole like fucking Peckham. Jesus. Now there are no southerners in London anymore because they've all moved out to Bath and the city is full of Croats, Russians, Poles and men from Croxteth selling bad acid and gang masters from Spalding looking for illegal labour to pick broccoli. Peckham I'm reliably informed is now "up and coming". Well back then the only thing up and coming in Peckham were the hookers' punters.

Anyway, there was a time when we rolled up darn sarf, with a twin-wheeled transit van full of musical equipment, cheap speed and some Pease Pudding stotties. What do you mean you don't know what a stottie is? Bloody poofs.

And there was a time when yer working-class, untravelled southern lady hadn't had a lot of contact with yer northern monkey. And some liked our unsophisticated ways even if our breath did smell of Cameron's Strongarm. Not for nothing were we called The Beer Pigs.

We were just such northern monkeys: leery; loud; uncouth; loveable; drunken; and in some cases, diseased. You'd have liked us. Honest. And so would your sister. But we were arrogant, puffed up with youthful delusion and lust. You'd have thought we invented chords E A and D; All fucking major chords too' none of your minor shit. But you need that just to get on stage with your bollocks crammed down one leg of yer jeans.

We were booked to play the back room of a pub in somewhere unremarkable in north-ish London.

We've just learned how to play Lights Out In London by UFO especially for the occasion, which if played right should sound like the four horsemen of the apocalypse are chasing a screaming banshee into hell. It involves a bit of nifty fret work by whoever is doing the lead guitar, which was usually me. We think we've got it licked, so we open the show that night with it instead of our usual opener which was 'Tonight' by Pat Travers. What do you mean who the fuck is Pat Travers!? Do you know nothing?

Naturally very few people were present, it was just another band playing noise to strangers. However, a small group of people were standing at the bar and as we went into the middle bit before the solo cranks up, two girls break from the bar onto the dark dance floor and start what was and indeed still is called headbanging. Now, if you don't know this song, you should really download a live version. It's a monumental riff, one of the under-rated classics and it lends itself to much freaking heed-the-ball head thrashing. As we're reaching a crescendo, these two lasses are thrashing in an almost epileptic manner.

192

It turns out that these two girls are sisters, though not in any way similar to each other. Well these two loved us. And from what we could see, they were better looking than the usual coalminer's daughter we regularly enjoyed. They went mental for the whole hour we were onstage and because of them a good crowd of 60 or so gathers to see what the fuss is about and to watch their big tits bounce up and down - well who wouldn't eh. C'mon. Tis' the way of the world and no amount of reconstructed sexual politics can make it otherwise.

We finish with Snortin' Whiskey, another Pat Travers classic. It's not high philosophy but its kick-ass rock 'n' roll for a Saturday night and don't let anyone tell you otherwise.

After the show, polishing our slaver technique we head to the bar dreaming dreams of the mutually appreciated exchange of bodily fluids that makes being on the first rung of rock 'n' roll's ladder so pleasurable

And there's Carrie at the bar. She's blonde and has watery blue eyes. She goes in and out in all the right places and has the full compliment of large mammary glands so desired by the superficial male. I was quick off the mark when I needed to be so I'm straight in there like a ferret chasing a cheese rabbit up a drainpipe knowing Hairy Tony would be up her before you could say Whitbread Trophy Bitter, the pint that thinks it's a quart'. He had to make do with the equally well-endowed if less pretty sister.

"Hey there, I'm Johnny. I play lead guitar," I said truthfully.

And she turns to me with 17 and natures queen if you know what I mean beautiful eyes all lascivious pupil dilating smiles and tongue licking off lips in the way that rarely happens to a bloke like me who, at the end of it all, is happy if he can just get a few minutes of pity sex. I'm going dry in the mouth. You know what it's like when you're young; you can do it anytime anywhere anyhow. I'd have had her up against the bar if necessary. It wouldn't have taken long. It was one of those moments.

All this is flashing through my mind in a nano second as I speak.

Then she opens her mouth. I'm just imagining what I'd like to put in there when I hear this noise. It's the sound of someone inserting a rusty gate into a seagull. It's horrible. It's frightening. It's her voice.

"Allo dahrrrlin," she said in an accent which was like someone had detonated a cockney Atom Bomb, so profound were the shockwaves. I thought my skin would peel right off. On top of this she had a speech impediment

"You were blaaaddy bwilliant" she said. She somehow pronounced UFO as Yoo-weff-oww. I hate to sound shallow, but this was not good.

Straight away I know there was going to be a battle between my penis and my brain. This is the worst of all battles because you know who usually wins and you know who always feels bad about it.

She sounds so appalling and on top of that she's astonishingly stupid. I mean, really, really stupid. The sort of person who thinks education is a character weakness. Worse still she thinks Northampton is well north.

I try and talk to her. I'm doing my best but the rest of the lads are taking the piss something rotten. Tony has it turns out got the uglier but smarter sister and has got it all sewn up already. Hunter drags me away and buys me a pint and a chaser. So I know something is up. He says something like," Look Nic, you're in there, you know that don't you....but I know you're a posh twat who likes to think he's got standards...and mind she is a total fucking plank....but if you don't want to hump her brains out, I fucking will - on your behalf like. Either way we're not leaving this fucking town without one of us having seen her naked and been up its tubes."

He was always a romantic Hunter.

But we're four bandits on the road away from home and we all have the in-built duty, where we learn it from I don't know, that says you must aid any one of your mates in copulating with ladies. Almost everything is secondary to it, even if it puts everyone out massively. It's a job that needs doing and we're all in it together.

Finally, there was talk of going back to their flat. So what did I do? Well what would you do? To dip or not to dip? That is the question. We worked it out.

Me and Tony went back to their flat for 30 minutes, Hunter and Lenny are under strict instructions to call the flat number - which we had got from them earlier - telling us we had to meet them 'cos the van was stolen or some other lie. This gave us just enough time to get there, for them to boil a kettle, make coffee, get pants off, inoutinoutinout and wipe it on the curtains. It worked like a dream. Within an hour of leaving the pub we were back with the lads in a late bar. If I'd just had ear plugs it would have been perfect. She even had a cockney orgasm.

You see, appearance and reality can be two very different things. And just as it is with heavy metal cockney girls, it can be with modern football. Ah yes. You knew I'd get there eventually.

Rio Ferdinand: Appearance; Modern defender, good on the ball, contemporary hair cut. Reality; Dopey overpaid bloke with gangsta rap fixation.

Wigan: Appearance; Pie-obsessed town with football team managed by similar pie-obsessed Scouser. Reality; Second best team in the land.

Jean-Alain Boumsong: Appearance; Fast, strong international defender. Reality; Barely able to play football at all. May play pissed.

Nobby Solano: Appearance; Peruvian goat-herder. Reality; Under-rated creative midfield genius.

Shay Given: Appearance; Half leprechaun/half bat-boy. Reality; Best keeper in the Premiership.

Liverpool; Appearance; European champions. Reality; European champions. But how?

Martin Jol: Appearance; A scary ugly bulldog of a wrestler. Reality; Best manager Spurs have had since Bill Nic, and charming with it

So the lesson: Don't be fooled by appearances!

41. STAND UP IF YOU DON'T WANT PILES
08/11/05

Look, I'm getting on now. Standing up is tiring and frankly, I'd rather be sitting or preferably lying down a lot more. But not at the football. This is an issue which makes my head steam with frustration because it's yet another example of how the game has been stolen from true fans on false notions about safety and spurious excuses about encouraging children and women to football.

Who thinks up these stupid notions? I wish I could lay the blame on someone specifically but it's become an endemic malaise right across all of football's governing bodies. And fans are just too often complicit. They keep their heads down and don't complain. They just put up with it all. If we turn up one week and we all have to stick a carrot up our arses before going through the turnstile we'll just bend over and insert.

You see, I don't understand why standing has been outlawed at top grounds. I have no interest in seeing the 70s-style Kop with its tidal wave of nearly 30,000 people and their piss flowing up and down the terraces. It was dangerous and if you were a short-arse you couldn't see a bloody thing and no-one wants to stand in a flowing river of urine as people relieve their bladders of eight pints of Double Diamond or Stones Best bitter.

But that isn't the only standing option. Standing doesn't have to be dangerous with a bit of organisation. But I think top clubs see all-seater stadiums as a symbol of their status and success. It's like a new Mercedes instead of the old Skoda.

To ask for standing to be re-introduced feels like we're asking for something terribly old-fashioned and out of date like socialism or mono records. But it's better and more exciting standing and anyway, fans stand up half the time as it is, even though technically we're not allowed. Football is notoriously unresponsive to what its customers want because as a business it's unique. People turn up in their thousands to watch crap in an environment they don't like that is physically uncomfortable and often open to the elements, just because we love the game so much.

So the authorities can point to healthy crowds and say, "look, they love it like this", but it's no more true than when the BBC say we love their football coverage and point to the big figures as proof. No. We love football and will put up with a lot to see it. Simple as that.

See, I told you it makes my head steam.

As I lay on my sofa enjoying the Man United game I noticed something unusual - Old Trafford was noisy, all the way through. There was a big atmosphere for a big game and it helped make it all the more exciting. But it's not the norm at most grounds now, not even at Old Trafford.

I know the TV mics can be deceptive but there are times when you can hear the coaches shouting above the paltry whimpering of the crowds, even at big grounds. Never mind the clichés, Highbury sometimes does seem like a library.

I've been at the Riverside when it's been so quiet you'd think we were waiting for a funeral, maybe for the death of football. Admittedly, Boro fans' natural state of mind is catatonic after years of boredom, pollution and cheap strong drink but this should not be an excuse. Silence is not golden.

There are times these days when the crowd seems to lose its collective focus and attention is distracted by something more interesting - like a nice arse, a hot pie or a passing erect nipple. There's a low mumble as we get disengaged.

Mobile phones haven't helped as there now appears to be a whole section of fans who are more interested in archiving their experiences than actually experiencing and wallowing in them - endlessly taking photos and texting people who aren't there while they ignore the person they came with.

But this isn't a recent development. Despite bigger crowds for the last 15 years, a lot of grounds have got progressively quieter. Fans seem to have changed. Too many are just reactive. That is, they only make a noise when something happens. So when nothing happens they sit there mute.

The art of the football song has all but disappeared. There was a time when every ground sang different songs. Now all you hear is the unambitious 'Champions League, you're 'avin a larf.' This was not always the case, especially when we had terracing and we were allowed to stand. Look at the old footage of crowds. They're almost hysterical. They almost lose control. This made football grounds places of almost frightening intensity at times. It made everything better and more enjoyable. It inspired players.

It's time we were allowed to stand again.

I'd like to see standing terraces introduced at all Premiership grounds again. Just at either end, you can leave the seats to the middle-class and the middle-aged who like their arse going numb on plastic seats.

But standing is a big no-no in the game these days. Everyone in authority is against its reintroduction but I think their arguments are fatuous and unreasonable and ignore what so many fans would like to see.

The argument that most annoys me is that all-seater stadia attracts more women and kids to the game, ignoring the fact that lack of standing makes many more stay away. For a start women and kids can still sit in the stands. So we're not excluding them. And I'm not proposing a return to the 70's phenomenon of 'taking an end' where several thousand fans would beat the living jobbies out of each other. I don't want that any more than some delicate peachy-pink girly wants it. We're not proposing all-standing stadia here.

It patronisingly assumes women, being sweet-smelling sensitive creatures, are just too delicate to stand - well that is utter bollocks. You know it, I know it, we all know it. It's sexist, condescending rubbish and it's uttered by people who have apparently never met women who like football.

And as for attracting more kids, there was always a family stand - but do we have to be subservient to what kids want? Really? It doesn't seem right to me.

It sounds very like the argument for child-friendly pubs, which is possibly the worst thing I can think of up to and including war. I don't even want to be in a pub with anyone who knows the words to Sugababes songs, talks about Big Brother, has corn-row hair or wears Burberry, let alone screaming little shit machines.

To everyone who tells us just how child-friendly cafes, restaurants and bars are in Europe I say 'well feck off over there then and leave me alone to have a pint or six and to put Thin Lizzy on the jukebox loud enough to make your kids' ears bleed'.

Sorry, I went off on one there.

The next argument against standing is that it's more dangerous. But that's just not true. No football disasters have been caused by standing per se. They're caused by poor policing, overcrowding, decrepit stands, poor fire safety etc etc. Standing doesn't make anything more dangerous as long as you don't pack too many fans into one end and don't have old-school metal crash (or crush) bars.

Advocating standing doesn't mean a return to how it was in 1975 - though I'd be prepared to take my chances even if it did.

We can create modern terraces with a modern approach to how we fill them with punters and how they're policed.

The real reason it's not considered, even though I would guess the majority of fans would like to see its return, is because those running the game have become wedded to the idea of sanitised, tidy, unemotional football for an increasingly middle-class audience. That's how they see it.

They can't get their small minds around the idea that we can stand for an hour and a half and it doesn't mean we want to fight, get crushed, steal each other's wallets or unleash a tidal wave of piss that flows steaming down to the pitch. We just want to jump up and down, wave our arms around and sing obscene songs without someone in a fluorescent coat telling us to mind our language.

It gets the blood pumping. It's healthy. It's one of the reasons we want to see live football and not watch it on telly. Don't they understand?

The current policy of the Football Licensing Authority makes no sense at all. We are apparently allowed to stand up when we get excited; when a goal is scored, when we see Mike Riley make another mistake or when we feel the need to stretch our legs after a nap during the Brum v Bolton game.

So the FLA think it's safe for us to leap up and down when we score - but that standing up all the time is way too dangerous. What exactly could we be doing that would be so dangerous? They appear to believe that more trouble will happen if we're standing up. But surely trouble happens when the nutters get going, whether it's seated or not. Does standing up make people angrier? No. In fact, wrecking seats is a good way to make yourself a weapon.

Do they really believe that a fan is going to go, "you bastard I'm going to twat you...oh, hang on that will involve standing up, I'd better not". It's plain daft.

Seating does not equal modern and standing does not equal old-fashioned. Introducing modern terracing isn't a step back. Encouraging passion, noise and giving the customer what they want is very, very important to football as a business. Or it should be. Fans pay the bills but we're forced to watch from nasty plastic seats. It's not comfortable at all. It's not more civilised. It encourages piles and frankly we're bored of it.

We all spend all our lives sitting in front of computers as our bottoms grow bigger and fatter. We could all do with less sitting down and more standing up. And if standing is viewed by the authorities as dangerous, why is it still allowed in the lower divisions in largely inferior, more decrepit stadiums? It makes no sense and it stands no scrutiny.

Why is it allowed at rock concerts? At gigs we're allowed to body surf, we're allowed to bounce up and down until sweat drips from the roof. All perfectly legal. Why can't we at football?

Even Lord Justice Taylor said in the report that kicked off the whole all-seater thing that standing wasn't intrinsically unsafe. It's all down to how it's managed. It's not hard to work out the capacity of a stand, only sell that many tickets for it and not let anyone else in.

So will it happen?

Will it bollocks. Football has been lured to a more sanitised, less visceral place and banning standing is crucial to that culture.

They want the kind of fans who buy the overpriced low-quality rubbish from the store, buy overpriced low-quality rubbish food, turn up sober, clap politely and then just sit there quietly until something exciting happens.

This is the ideal modern fan. Not too noisy, respectful, doesn't swear and has plenty of money to spend on merchandise.

This isn't me. And it probably isn't you.

They're taking the pish out of us. They have taken our money and they are not giving us what we want.

What those in authority seem unable to realise is that the atmosphere at a ground is crucial to the enjoyment. We don't just go for the football. We like the whole experience - or we used to before you could get thrown out for swearing or standing up too much.

Football culture is strong and resilient, atmospheres at certain grounds are still good, but it's slowly becoming less the case. All-seater stadiums are a further illustration of the neutering of football and a whole generation has now grown up without ever knowing just how great it was to be on a packed terrace at 3pm in a Saturday afternoon with a low mist of Bovril, breath and baccy in the air as thousands of damp parkas gently steamed. This was life lived more fully. It gave you a tingle, a spark of the immortal, something that sitting on a plastic seat will never, ever do. But hey, who am I? I'm just the schmuck who pays the bills.

We all knew Bestie was dying. It took longer than some had thought. He hung on and hung on but we knew it was soon a matter of 'if and not when'. Even now, thinking about it, it fills me with tears. I know that it did the same for far harder men than me. As the old bloke of F365, I was probably the only person to have seen Georgie play in real life. I was the only one who had been of the right generation to understand his impact, not just on football but on popular culture. So it fell to me to write his obituary. People under the age of 30 sadly think of him as an old loser drunk who popped up looking the worse for wear on talk shows. I can tell they don't understand our worship of him.

Some people said a lot of harsh words about him around this time and I suppose if you hadn't grown up with Bestie, you couldn't feel empathy for him. It was different for me and millions like me. He wasn't just a man who played football; he was, in the truest sense, an artist. He wasn't normal. He was a freak and I am almost always on the side of the freaks. All the talk about whether he deserved his liver transplant was a disgrace. He had already given us so much. He had made life worth living just to see him play. Who amongst us can say such a thing?

It was a perverse twist of fate that his surname was so perfect a description of his talent and yet it seemed fitting for a man so uniquely blessed. I found myself shedding tears during his funeral and I never even cried when my dad died. The only comfort is that like all greats, he will never really die. Whenever football fans get together for decades to come his name will be spoken of in reverential awe.

Gone but not forgotten. It's a glib phrase that's trotted out too often on occasions like this. But for once, it's true.

Georgie Best touched me and my generation's life in the same way as The Beatles, Bob Dylan or Jack Kerouac. He was that important.

He was far, far bigger than any footballer today, even in this era's massive over-exposure of players. It may be hard for younger fans to understand just how profound the impact Bestie made from the mid 60's onwards. It was as though he invented modern football all by himself.

He didn't even look like any of his contemporaries. Put him in the Man United team today aged 18 and he would look and play like a modern footballer. He was that ahead of his time. He was new, exciting and utterly, utterly brilliant. A man without peers.

Bestie invented the 'footballer as rock star' concept without really trying. It was all natural. In an era of stout men of grit and muscle, Bestie was a thin sliver of a boy blessed with ball skills that were breathtaking. The old films show him bamboozling defenders like a magician doing tricks. It was all the more remarkable because he did it in an era when you could hack someone down and get away with it. But Bestie was rarely injured, he'd gone before they could get near him.

And what the old films don't show you is the effortless way he moved across the pitch with or without the ball. He glided through the air like a ghost. It was perpetual poetic motion. No other player I have seen since could run with the ball as easily as without it. He ran with perfect rhythm and poise. He seemed to barely touch the pitch with his boots. And no-one needed the benefit of hindsight to realise we were witnessing a genius. It was in your face, you couldn't ignore it. Whoever you supported. We all knew.

His European performances in the 60's in particular were monuments of the highest art. No-one could quite believe it. He was so much better than any of his contemporaries and it was all so effortless to him.

But of course it wasn't just the earth-shattering football that Bestie will be remembered for. He was a fashion icon, even despite being in Gratton's catalogue and on knitting patterns. He had great hair, great side-burns. Like all rebel spirits, he wore his shirt untucked and socks rolled down. He was the very epitome of rock 'n' roll football and there will never ever be his equal. Ever.

Maradona had all the talent and the addictive personality to match but he was never a charming, beautiful man. He didn't have the swagger or the poise of The Great Man. It's worth remembering that he retired when he was just about 28. Yes, there were all the adventures in America, Fulham and even Barnet but in a way, they didn't count. When he left Man United his real career was over.

How hard must it have been to be a shooting star? To burn so brightly for little more than ten years and then have to live the rest of your life knowing it would never really be as good again. The pressures that would bring to bare on your soul is something we can't understand.

And of course as we all know Georgie had his problems; problems that eventually took him from us. At the highest levels of the arts, people are different; they're not milk toast folk who are always easy, pleasant or accommodating. The spirit of genius doesn't always allow that. Maybe they feel too deeply, have too much vision and see the world differently to us.

You can excuse it or condemn it but it doesn't alter the truth. Artists are different and Bestie was an artist of the highest order. He was imbued with the spark of the divine; the light of the immortal. But the deal between God and the Devil meant that to have this genius, he was possessed by the demon of alcoholism.

None of us is perfect. We fuck up. We do the wrong things and behave badly and Georgie was no different, but the reason so many of us can't bring ourselves to say a bad word about the man is because he gave us so much in his playing days. In fact, I still feel like I owe Bestie something personally for all the awesome entertainment and artistry he gave me. I just feel grateful to have seen him.

He was a poet, a rebel spirit and footballing aesthete the like of which shall never grace our lives again. He made life better.

43. A MINUTE'S SILENCE FOR THE DEATH OF THE MINUTE'S SILENCE

28/11/05

This attracted the second-most mail I've had in nearly six years. All but one was in agreement with my position. Sadly, things haven't really changed and we still have these pointless minute's silences for non-football-related things at the behest of some mystery minute's silence mafia.

Briefly there was a rebellion and people decided to clap instead. But we're all so hung up on doing the right thing and no-one wants to do the politically-incorrect thing even if it more accurately reflects their feelings. It would appear that the public expression of an emotion is somehow considered important, as though it blesses humanity on us all collectively if we all feel our pain together. We are under the tyranny of people who have assumed the moral high ground without ever having to justify it.

It's all just too unbearably shallow, childish and plastic to me. What are we doing and saying with this kind of gesture and why do you want to include me in it without asking me? The World Cup 2006 started with an attempt at a minute's silence 'for the FIFA family', boomed the tannoy. The what sir? The German fans rightly saw this as a disgusting self-indulgence and made a lot of noise, thereby ending it after ten seconds.

Maybe people like this sort of thing these days. Maybe people don't know what to feel until they're told what to feel in public. I do know that there are thousands of people out there who think a football match is no place for this kind of thing. They're right

Some of you will think after reading this that I'm some sort of cruel, morally-vacuous creature with no empathy for my fellow humans' suffering. Trust me I'm not, I deplore bigotry, cruelty, war and being beastly to animals. I want a world based on love and generosity, not on hate and violence, and it's precisely because of this that I want our football grounds to stop observing minute's silences.

Who decides about these things? The latest one was for Ken Bigley (though apparently not for the two Americans who also suffered the same fate - are their lives different in some way?) and good old Brian Clough got one.

Are we supposed to equate these two things? What does it all mean? What are we doing holding a minute's silence at the football? Are we showing respect? If so, is it to the victim or to each other? It must be the latter because otherwise why would we be asked to do it in public? And what happens if you didn't like Brian Clough? Are you obliged to be quiet or can you express your disagreement? No of course you can't. There's some kind of collective if synthetic moral outrage if anyone breaks the silence by shouting, say, "come on Wales" or "fuck off Wales" as they did on Saturday.

The way these things are forced upon us feels wrong. It feels like I'm being told what to do and what to think. It's prescribing my emotions. I can't feel sadness and empathy for every human tragedy - I just can't - and the truth is, as terrible as many things are, if you let yourself get too caught up in them, you'd become a weeping wreck and utterly dysfunctional. So maybe this minute's silence thing is to give us all a chance to pause and think 'thank God that didn't happen to me'.

We've had minute's silences for the horrors in Beslan (I couldn't work out if I was supposed to be silent just for the children, or the adults as well - it wasn't made clear). We had it for Holly and Jessica. What good does it do? Does it show we care? If so, why do we need to show each other? You can't make yourself care about anything. You do or you don't. It's in your heart or it isn't. I think it's often nearer the truth than we care to admit to say that we don't really care that much, but we're trying to show we really do. This doesn't make us heartless bastards.

People have just been killed in hurricanes in USA - no minute's silence for them though. What about the killing in Sudan? Are they deemed less worthy than the kids in Beslan? What criteria are being applied here? Does the amount of people killed matter? Is beheading worse than shooting or getting run over by a drunk driver? Is it the colour of skin or their nationality? And just who is judging who deserves our silence?

It's certainly arguable that the minute's silence for Mr Bigley was doing more work for terrorists. Look at the effect they've had on us all. Maybe they'll want to do it again just to see if they can repeat the same kind of coverage.

My dad had three brothers killed in WW2. His own role as a gunner in the Battle of El Alamein scarred him emotionally for life and that was not without consequences for me. From time to time I think about them and what they went through and why, but I don't need to do it with 30,000 other people before seeing the Boro. I don't need to do it collectively or while inhaling the cheap Albanian fags the bloke in front of me smokes and I would object to being told that I should. I don't expect anyone else to feel like I do about my dead uncles and I would never ask that anyone should.

It's like when politicians make sweeping statements about our lives, telling us what we think. Last week Michael Howard told me that I thought the NHS wasn't working and that crime was out of control in my area, which was a bit odd really since that's not my experience at all and I think the exact opposite. But thanks for telling me what I think, eh.

But that's the same as an enforced minute's silence isn't it? It assumes we all feel bad so we shall all stand and feel bad together - if you don't feel bad then there must be something wrong with you.

And just what is so respectful about silence anyway? Why is silence the expression of our empathy? I loved Brian Clough but I didn't want to be silent on his death, I wanted to be noisy and to have some drinks in his honour.

An obligatory minute's silence does not show respect. It doesn't show what is in the hearts of those present. We're told to do it, so most do for fear of being slagged off. It's vaguely fascist and it's an emotionally childish response to events that have been on the telly.

And that is at the heart of this. It's all a response to stuff that's on the telly. And that's what these minute's silence really tell us - if you want to get public respect, die on the telly. Get some coverage in the papers. It's like a macabre extension of celebrity culture. It's as though those who perpetuate the concept are saying 'don't make it hard for us to find out about your tragedy or the reason behind your suffering because we can't be bothered and we're too shallow'. I don't think that's true. Football fans are not all knuckle-dragging idiots and we have emotion, empathy and soul, but a football match is not the place for us to collectively or individually prove it to ourselves or each other.

44. THE MYSTERY OF THE STEWARDS
05/12/05

Stewards are on that growing list of things that have become such an institution that no-one questions their presence any more. But if you go to any game, pay close attention to what they actually do. More often than not they're just standing there staring into the middle distance bored witless. They're employed to stop trouble and to eject people who are swearing too much, or who shout too loudly about the latest tactical system they've dreamed up, or have the wrong coloured trousers on. But they hardly ever have to do any serious work as the police sort out any real aggro, the stewards not being allowed to wade in and crack heads.

The one thing they are supposed to do is stop people getting on the pitch, but they are pretty powerless to do even that, as this incident last season proved. These are not crowd-control specialists; it's just someone in a High-Viz jacket.

Now you know me, I'm the hairy bloke at the bar who smells of drink and curry. But that aside, you know I like to ask questions that get asked all too infrequently. Like why are thongs supposed to be sexy? Why is The Darkness's second album so awful? Why does anyone believe anything Harry Redknapp ever says anymore? And, oh yes, what exactly do stewards do at football matches?

I ask after the hilarious incident at Stoke this weekend where a fan managed to get on the pitch and engage in a proper wrestling fight with QPR keeper Simon Royce just after the full-time whistle. Now, if you didn't see this, Royce is a massive bloke and the fan is trying to pull him down and crack him one, but Royce has an iron grip on him the way you might have on a daddy long legs as you throw it out of the window.

This is all happening in the back of the net, which is getting torn to pieces in the ensuing melee. Eventually Royce throws the bloke to the ground with a weary frustration that you might feel after a puppy has been knawing at your ankle for an hour.

This goes on for some time without any officials doing anything. Then along come the fluorescent stewards waddling like the Keystone Cops with looks of sheer fear and incredulity that they have to do something for their £20. However, instead of trying to get hold of the intruder and dispose of him, they seem far more concerned with keeping the players apart and away from the fight. Some of them are dancing on their toes like they're up for a fight after ten Stellas on a Friday night.

Meanwhile, another fan is on the pitch and having a pop at QPR players and it's all kicked off in grand style with players pushing each other and everyone else instinctively wanting to fight. Meanwhile, Royce has walked away from the fan who still wants a piece of him. Eventually, there are so many stewards there that they wrestle the intruders away. It's all taken many minutes.

I thought this was exactly what stewards were supposed to prevent. Fans getting on the pitch is the one easily-identifiable thing that is not allowed, and trying to twat the goalie is especially illegal and just the sort of thing they're supposed to stop. But they were blissfully unaware that someone wanted to kick seven bells out of Royce even as he was caught up in the net like a particularly large bloater in a fisherman's net. And when they awoke from their pie-induced slumbers they were clearly wholly unable to deal with the situation.

I've nothing against stewards as individuals but they annoy the hell out of me - the way they stand when a goal is scored and everyone is jumping up and down, seemingly looking in the crowd for someone who is enjoying themselves too much, trying to look like they're on their toes for any over-exuberance. Essentially they just try to look busy but do nothing.

213

Occasionally they'll throw someone out for swearing. That's really helpful. Thanks for that.

Most of the time they're trying to surreptitiously sneak a look at the action on the pitch, or have given up all pretence of stewarding altogether and are just watching from their primo position. I have no proof of this but I suspect a lot of the stewards have just pitched up at the company that has the contract in the morning and got the job for a few quid that afternoon.

There is no national training scheme or standard for stewards - essentially you turn up, get a coat and look serious. That's about it. They can chuck people out of the ground for breaking club rules and policy, which the police apparently can't do. So perhaps it's club policy at Stoke to allow opposition goalies to get a good kicking from fans? But really they're just a cheap police-lite.

And if a lot of trouble really does kick off, what is the steward's role? Do they wade in and dispense justice or stand back while the police sort it out? At every game you'll see lines of stewards lined up at either end to stop fans coming on the pitch but they're almost always powerless to stop those who really do want to get on there. Then you get the comedy chase as they run after the invader, who may well be naked. We're not allowed to see this on telly anymore as it's deemed to be in bad taste and giving them the oxygen of publicity, when it's really the only thing we really want to see. Everyone enjoys a naked pitch invader and frankly, if I've paid £50 I want to see some entertainment, even if it is a very drunk man with a micro-penis being chased by 37 men in bright yellow day-glo jackets.

The FLA says: "Each club needs to provide a given number of suitably trained and qualified stewards to enable it to fulfil the requirements of its safety certificate and to ensure the safety of spectators. The number and deployment of stewards will vary according to local circumstances."

But this rather typically seems to me to be written to mean all things to all people. How many is the 'given number'? What does 'suitably trained' mean? What does 'qualified' mean and who is judging whom against which standard? And since the number and deployment of stewards can vary from ground to ground, that seems to me to mean that you can set your own rules and standards.

Presumably this is why some stewards are simply spectators to the game and others are draconian wardens of the English language, ever alert for an expletive. However, they all seem to be prepared to tolerate any amount of hand gestures and general slagging-off of nearby opposition players. So what are those stewards doing again? Yes, they're looking at us. Well sort of. The lights are on but no-one is home. Frozen half to death and bored witless, most are just staring into space and dreaming of the first pint of the night.

The only reason stewards exist is because it's cheaper to contract policing out to security companies than it is to get the professionals to do the job. And I'm sure in truth it's more for PR reasons than anything else, just so the club can say, 'look how effectively we're policing the crowd', to the local authorities. But as proved at Stoke, when there's any real work to be done, they're woefully inept, and slow to do anything at all.

No number of stewards will stop the odd nutter wanting to get on the pitch and have a slap at a player. It's no-one's fault but the nutter's. By and large football crowds are not going to want to get on the pitch, but if they do, the presence of stewards will not stop them en masse. A few coppers with the aid of CCTV can easily identify racist abuse from punters and throw them out, and if real violence kicks off the stewards are sod all use because they can't arrest anyone, nor than they whack them with a rubber truncheon.

So what is it that the stewards do again?

This is the longest column I have ever written for Football365 and it was also the piece that attracted the most mails. Boro fans contacted me from all over the globe to tell me I had somehow crystallised all their own feelings about the club and about football in general, which was incredibly exciting and gratifying. For that reason I consider it the best, most successful rant I've ever done. It even got me onto Radio Tees. Now there's true stardom for you.

Oddly enough, after I wrote this and after the lad threw his season ticket at Steve McClaren when we were creamed 4-0 at home by Villa, things got much better. I have been told by some insiders that the fact that we, the fans - who at Middlesbrough are a notoriously patient and undemanding bunch by and large - had just had enough of the terrible football played by half-arsed mercenaries actually finally motivated some of them.

I think it was a wake-up call and to some degree it worked. Reaction to this piece showed me that fans feel their clubs in their hearts far more than their heads and time after time I got mail from people saying they felt their club had been stolen from them by money-grabbing players who cared nothing for where they played or the traditions of the club. It almost physically hurts fans.

We have a superb youth system at the Boro and some great young talent. I only hope that the underlying culture of trying to buy in expensive overseas players changes because if it doesn't, fans will start to stay away and spend their money on things which give them pleasure instead of handing Mark Viduka £60k a week to make himself fat. How galling when he then turned out for Australia at the World Cup looking half the size after just a month's training - training he could not be arsed to do for the club that pays him so lavishly. There's your trouble. Right there.

Fresh from FA Cup humiliation at the hands of Nuneaton, I feel compelled to dwell this week on my own club's private grief, because I think it illustrates a broader, more universal problem with many of our clubs in the modern era.

Essentially it boils down to this: Our clubs are too full of twats who rob us of our money, our identity and ultimately diminish our passion for the club.

Middlesbrough FC is a great old club with a few lower-league titles to our name. We've been in the Premiership since 1998, in Europe for the last two seasons, had a League Cup win, and regularly get crowds of between 25 and 30,000. Historically this is a period of unparalleled success the like of which we have never before known.

So why doesn't it feel like it?

Why do I and other fans feel a bit hollow inside?

Why in only our second season in Europe can we not fill 75% of the stadium?

Why are this season's attendances the lowest since we opened the Riverside?

Something is wrong and it's not just being fifth-bottom and unable to beat Nuneaton. It's a deeper, wider malaise in football that Middlesbrough serves to illustrate perfectly.

I first went to Ayresome Park in 1973 to see them play Hull City. It was 1-0 to the Boro. A Mills goal. Just over 9,000 were there. Most of us stood in the Holgate End on flaking concrete terraces. The players were balding, chubby, long-haired and some had thick bushy sideburns that you could hide an owl in. We didn't go for the glory; we went because it's always been a laugh. It's always been fun. But it's really not anymore.

We should be joyful at our current relatively high status. But many of us are not. And be warned, all of you who support teams striving for that European place, this can happen to you; for we at the Boro are, like California, a few years ahead of the game.

This is the problem - we're so bored and discontented by the football we play, how it's played and a lot of the players who play for us that all the passion, attraction and excitement is getting sucked out of the whole concept of going to the match.

We have been one of the most consistently boring clubs to watch for at least ten years now. This isn't a knee-jerk reaction to a few dodgy games; this is a whole extended culture of football tedium. If we're coming to your club to play you, I bet you groan. Middlesbrough is a by-word for boring, and this season is just as rotten.

This is bad enough, but on top of that we have possibly the worst reputation for buying over-priced, over-paid, under-committed players. This really needs saying. We shouldn't try and pretend it's acceptable.

Most of them have been little better than average, some of them have been appalling; others have just taken the piss out of the club financially. But they all shared one thing. They didn't give a shit about the club and just drained us of huge amounts of money and left as soon as they were offered a job anywhere else. Now I know we don't suffer uniquely from this. But it has become a way of life at the Boro.

This endless catalogue of footballing mercenaries has slowly rotted the guts of the club and is slowly separating the fans from their team so that the club doesn't feel like it's ours - instead of the love of our life it feels like its some kind of hooker who's taking it up the arse from legions of sex tourists.

And yet we have one of the best youth teams in the country and are bringing some of them through to be regular first-teamers and in James Morrison, Stuart Parnaby, Stewart Downing and a couple of others, we have the only members of the team who seem to actually give a fuck - which is because they're local lads and surprise, surprise, care a bit about their team. But they're dragged down by the mercenaries and the lazy good-for-nothings and will continue to be so unless we change the rent-a-footballer culture.

The plain fact is we don't really care about the UEFA Cup adventure. With a crowd of just over 9,000 I think we proved this conclusively. We didn't care much about drawing with Nuneaton. A lot expected to lose. We won't fill the Riverside for the cup replay. It may only be half-full.

People who feel like me don't care much because we suspect most of the first team don't actually care much. So if we win we don't care, because it's the same load of shit-eating fuckwits who've won and we secretly hate most of them. I'm just saying what a lot are thinking. Who at the Boro has affection for Viduka, Rochemback, Doriva, Pogatetz, JFH and Yakubu? No-one. Occasionally, like with Frank Queudrue, we buy a player who does put his shoulder to the wheel. Sometimes we get it right. Not often.

Our relative success feels hollow because it's being achieved by players we by and large don't respect.

And you may point to the 4-1 Man United victory and the 3-3 draw with Spurs and say 'look how great those games were'. Well, you'd be right, but that ultimately doesn't make any difference because, after all these years in the top flight with Gibbo's money buying so many desperate money-grabbers, we find it hard to really feel good about any performance anymore.

Rather, it compounds the problem because, to me, it looks like some players are only interested in playing against the top clubs and that makes us feel even more disenfranchised and furious. Remember we lost to Sunderland. That tells us something important.

Our policy of buying old has-been or never-were strikers is unparalleled. Every season brings a new joker who takes our money and then laughs at us as they leg it back down the A19. It started with the evil white-feathered goblin Fabrizio Ravenelli of course but there are many, many others. Hamilton

Ricard, Alen Boksic, JFH, Viduka, Maccarone, Nemeth...and that's just a few of those who ride the Boro gravy train before getting off with their pockets full of our money and a smug look on their face.

Most of the time they play rubbish and only get picked because McClaren has wazzed so much money on them that he has to justify it by picking them. But occasionally we resurrect players like Christian Ziege or Bolo Zenden's career and what do they do? They repay us by fucking off as soon as possible.

And something tells me we'll find Yakubu doing the same soon enough if he has half a chance. I don't trust him. He'd be gone before the end of the month if it suits him. We seem addicted to players who disrespect us, like a wife who returns to her abusive husband for another slap.

Okay, you say, no-one who's any good wants to move to the unglamorous Ironopolis of Middlesbrough unless no-one else will have them - fair enough, then, sod them all. Let's just use the youth team and a handful of good British players who understand the value and worth of the industrial heartlands of Britain. I really don't care.

I genuinely believe that the gradual effect of all this abuse over the years has been to freeze our hearts. But McClaren doesn't seem to realise and keeps on buying these muppets. I despair of him. He makes one good buy in every six. He might, might be okay as a football coach but as a manager of the club he's lightweight and quite rubbish really.

Okay, we've had some success and we're a stable Premiership club, but the price for that has been selling our soul to a revolving door of mercenaries who use and abuse our club. That's too great a price. Are you really surprised so many stay away now? We're numbed by it after all these years but deep down it's a bit humiliating.

We're dying inside. The best signings we've made in recent years are almost all British players. Southgate, Ehiogu, Riggott, even old Ray Parlour has been better than the likes of Doriva.

Have you seen Rochemback? He's surely one of those not-really-a-footballer ringers that only Souey gets fooled by. It's not because they're foreigners per se, God knows we've rubbish British players as well - remember Robbo bought Brian Deane, Noel Whelan and Dean Windass - but it's undeniable that we have attracted some of the worst imports. Not just poor players - some of them can kick a ball when they feel like it - but just woeful attitudes. We've had them all going back to Emerson and his unhappy wife drowning in our money.

Personally, and this is a radical point of view I know, I would rather be relegated playing our youth team then stay mid-table with the bunch of football hookers that we have season in, season out. I'd rather have a purge of all the lazy leeches. I'd rather have good honest pros and not feckless egomaniacs, wherever they come from.

I fear that younger fans now think this is the only way you can run a football club as one big name after another is touted as our saviour. Maybe it works at other clubs, I don't know, but to me, at Middlesbrough, it all seems dreadfully inappropriate.

I hope Steve Gibson realises why the stadium has big bare expanses all the time now. He's a man of great integrity and the fact so many of these twats have taken his money and laughed in our collective faces as they run off back down south really angers me. It's time to stop this now.

During this transfer window I don't want to see any more of it. No more half-buying half-assed players who are mysteriously injured for four months a year or who are 34 and looking for one last big pay day. If we've got the money, why not gamble on promising British players? They cost less in wages than bloated tarts like Viduka and might actually bond with the club which has given them a break.

Players arrive and clearly loathe the place like Pogatetz. I wonder where he thought he was going. Misquoted my arse. He hates the place and will be gone as soon as he can. I wish he'd go now. Imagine if you turned up at work and said in front of your paymasters: "This is a right dump, now pay me."

We're not the big city, glory-hunting prawn sarnie mob at the Boro. We'd take love over money. We're not flash, we don't want to be flash - we want true grit to make the pearl, not another donkey-choking wad of cash paid to strikers who can't get a gig anywhere else because they're lazy fat fools. It's time the manager realised this. He may be the last man on Teesside who doesn't.

Southgate and other players have been asking fans for more support - hey Gareth, thanks for that, but remember you are getting paid to turn up, we're not. We're not discontented for no reason. It's not knee-jerk fickle fans here. This has been a long, slow process of disillusion. Win or lose or draw, a lot of us feel too distant, cold and alienated from much of the team who in turn hate playing in front of us.

And it was you Gareth, who revealed the extent of Boksic's pampering. It sickened me. So don't lecture us please, son. We've been Boro for longer than you and will be so long after you hang up your boots. We're the experts. Not you.

Can we please have our club back from these slippery characters who seek only to cream us up one last time? These jokers are not fit to wear the shirts that once belonged to real men like Alan Foggon, John Hickton or even Bernie Slaven and Paul Wilkinson.

I'm not depressed because we're fifth bottom and can't beat Nuneaton. It's weird but the results don't matter to me now. It's bigger than that.

Is there anything wrong with wanting a team of mostly-British players complimented with one or two top-class overseas players? Is that such a bad thing? Wasn't that actually how it was supposed to work? Are you really telling me we can't find a lad in the north east who can play just 1% better than Rochemback? A drunken monkey could play better.

The irony is that because of a good youth policy we have the chance to do something shocking. We could have 75% of our first team as home-grown talent. Top it up with a few judicious buys and we'd all be much happier. Is it really so shocking to think that might be the answer? Surely, that is the future and all this buying in a striker from Machu Pichu will be seen for the foolish delusion it is.

Would it be so shocking to try? I'd rather be relegated with that team than stay up and have to look at Viduka's big square head and JFH's ridiculous big sticky-out granite horse's arse every week.

Maybe I'm just old-fashioned. Maybe. Or maybe it's the most modern of thinking. But Middlesbrough should be a warning, an illustration of what can happen if your club is one of the many unfashionable, out-of-the-way clubs who are trying to pretend to be a big boy.

If you have some money and resources and moderate success, you too might find that you feel very disillusioned. That for which you have struggled for years is not the Promised Land after all, because your club has been flooded with desperados.

We're losing all our highs and lows, ain't it funny how the feeling goes away?

This piece was published in the wake of the latest Sven scandal when a newspaper caught him (well, set him up) with that most British of things, a fake sheik.

You can argue all you like about how good a manager Sven is or was for England but he got us as far as and a bit further than his two predecessors with relative ease. We would not have qualified for the 2002 World Cup were it not for him stepping in after Keegan. With a bit more luck on occasions and by being bit less conservative we might have reached a semi-final or final. Who knows?

But regardless of any of that, in the last two or three years of his tenure he was treated by some sections of the British media as though he was some sort of oaf, retard or deviant. He was abused and pilloried even though he was essentially doing nothing wrong. He was criticised for not being value for money but such accusations should have been directed at the FA, not Sven. He just took the money put on the table as we all would have done.

Slagging people off unreasonably is a national sport in Britain and, while I like a pop as much as anyone, with Sven it became ridiculous as the press united to drive him out of the job. I don't blame him for wanting to leave. I don't blame him for not caring that much about England after the way he was treated by the press, who disrespected him terribly, and by the FA, who were witless buffoons who caved in under pressure from the press.

It is so hard for anyone to do their job in Britain if they're in a public position because eventually, when the time is right for a media campaign against you, any flaw, mistake or character trait not deemed to be currently acceptable will be ruthlessly exposed and dwelt upon for days, weeks and months until people who haven't really been paying attention think all this distortion, lies and half-truths is in fact all true, and by then the person concerned has lost the will to fight anymore. It's undemocratic and it's despicable.

You'll never find anyone who is whiter than white to fill any public position and, even if you did, it wouldn't be long before the press had a pop at them for being boring and characterless and unfit for the job by dint of being out of touch with ordinary people's lives. But as soon as you get someone in a public position who has led an ordinary life, their typically ordinary mistakes and misjudgments are all dragged out to prove how unfit you are for this high office.

In sport and in politics and other branches of public life, 'whatever happened to all the characters?' is a question that is often asked. Well you fucking hounded them all out of public life didn't you, you bunch of cunts. It wasn't always like this. There used to be a bit of privacy for prominent people. Now it seems to have gone in favour of making life into one big fucking reality show created just for fleeting moments of titillation. It makes me howl at the moon.

The best programme on TV right now is Life on Mars, which transports us back to 1973 - not least the rough-arsed, hard-faced way a lot of us lived back then in the north. Life was really tough for a lot of people. Much harder than now. We lived in cold houses, food and drink were relatively much more expensive and there were only three TV channels.

Of course, to me the music is superb - featuring Deep Purple, Thin Lizzy and Blue Oyster Cult amongst others. This is real get-a-blow-job-during-the-drum-solo rock 'n' roll with riffs so big and heavy they drove them around on the back of trucks. Razorlight it ain't.

Heavy rock always went down well in the industrial cities of Britain - perhaps because it sounded like machinery. It wasn't just entertainment for a lot of us; it was a way of life in a way that the MTV generations can never imagine. We had so little exposure to rock stars. They were almost never on TV. They didn't have videos and they only appeared in the rock press once a year when an album was out. So your only chance of seeing anyone was to see them live. If they didn't have photos of the band on the album covers, you frequently wouldn't know what most of the band looked like until they shuffled out on stage in a mass of hair and beards.

But back to Life on Mars. Of course it has Sweeney overtones, especially as the coppers dispense their own form of justice. Is fitting up known slags to stop them going back out on the streets to commit more crime a good or bad thing? That's the dilemma. Does the end justify the means?

Life on Mars raises that issue, and in an age of knee-jerk media hysteria and the crippling over-sensitivity we all have to show to everyone, it's refreshing to see a time when things were different. Not a perfect time - except musically - but a very different time certainly. Yes it's sexist, and sometimes violent and unsophisticated, and yet I find myself wanting that kind of honesty back again. This was a time when you could be wrong, you could be flawed and imperfect and not get a merciless slagging for it.

Trial by media is now a way of life for everyone from the top coppers down to benefit fraudsters. You can't commit a crime these days without someone making a reality show from amateur or CCTV footage. You can't grope a lass in a shop doorway without the video being sold to Bravo for a show. You can't do anything without someone passing judgment or having a wank.

So it's been with the latest Sven business. I found it very interesting to see baby Jamie Redknapp sitting on Sky this weekend, speaking increasingly like his father, gripping the arms of his chair tightly, as though he was trying to dispense a very large obstructive turd, pontificating about how Sven should go and we could do just as well or better with an English manager. Obviously, he's an impartial judge in such things and we really value his input, don't we? He lives his life at the coal face, doesn't he? Yeah right. Just like we value the opinions of Mr Le Saux.

But I was even more surprised to see Andy Gray saying that the England fans might just have had enough of Sven now. I was surprised because I thought he would have judged the public mood better. Maybe when you live in the telly world you lose track of real life. Because with this story as with so many others, our bullshit and hypocrisy alarms start ringing right from the start.

Increasingly, we despise the purveyors of news more than the subjects of the news - regardless of the issue, regardless of whether we think Sven is right, wrong or stupid or if we just don't care, which I suspect is true for most of us. We don't care. We've got more important shit to worry about. We just want England to win. We've won a lot of games under Sven. That'll do for us for now.

And as the hyper-ventilating media drone on about whatever it is this week, we just tune out. They don't seem to have twigged this. The more they go on about things the less we believe them, often because we meet people who believe everything they see and read and we know just what knuckle-draggers they are - and we don't want to get to that level, do we?

And what does my head in is that behind all these issues is some implied or stated judgmental attitude which is trying to tell us who is right and who is wrong and what we should really think. In this climate, pressure is always 'building', it's always a 'crisis', people are always 'under pressure'. Who from, like? Me? You?

I mean, this week I bet you've just gone to work, had a few beers, listened to the radio, bought an Aerosmith live album if you're lucky and got your end away. Have you been putting pressure on Sven? On Ruth Kelly? On John Prescott? No. And even if you wanted to, how would you do that? We've got our lives to be getting on with. But the media have spoken for us, apparently. Well, thanks but no thanks, pal.

Unlike the world on Life on Mars it seems people aren't allowed to make mistakes, or an error of judgment or just fuck up like humans do without the full weight of the press and TV falling on them as though they were responsible for starting World War III. Even if they were trying their best or just did something very innocuous in the overall litany of human deprivation. It matters not.

So far Sven's crimes against society have been to talk to some people about a potential job, be conned by a bloke in a tea towel into making bland comments about a couple of footballers and have sex with some women and err...well, that's it. How criminally stupid and evil, eh? Give me a break.

Funny how the really important issues such as financial irregularities in the game are not subjected to such endless in-depth scrutiny by the tabloids, isn't it? I can't imagine why they'd want to give a free ride to the rich people they rub shoulders with in their everyday jobs, can you?

It's exactly the same with the issue of corrupt officials in football. We're not even allowed to mention that can of worms. Don't go there. They're just inept, not corrupt you know. Of course. That's always true, isn't it? Yes. I am a robot. I will do what's right. It's the Brave New World.

Let's spend all our time and money on making a fool out of someone instead. Either that or let's make a programme or write an article crucifying some poor sod's lifestyle, diet and clothes just to make people feel better about themselves.

228

I hope it's not just me who's tired of it all. I hope it's not just an old bloke moaning. If it is, I apologise. But there are a lot of us out here smelling a bit of wee and listening to old Blodwyn Pig albums.

Ironically it was in 1973 that the FA sacked Alf Ramsey for not getting us to the 1974 World Cup and appointed Don Revie instead - a man who a couple of years later ran off with his pockets full of cash to Saudi with some real sheiks. Funny how that's rarely mentioned these days.

Gary Neville is one of my favourite footballers of the last decade. He's a superb full-back, solid and reliable; the kind of player you don't realise you rely on until he's not playing. But apart from that, he embodies so much about what a modern footballer should be.

He's a one-club man and he loves his club. He stands up and is counted. He plays the game with an innate honesty and work ethic that most players just don't have the guts or the fibre of character to do. He is mentally tough and glories in his side's victories because he feels it in his heart and soul. It's like he's a fan on the pitch. He is, in a very real sense - as opposed to the shallow celebrity Hello magazine sense - living the dream. He is Citizen Neville. He is the ordinary man. He is you and me out there.

When England lost to Portugal in the World Cup, while the supposed hard men like John Terry were on the ground weeping like children, Nev was walking around the ground with his chest puffed out applauding the England fans. Not for him the self-indulgence of publicly-shed tears. To his enormous credit, he took it like a grown man should and he shouldered the blame. He said it wasn't acceptable and they had let themselves and the fans down. He didn't hide. He faced up, fronted it out and told it like it is. It takes real balls to do that, it takes strength of character that too few contemporary players could match.

You don't have to worry about Gary; fiercely loyal and incredibly self-motivated, he'll pull his tripe out for you week in and week out. He gives everything and that's all you can ask of any man. So when there was a furor about his 'incitement' of Liverpool fans after Rio headed in a last-minute winner, it made me very angry, because the very essence of what he was expressing and the way he was doing it is precisely what is good about football and it felt as if the world was being turned upside down when he becomes the villain. They were picking on the wrong man.

Why are there not more players like him? Where have the real men gone? I think I love Red Nev...even if he has rather worryingly started talking about himself in the third person. Johnny gets scared by that.

Let me incite you for a moment. Feel free to run amok in the streets and then blame me.

A 90th-minute winner in a long, tedious game against your most bitter rivals is always a great thing. If now is not the moment for a bit of chest-thumping pride, a bit of honest to goodness 'fuck you' piss-taking, then when would be the right time?

So there's Citizen Neville, taking the piss out of Liverpool fans, thrusting his groin at them in what were amusingly later called 'sex actions'. It's all fair enough isn't it? After all, that's what you've been doing to him all game. 'But surely he's supposed to rise above that', I hear. Isn't the deal that fans berate and abuse players, who in turn smile sweetly and take the money home?

Well at Middlesbrough that's certainly the case - except that we're abusing our own players of course. But come on, think about this for a minute. Football is still occasionally tribal and visceral, only occasionally, but Man United v Liverpool may well be one of those few occasions. If you're seriously telling me that the Nevillista pumping his arms up and down, kissing his badge and angrily displaying his sparse Three Musketeers facial hair at you is going to legitimately cause you to do anyone else any harm, which is what I take 'incitement' to mean, then I must politely tell you that you are freakingly out of your mind, son.

And answer me this. Is it you he's inciting? Are you really going to leave the ground and kick off a fight because of Gary's behaviour? If it's not you being incited, then who is it? Other fans? That'll be other less mature and responsible fans than you, will it? So what you're saying is you can't trust your own supporters not to kick off outside because Presidente Nevillo has flicked his 'tache at you?

He's driven them out their minds, hasn't he? Driven them to the point of insanity. They are not culpable for their own behaviour now - it's all Gary's fault...they've got a free reign to do what they will because they have officially been 'incited'.

Christ, is that what you're saying when you run to the phones to complain? It's - and let me say this very slowly - absolutely, utterly, totally pathetic. Stop saying it. Stop saying it now. That includes you Alan Green. Even though you're a Liverpool fan, I expect better from you.

It must be especially galling for the vast majority of fans who don't care about 'incitement' and are embarrassed by those who whine about this sort of thing. I know that's the vast majority.

But where will this stop? It's a slippery slope. Do you want social workers on hand at the game to report how upset you are and how this makes it more likely that you'll slap your kids around? Where does incitement stop?

Because you know, you're not just affecting these two clubs, you're affecting all of us fans. You are, by making these 'incitement' claims, directly responsible for the downgrading of football as exciting entertainment. Yes, you're culpable in the decline of the game as a spectacle because you're giving the FA more reason to treat football like hysterical girls.

They've already outlawed the more expressive forms of player celebration, and now by indulging in accusations of 'incitement' you're just handing the game over to the blazered old farts even more. You're directly responsible for the further emasculation of the game. Do you really want football turned into a polite sport where no-one feels anything or shows any emotion just so you can indulge in the popular contemporary sport of 'where there's blame, there's a claim'?

Don't you realise that of all the overpaid dancing monkeys on the pitch playing for Man United, only Citizen Neville really felt it in his heart? Can't you see that is actually a good thing? He's a player who feels his club to his core, who takes pride in beating you. That's a really fucking good thing. Shit, I wish we had a bit more of that at the Riverside.

Regardless of who the player or club is, do you really want footballers to be emotional robots? It's shameful that anyone should want to take away The Neviller's right to briefly lord victory on his home ground. You've just got to take it. Your lot can do the same when the occasion arises.

All this talk of incitement is self-indulgent hypocrisy and frankly, if you can't take it, don't give it out. Is this what we've come to? Are we such a nation of wet farts now? Fucking hell!!

Football isn't reality TV you know. The performers can and should be allowed to talk back to you. You're not watching it on the TV where no-one can hear you scream. The question that needs asking is, do you really just want to hurl abuse and take the piss out of a player for an hour and a half without it having any effect? Aren't you trying to put him off his game?

So when he kicks back a bit after beating you, have the good grace, the balls, and the guts, to take your medicine from the man you have abused so merrily. Not to do so is just plain wet. Don't start ringing up the radio phone-ins and start weeping about it.

Are you going to tell on Nev to the police? Are you going to get him reported as a social revolutionary, able to incite a crowd into violence at the twitch of his hairy lip? Who do you think he is? Malcolm X? Do you want all of these authorities involved in our game further telling us what we can and can't do or say?

Maybe you'll want to sue him for emotional upset. It was so hurtful, after all. Ah diddums. Why do you care what Neville says or thinks about anything anyway? You love him really, don't you? You do, you love him.

This is nanny culture of wussy, pathetic, limp-wristed proportions and we should have nothing to do with it. You know what you should have done as Nev is kicking off - just call him a wanker, a fuckwit, anything you want and go home happy that you have done so. He'd expect it. He won't be reporting you for hurting his feelings. He's a grown man.

It all made me love D'Artagnan Neville even more. I don't want such emotion to be outlawed, made illegal, suppressed or punished just because some people in the crowd have found an excuse to be upset by it. If you really do think he was wrong and think he really was inciting the crowd to, to, to do what I really don't know, then I in turn shall accuse you of inciting real fans into apoplectic anger at your girly behaviour.

Oooh, I shall scream and scream and scream and scream until I'm sick.

While Peter Osgood didn't have the same cultural impact as George Best, nonetheless he was one hell of a player and, to me, he was part of that late 60's and early 70's football party mafia who lived high on the hog and set a fine example of how to have a good time while doing something you love. It's an example I have always striven to live up to. He belonged to a different era in every way to today's footballers. It was an era when the emphasis was on entertainment and having a good time and isn't that really what the game is all about? Isn't that what life is all about?

These were lads who were a bit flash, splashed their cash and lived the birds 'n' booze lifestyle as all working-class lads who make good are entitled to do. But it wasn't like today when players are super-rich and their idea of a good time is flying out to their own private island with their mates rather than sharing a couple of bottles of champagne in the local nightclub. Ossie's generation lived their lives in a way we could still relate to, but these days when a player earns more in two days than the average punter will earn in a year, the gap is too wide for us to properly empathise.

He should never have died of a heart attack aged 59. That should be a warning to us all to realise that we are not immortal. I raised a glass to him that night. Cheers big man.

So another legend has gone.

Even for a devoutly northern lad like me, who was gutted when Chelsea beat Leeds in the FA Cup final replay of 1970 - a game in which Ossie scored - it was hard not to admire the Chelsea team of that era. Ossie, Charlie Cooke, Alan Hudson and the rest were the very epitome of the flash, Kings Road football lifestyle of the late 60's and 70's. Like a footballing version of The Sweeney, it was all balls, booze, birds and sideburns. Working-class lads made good. And if you came from the kind of town I came from, no-one could resent a boy from the streets filling his boots when he had the chance. We'd all have done the same.

As Chelsea's number nine, Peter was a big bugger. At 6' 2" he was a consummate header of the ball. Powerful and strong in an era where the centre-half could chin you and get away with it, Ossie was also blessed with good ball skills and had a bloody powerful shot on him as well. He was a class all-round number nine, the likes of which the game no longer produces. Hard but skilful. There was a joy in seeing a big bloke throw his weight around and lash the ball in the net. It's what made football great. It's what made Ossie great.

He only played four times for England - probably because Sir Alf didn't like his West End flash. He should have been seen on the international stage much more often. He won the Cup-Winners' Cup in 1971 with Chelsea but I always felt that for his generation and class of player it was less about winning things and more about having a good time. And that is a great lesson to learn.

And for a man who liked a good time, Ossie was playing in the right era. He was in the entertainment business and he knew it. And if he was having a good time, he knew that the fans were probably having one too.

He scored a goal about every three games and he never lost the affection of the Chelsea fans (and later Saints fans) and will always remain one of their all-time true greats. And rightly so.

He died on a day when a modern Chelsea player, Joe Cole, delivered an England performance he would have loved. Full of flash and swagger and a cross he, like Crouch, would have loved to power into the net and score - a brilliant old school goal.

Ossie's death really knocked me cold. Maybe it's a lesson to all of us who are not kids anymore to go to the docs more often. If only so we can watch more great footballers like Ossie for longer.

One Peter Osgood, there's only one Peter Osgood.

Nice one son.

As I mentioned earlier, there's probably some deep, psychological reason buried in my subconscious why people pissing in sinks sticks in my mind so much, but frankly I can't be arsed to think about it for long enough. I'm of the school of opinion that says the more you pick at your psychological and emotional scars, the more they'll bleed. Better to swallow it all down (not the piss) into a dense, hard, bitter ball of bile in your guts until you can't tolerate it any longer and have to get up on the roof of your local shopping centre with a sniper rifle and make the kind of news that ends with the words....'before turning the gun on himself.'

There's no point in fretting, so just have another drink. That's my philosophy and it's kept me relatively happy.

When I was writing this I realised just how blasé we'd all become about things which used to be taboo. When I was a teenager I used to try and sneak a look at Page Three in The Sun and the illicit thrill of the nudity was fantastic, made all the more exciting by the fact that, because my dad bought the Daily Express, I could only see The Sun round one of my mate's houses. It was therefore a rare pleasure and got me through the long dark nights of puberty.

If I was 14 now I would have my Google searches unfiltered and I'd be looking at gynacological porn until my eyes melted, I know I would. But I bet I'd get jaded much quicker. Surely, like all of life's pleasures, it operates on a law of diminishing returns. There is much to be said for the concept of 'less is more', except when it comes to pies, mashed potato or beer, of course.

If you ever drank Dryboroughs Keg Heavy the experience will no doubt have impinged itself indelibly onto your taste buds. It should have been preserved as a gold standard of just how not to brew beer. It was the very apex of the mass-produced chemical beer revolution of the early 70's which turned our pubs into dispensers of thin, fizzy, bitter, characterless brews. It's all changed now and beer has never been better in Britain.

The best thing about being a nation of alcoholics is that every off-licence and bar is stocked with dozens of delicious falling-down water. This week alone I've had Latvian lager, Belgian cherry beer and Scottish beer from Deuchars - it's like going round the world without leaving your sofa. Who says drinking makes you an uncultured slob?

I'd been staring all night at this lass who was wearing tight bright red corduroy dungarees really skin-tight up her arse. It was doing my head in. These days dungarees on a woman are usually a sign of a clog-wearing, wholefood, high-fibre, wet liberal type or it's the uniform of the lentil-loving jumper-wearing crusty anarchist with a penchant for sitting up trees and smoking roll-ups - after all, what is more anarchic than smoking fags you've rolled yourself, eh?

But there was a time in the late 70's when women wore dungarees without it being some sort of political statement.

We were at a Slade gig at Newcastle Polytechnic in 1980 and many pints of a strange, almost tasteless, very cold beer called Dryboroughs Keg Heavy had been consumed. Unlike most lads aged 18, at the time I had been drinking quite heavily since the age of 15. And I really bloody liked it. It gave me a place to call home. Consequently I could consume loads of the relatively weak ale without falling over. The strongest beer you could usually get on tap back then was Carling Black Label, which was only 4.1%, but a lot of it, like Harp and Heineken, was 3.5% and so you could easily neck ten pints of the stuff over a night and still be able to remember your name and which planet you were on.

Anyway, so I'm necking this bloody Keg Heavy stuff all night and eventually, after the gig and three hours of staring at the girl's apricot-shaped arse crammed into these red dungarees, I have finally got enough courage to go up and give her the infamous Nic slaver...which at the time usually just involved talking about UFO and beat poetry. Nothing's changed.

And it turns out she's a Geordie, likes drinking cider and blackcurrant - which I think was called a Red Witch back then - David Bowie, has a Ten Years After album and smells of frangipani - all these things cause me to fall in love with her immediately.

As I go to the bog to empty my Keg Heavy bladder I meet Hairy Tony (this was eight years before he became our bass player) coming out and he tells me that the lady in question will most likely offer me some physical gratification at the end of the evening ("they say she gans like", was his post-feminist analysis of the sexual politics of the situation.) He grins and hands me a plastic pint of more Keg Heavy. He's with an innocent-looking young lass from Whitley Bay who seems about 15 and from a good home. She smiles at me nicely. Tony grins and I know what he's thinking. He's thinking he's up her tubes tonight - his words, not mine. He was. She had no complaints.

And as it turned out he was right. She was about as wild and rock 'n' roll as a Geordie lass got in those days. Later that night in the halls of residence a mutual exchange of the appropriate bodily fluids took place to the complex rhythms of Rush's 2112 album.

The trouble with these rooms was they didn't have a toilet, you had to go down the hall for a slash. So obviously no-one did, you just lobbed it in the sink instead, especially at four am. What I had not thought about, being a naive young lad, was that girls also suffered this same problem. So I'm lying there in a post-coital warm glow of achievement when suddenly I'm shocked to see her climb onto the sink, position her arse between the taps and take a long, hissing piss. It was quite a gymnastic and tricky thing to do because these were not big sinks, they were set back into an alcove and she'd been drinking all night.

Back in 1980 we didn't have all forms of human perversion available to us on computers, so consequently a lot of us were, if not exactly innocent, certainly living more sheltered lives than kids do now. For example, I was 15 before I learned that a blow job did not involve any actual blowing. Previously I had assumed it was something akin to glass-blowing and was vaguely frightened that my balls might be inflated and burst and on balance, that didn't seem to offer much pleasure at all.

So seeing a girl performing a basic bodily function on a sink was a secret illicit thrill to me, even though I tried to pretend I was cool about it at the time, as you do...

I know this may seem a lame nowadays when your average 18-year-old is so jaded that anything less than a night out smoking crack with naked dwarves while simultaneously being anally penetrated with a banana by a team of exotic limbo dancers from Mexborough and having your scrotum shaved by drug-fuelled super models is considered rather conservative, but at the time it was probably the most rock 'n' roll thing that had ever happened to me.

Sadly, if it happened now it would just seem quite normal, as it probably does to you as well. Weary and jaded by a lifetime of exposure to life's naughty stuff, it would hold none of the thrills that hearing that first steaming hissing stream did. Indeed now, I'd probably just hope she didn't take a shit and try to force it down the plug-hole with her fingers.

And that's why it reminded me of the cup final.

As I listened to fans under the age of 25 say it was the best final they had ever seen, it was like they were innocent kids

241

who had been exposed to their first insight into the thrilling rock 'n' roll experience that used to be cup football.

Fans get jaded by too much unexciting, unambitious football. FA Cup finals are almost inevitably terrible, cautious and tedious affairs, either totally one-sided or a stalemate. So when a truly exciting game comes along, it's a really new, unique experience for loads of people. It's hard to convey to anyone under the age of 25 just what a massive day the cup final used to be, partly of course because we had so little live football on telly in the 70's.

In fact, to win the cup seemed like a bigger achievement than winning the league. It was more glamorous and dramatic and even if the game was a bit dull, it was still a really big drama that kept everyone off the streets and glued to their new colour TVs. And as the calls came into the phone-in programmes eulogising about what was a superb game by any standards, it was great to realise that football could still excite and shock fans, even fans that have grown jaded on almost two decades of rubbish football.

Now if we could just make the Champions League like the old European Cup by getting rid of the league stages, we might all start getting our rocks off on cup football more often. Or am I just pissing in the sink?

This was written after England had beaten Ecuador in the World Cup and a few days before they lost to Portugal. We all know now England didn't play very well and went out tamely to an ordinary Portugal side, but that's football for you. It's annoying but it's not the end of the world and it was all to be expected really.

However, for the last two years or more this 'Golden Generation' theory had been touted by all the press who wanted Sven out. I saw it for what is was from the start, a stick to beat the man with. It was always a lie but it was all too eagerly eaten up by fans who for whatever reasons were unable to see the reality behind the rhetoric.

And now the prophets of doom would have us believe that we'll never win a World Cup again. It's all over the top. Cup football is too fickle and is decided by too many marginal decisions to make any meaningful predictions - the 2006 World Cup proved that as Brazil and Argentina went out in the last eight after being favourites. I just wanted England to win and I wasn't bothered how it happened. And that's what it'll be like for me next time too.

Oh dear, things are getting very weird. And no, I've not been eating those funny little mushrooms again.

Listening to far too many phone-ins and reading too many reports, one thing stands out - delusion. If you think the Golden Generation exists, you've been sold a lie by the press, who created it purposefully as a stick to beat Sven with and to give themselves plenty to write about without having to make much effort.

Once the concept was established, the critics couldn't lose; they'd always have an easy position to take. It was clever really.

And it worked. Time after time you hear fans reiterating the propaganda: "This is the best squad of players for 40 years."

It was never true.

But it worked.

If England don't win, they're under-performing idiots and it's all Sven's fault for bad tactics, selections and team talks and it must be so because this is the Golden Generation, who are so much better than this.

If they do well they're the Golden Generation and therefore it's nothing to do with Sven, they're winning despite of him not because of him. It's a perfect Catch 22. It was set in place to get him out of the job and it worked because enough fans fell for it.

And once the Golden Generation notion was established it provided a seedbed to grow all of the innate negativity that runs like a thick seam through English football culture. Players have suffered terrible criticism for not performing well enough based entirely on an initial false assessment of their talents. They have been set up as footballing gods but they never were that. They have not let us down. They have simply been built up to a level way beyond their ability to regularly deliver. They're good players but mostly not great.

Why does anyone expect England's players to play like they do for their clubs when their clubs are largely full of overseas internationals with better technique and skill? This doesn't mean players like Frank Lampard are rubbish. He's a really good player, just not a great player. But at his club he has all the advantages of a great defensive midfielder behind him and the space created by aggressive strikers up front.

England are not Chelsea, so why would you think Lampard would play the same way or be as effective? At least he got into positions to score even if he did miss 198 times. That should be applauded and not so viciously criticised ad infinitum. Lampard has been massively over-rated. Too much was expected of him so don't go over the top slagging him off. It's your fault for over-rating him.

244

It's not their fault they're over-rated or overpaid. They just take the money. The same goes for Sven. He didn't say he was worth five million quid, they just offered it to him, he took it. The money he receives is a reflection of the FA's stupidity, not Sven's.

Having watched all the World Cup games it is obvious that the vast majority of major international countries are loaded with excellent players. Just because we haven't heard much about them or only see them occasionally doesn't mean they are not the equal or greater in talent than the majority of our players. For example, a central defender like Mexico's Rafael Marquez is a better player than any of our back line.

We have a thin veneer of quality players and they cannot be expected to carry the team all the time or stay fit all the time. This is not the same thing as a Golden Generation.

It appears that some of English football culture cannot strike a realistic view. We are either brilliant or rubbish. Either 100% great or 100% bad. This kind of bipolar disorder is very destructive to our players. They are vaunted as geniuses one week only to be scorned as fools the next. This is why they play with such tension and fear. Until we learn to keep our heads and not go so over the top one way or another, this will continue to happen. These lads are people like you and me, how messed up would your psyche be when you are lauded as a god one week and then destroyed as a liability the next?

Genuine belief in the players' actual talents seems to have been replaced by a blind passion that veers between love and rage - often within a few minutes.

And I think this is at the core of what is wrong with English football. We are far too negative about almost everything and the press and media are complicit in perpetuating this national characteristic. We seem to love to wallow in our own crapulence. We cut ourselves up over inadequacies, real or perceived, slashing at our skin with razorblades of self-loathing.

Some fans' first reaction after we won the Paraguay game was to say how the likes of Brazil and Argentina would be laughing at us for this pathetic performance. They seem to love to twist the knife in their own guts; to feel the pain; to see only the worst in things and never the good. Some even seem to be saying that by playing as we are and winning, we're insulting countries like Mexico who have been knocked out. It's outrageous really. It's a cup competition; the best sides often don't win cups. Has no-one been paying attention? It's not an exercise in football democracy. If one side plays bad but wins you don't get less points. It's not a beauty contest. The only reason anyone would say this kind of thing is because somehow they enjoy making themselves, and by extension England, feel bad.

I caught a bit of 606 after the Ecuador game and it's exactly, exactly as I thought with Greeny at one point saying if England won the World Cup playing like that it would be just wrong. This is madness. Crazy. And to be fair, there are a few callers who are equally as bewildered, not just by criticism but by the level of bile and anger directed at Eriksson.

One bloke was getting so worked up and seemed on the verge of blaming Sven for the rise of Hitler, the atom bomb, mad cow disease and the fact that his cock is too small. All of which might have had some weight if we hadn't just won. It's as though they've all got this standpoint worked out in advance and deploy it anyway regardless of the result.

There's a perverse delight in hearing all these frustrated people who, for two or three years now, almost in denial of our victories, just treat every game as a further national humiliation and further proof of how rubbish Sven is even though we've reached the last eight again.

It must drive them bonkers that we keep on qualifying when they say we won't; that we keep winning when they predict a thrashing. Eventually, when we do lose, they must be ready to cream their pants in joy.

I can only surmise that this is some personal inadequacy they're trying to deal with vicariously through the football. So bizarre, extreme and misplaced is it.

You don't have to be an expert to see that Argentina play a more skilful, agile and quick game than we seem able to do. But anything can happen in football which, if you've been watching for a while, anyone would know. Every game is so different against such different opposition that you cannot extrapolate from one match to another. And by the way, I saw Riquelme whack the ball over the bar and wide plenty of times. I saw him misplace passes too. All footballers make mistakes. England's mistakes seem to be judged more harshly by some who are equally blind to other nations' players' deficiencies.

I'm not saying we shouldn't be critical on occasions but we do need to keep it all in perspective. We need to keep some light of positivity in our souls.

We've got to the quarters again. We're a top-eight side - results show that - anything else now is icing on the cake. We're not great but on the odd occasion we could be. Cup football is timing those occasions with the big games. This is the extent of England's talent and form. It's okay. It's not the end of the world. The sun is still in the sky.

If you want to see free-flowing, passionate, attacking football we need to create a day-to-day football culture that allows that to happen. We need to not worry about losing in order to win. We need to allow them to play without anxiety because right now, they're knotted up in fear of the lambasting they'll receive for anything less than a perfect game. It's wrong.

Just wallowing in all the flaws, viciously attacking players and basking in the pain and not celebrating the good, we're forever tied to this way of being. England are doing alright. To me, after 40 years of losing I just want to win. By any means. In any way. Nothing else matters to me. So, all in all, I'm loving it.

247

New Writings

1. WHAT'S WHAT: A ROCK 'N' ROLL GRANDDAD

As odd as it may seem, and it seems very odd indeed, people write to me for advice on all sorts of things. This is as varied as how to get into journalism, what are the chords for the middle bit of 'Don't Fear The Reaper' by Blue Oyster Cult and why does my cock burn so much when I have a piss? I could only answer the last one.

But the oddest question came from a guy in Keighley and, as befits a Yorkshireman, it was short and to the point. "How come you ended up such a mad fuck?" Good question. This is one of the many reasons:

Fred. It's not a glamorous name. It's functional. Frederick is a posh name that posh people give to their posh kids. Fred isn't. Fred is working-class. Or at least it used to be until the middle classes recently started giving their offspring working-class names like Alf or Doris as though to take on some quaint credibility.

This particular Fred was my granddad, but the name became synonymous in my mind with his character. There were things that were clearly Fred and things that were equally obviously not Fred at all. Rugby league was Fred, as was creosote, potatoes, mint imperials, horse muck, penknives and bags of nails. Horse-racing wasn't Fred in the slightest - "for stuck up folk and those that wish they were". Soft toilet paper wasn't Fred - "tell me what's wrong wi' newspaper, it does the job champion" - and southerners were not Fred. "Full of wind and piss jus' like their beer," he'd say with a grin. He didn't mean it really. Only he sort of did.

But Fred wasn't normal. And that's why I loved him. Fred showed me that it was usually a good idea to do things your own way and not take too much notice of what he'd call 'neatly ironed' people. And he didn't just mean their clothes.

He took me to my first football match, my first rugby league game and he set an example that I never forgot. All of my passion for football, rock 'n' roll and all the other good things in life were awakened in me by Fred. So in a way, everything in this book is in part all due to him.

Fred was born at the end of the 19th century. His dad was a miner in a pit just outside Castleford. A place called Friston. Fred lived all his life in Castleford and never, ever left Yorkshire in his whole life and for most of that life he worked down the pit hacking out coal with a bloody big pick and shovel. He was hard as nails - you had to be to work three miles underground stripped to the waist for five-and-a-half days a week - and yet underneath he was as soft as shite.

His hands were rough and leathery from years of graft and were missing two fingers he'd lost down the mine. His lungs were full of coal dust and when he breathed it sounded like a train pulling into a station. He didn't just wheeze, he rattled. It even made him laugh:

"Bloody 'ell, listen to me, I sound like a pigeon stuck in a chimney."

Fred's last years were his best years. After he retired he went on a kind of spiritual journey to discover all the things that he'd been too busy to discover before. He became, much to the amusement of everyone who knew him, a kind of West Yorkshire renaissance man and to me, as a kid growing up, he was a hero because he was the only grown-up I knew who behaved like a kid.

He didn't patronise me the way other adults did. He'd treat me like I was his little mate and he showed me enjoyment in life's simple things. Whittling wood, digging a garden and sitting on a fence in such a way as to make your farts come out in a high-pitch squeaky manner were all arts I learned from the old bugger.

Fred was a widower when he married my mam's mam some time in the mid-60's. I could never understand what he saw in her. She was a sour-faced old woman of the kind so common in Yorkshire. She thought she was a great cook but she wasn't. She thought she was a great knitter but she wasn't. She thought she knew a great deal about almost everything but she actually knew almost nothing about practically everything. She was never short of an opinion but it was almost never right.

She made judgements on the characters of both neighbours and people she saw on the telly based entirely on how well they spoke. I think this was why she always voted Tory.

"He speaks the Queen's English as it ought to be spoken," she said of Edward Heath. She saw it as elevating herself above the working-class mire of council houses, the pit and the miners' welfare club. But in truth she was a snob. I wouldn't have minded but she was just so dour and miserable most of the time. The snobbery gave her no pleasure and it didn't elevate her social status anyway.

Like a lot of Yorkshire folk, who wear their misery like a full-length winter coat, she was suspicious of any positive human emotion. If she heard someone laughing loudly in the street she'd peer out of the window and say,

"What's all that noise? What's he got to laugh about?" as though laughing was a character weakness, something that any right-thinking folk should feel guilty about.

If someone, especially a woman, was interviewed on the local news and she had a strong Yorkshire accent, my grandma would shake her head and say,

"Oh she's so common" or, "What does she know about anything? And her in that old cardigan as well!"

Style was everything to her and content mattered almost not at all.

"She'd have voted for Hitler if he had the right accent," Fred once told me after a row over the quality of her dumplings. It had started with a casual remark that they were "a bit solid". Solid? It was like eating small, salty rubber balls. But gran took offence, what with her being a superb cook and everything.

There was much talk about him not knowing good food when he saw it and how he had 'common' tastes and other such snobbery. Fred was unimpressed but he never argued. He went a bit quiet and sat in his shed for a few hours, but he never argued.

"Why don't you ever argue with her? I would if I was you," I said.

"There's no point lad. All arguing does is pour petrol on a smouldering fire. Then boom, you've got singed eyebrows. I wouldn't want your gran to singe my eyebrows now would I?"

He had a point.

Maybe she had some self-loathing issues or maybe she was just a genuinely unpleasant person, but all I knew aged ten was that she was no fun to be around. I didn't respect her enough to fear her but I feared being left alone with her because I had no idea what I could possibly say that wouldn't be met with disapproval. Perhaps I should have declared myself the prospective parliamentary candidate for the Conservative Party. Though if I had, she'd only have said, "What, with you dropping your aitches all the time. Never!" Even when I got into grammar school her reaction was to comment that "standards aren't what they used to be at schools these days". Thanks Gran.

Even at the age of eight I thought they were an odd couple, but I just assumed that was the way of the world, especially as my own parents were hardly Darby and Joan themselves. In fact, growing up in Hull it seemed that all adults were a bit miserable, though that may have been to do with the fact that the whole town smelled of fish when the wind blew off the sea.

Being born in the early 60's to parents who were born into back-to-back, three-to-a-bed working-class stock meant that I was destined to be pushed socially upwards into the new lower middle classes. It was my parents' ambition to be part of the new Marks & Spencer-shopping, car-driving, mortgage-owning, well-spoken class. They actively rejected any of their roots where at all possible.

Even baking cakes and pies was sacrificed in the 1970's when it was financially viable to buy them from the shop. I was brought up with the notion that shop-bought was always better because it showed you had money. Doing it yourself was what they'd had to do when they were really poor. How times have changed - back then the only fat people you saw were aristocrats and upper-class types, the poor were always stick-thin and wiry. Now it's the other way round.

My mother - having learned her culinary talents from her own mother - was a distinctively average cook, so it was always a truism that shop-bought was best in our house. Everything she made was too bland, too stodgy or too dry and she was extremely suspicious of anything she suspected was foreign food. Foreign food was always declared to be 'muck'. I thought this must be true.

"I don't know how they eat that muck," she'd say if someone was cooking with garlic on the telly.

"It makes them go mad," she'd say if anyone going even a bit mad appeared to be from anywhere east of Belgium or had a skin tone not bleached white by the winds that blow off the North Sea.

"It's poison to us is that," my gran would chip in as someone - probably the Galloping Gourmet Graham Kerr - deseeded a chilli pepper or poured olive oil onto tomatoes.

They were so consistently vehement you'd have thought they knew something. Let me tell you, they knew nothing. I had heard that potatoes were in fact foreign food as they'd come from the hills of the Andes. "Aye but it took the British to learn how to cook them properly," she said quite untruthfully.

"What about tea then mam? Tea comes from India so that's foreign as well."

"Tea doesn't count - they wouldn't even have it if it wasn't for British rule," she said with blithe certainty. Even aged eight I thought this sounded a bit odd.

"But it grows there mam - we did it in geography."

"Shut up our John. No-one likes a clever clogs."

I got a lot of that; being told to shut up for actually knowing something. Education is a threat to stupid people. I spotted that early on. So I shut up. No point in getting my eyebrows singed and anyway, I knew that some did like a clever clogs. Fred liked a clever clogs because he was one himself and I grinned to myself at the thought of that.

"What are you smiling at?" snapped mam.

"Nothing," I said innocently.

"Well don't then." She had inherited her own mother's miserablist tendencies.

"Say nowt and then do what you want anyway," was what Fred would say to me. It's not a bad philosophy.

This obsession with foreign food was to take a strange twist. We were visiting Fred and Gran over the Easter holidays and one of the things I liked to do best on these visits was accompany Fred on what he called 'his rounds'.

'His rounds' was his way of saying he was going for a walk, but it was much more than sauntering the streets. He'd go down to the allotments to see his mates - all of them ex-miners - and he'd pick up a cauliflower from one and a pound of carrots from another. He'd have had a walking stick whittled up for someone else and that had to be delivered. They'd all do stuff for each other - some brewed beer or pickled their own onions - and they had this sort of barter system. They didn't have much money so it's how they got by. It was, ironically enough in the late 60's, a very hippy thing to do. Not that they would have entertained such a notion, if they had even heard of hippies, which they probably hadn't.

He'd go up the shops for his ever-present quarter of mint imperials and he'd pop into the Miners' Welfare for a pint or two. He'd take me in and buy me pop even though of course I wasn't allowed. Rules like that didn't bother Fred, he always knew someone who would turn a blind eye.

I liked to go with him because everywhere he went he seemed to make things interesting. He'd point out birds and tell me what they were. He'd show me funny little beetles that were eating his cabbages, he'd nip into the chippy and get me a bag of scrap batter for nothing. And it seemed to me that the people he knew were all real characters. Odd some of them were for sure, but characters nonetheless. In my mam and dad's socially-aspiring world the very opposite was true, people were polite and well-mannered but they had nothing about them. They were as bland and stodgy as mam's cooking.

Fred's mates were often rude and boisterous. It was as though they all belonged to this male club. They all had the same nagging wife. They all got the same dinners cooked equally as badly. They all dressed the same in a dark wool jacket, baggy pants, waistcoat, white collarless shirt and a checked flat cap. All of them. They all looked identical. You had to be a character to stand out when you looked and sounded identical to everyone else.

That Easter holidays I went with Fred on his rounds. First stop was Harry's house as Fred had carved him a knife handle. As usual he knocked on the back door and walked in. He did this everywhere. My mam would have thought it was the height of bad manners, an invasion of privacy, but Fred and his mates seemed to be oblivious to the notion of privacy.

"Harry! Is thee in?" he shouted from beside the old cream Belfast sink.

"Aye I'm 'ere, tha's no need to break me windows wi' that foghorn of yours," said Harry, coming in to the kitchen. He was small and thin but strong. His skin was all leathery and pitted like Fred's. His lungs rattled like Fred's as well. This hadn't stopped him smoking though; a Woodbine hung on his lips.

"Ah, I see you've got the lad with you. You keep him out of mischief, lad. He's a right bugger is this one tha knaas."

I laughed and nodded, though I didn't really understand. It just sounded right somehow.

Fred gave him the knife handle.

"By 'eck Fred, this is champion," he said, rolling the carved piece of ash around in his hand: "Nice bit of work is that."

He reached into a cupboard and took out four beer bottles made of heavy dark brown glass and stopped with a cork.

"There you go, Fred. Four bottles of Harry's Best Bitter."

"Champion," said Fred and he licked his lips and made a funny, delighted face in anticipation of the brew. As he put them in his grubby bag, Harry whispered conspiratorially:

"Don't make a noise with them bottles, 'else Eileen'll know I've been brewing again."

These men spent their whole lives in fear of their wives and I could never understand why they were married at all. They clearly enjoyed the company of men far more than the company of women, and it looked like the women stopped the men from having a good time. The women thought the men were daft and the men thought the women were killjoys.

"Is thee goin' dahn to Wilf's?"

"Aye, I thought I'd take a saunter down theer and see what's what," said Fred, 'seeing what's what' being one of Fred's favourite hobbies.

"Aye, well you wait till you get down there. The bloody smell - it'll take your breath away."

"The smell? 'As he been on that bloody syrup of figs again?"

"You'll see soon enough," laughed Harry.

So off we went down the road, through the council estate, across the recreation ground and down to the allotments.

Fred had an allotment that he shared with Wilf Wilkinson. Allotments were like gold - you had to get on a waiting list and then hope someone died or moved away. It was usually the

257

former as no-one ever seemed to move. Fred had a garden in which he grew vegetables and a few flowers but the allotment was massive and it was mostly dedicated to growing potatoes. Fred and Wilf were self-sufficient in potatoes all year round.

They had a small potting shed which had been one half of a pigeon loft at one point in its shabby existence. It was nailed together with apparently random pieces of wood and partially covered in tar-paper and creosote. Wilf was sitting in a fold-up chair outside the shed as we arrived. He was also a short, muscular thin man - very similar to Harry except he was quite bald but for a short bristle of grey hair around the back of his head.

"Aye aye Fred. Now then John, lad. Come to see us 'ave you? Got a grand crop of earlies coming on."

He gestured at the young potato plants all standing in neat rows, little mounds of earth either side of the stems. It was Wilf who had taught me about the Andes and potatoes.

"Harry says you stink," said Fred, chuckling. "I knew that already but he reckoned it was extra special today. What's what Wilf? Are we cooking?"

"What's what? I'll tell thee what's what," said Wilf, getting quite worked up. "That Harry Casson is what's what. He knows nowt that man, nowt whatsoever. If owt's a bit different he thinks you've gone mad. He was down here shouting the odds. I told him 'shut thee mouth before I shut it for thee'."

Fred just laughed loudly. I was confused. All that 'what's what'ing was hard to follow.

"My God!" Fred exclaimed from inside the potting shed where he'd wandered to get a shovel. "Bloody 'ell Wilf. He was right. It's powerful enough in 'ere."

I followed Fred into the small wooden shed. As I entered, a smell caught my throat and made me cough. I veered away from the door and back out into the fresh air, my eyes stinging.

"There's no need for all that fussing John lad. It's only a bit of curry," said Wilf, clearly annoyed at me for making such a show.

"Oh," I said, trying to get my breath. "What's curry? Do you use it on the garden?"

They both erupted into roaring laughter like a pair of asthmatic bellows. Fred leaned over and put his hands on his knees, his whole body rattling with laughter. I wasn't sure whether to join them or run away for clearly making a fool out of myself.

"Well I'll say this John lad, it is food, but not for the garden - it's for us," he said, wiping a tear from his eye with a snot-crusted blue handkerchief.

I hadn't heard of this thing called 'curry'. It sounded a bit like 'slurry' and I'd heard of that so supposed it wasn't a bad guess that you'd put it on the garden. I couldn't believe that whatever was giving off that smell could possibly be edible. It was acrid and choking.

I went back to the potting shed to take another look. Now that the door had been left open there was better ventilation and the odour wasn't quite so overpowering. On the bench stood a little camping gas stove and on top was what I thought was a dustbin lid, but on reflection it must have been a make-shift wok-type arrangement.

I peered nervously into the lid as it bubbled away - it was bright red, the colour of molten lava - molten lava full of potatoes and chicken. It smelled like nothing on earth that I had ever smelled before. It wasn't actually that unpleasant, even though I was sure it was making my throat sore. My eyes were watering too. It was all most odd for a boy who had been brought up on milk puddings, mashed potatoes and boiled vegetables.

"Go on lad, 'ave a taste, it'll not hurt thee," said Wilf. He dipped in a big spoon and offered me the steaming miasma.

Fred encouraged me: "I'll tell you summat for nowt, your gran would definitely not eat that, our John. Definitely not. Now if that doesn't give you a reason to try it, nowt will."

That did it. Tentatively I sipped at the bright orange concoction. It exploded in my mouth. It had so much flavour it actually hurt - salty, sour and sweet all at once. Then came the burning sensation. I panted to get cool air to relieve the pain. The old men couldn't stop laughing.

"Is it supposed to hurt you?" I asked, unable to believe anything edible should inflict pain, though my mam's pastry had been doing that all my life to my gums and gut.

"It's all part of t'pleasure of Indian cooking," said Wilf, taking a spoon himself. "It makes you feel right 'ot."

"Champion is that," said Fred, helping himself. "Clears your passages - both ends." They both roared and laughed.

"Aye, you'll be redecorating the lav after this lot," said Wilf, his face red and dotted with beads of sweat.

Apparently Fred and Wilf had developed a taste for Indian cuisine after being introduced to it by Mr Singh, a fellow allotment-holder, but neither of their wives would let them cook it in the house...so here they were cooking on a camping stove in the shed. Both old blokes had such a look of joy at the illicit food cooking on the stove, you'd have thought it was illegal.

Wilf took the beer from Fred's knapsacks, pulled out the corks and poured it into the two big chipped white-and-blue enamel cups that lived in the potting shed. Fred spooned out curry onto two enamel plates and cut three bug hunks of bread from a loaf with his penknife.

"Go on, dip tha' breed in the gravy," Fred said to me. "It's tasty stuff - delicious, lad."

I didn't want to be seen siding with my disapproving gran so I did exactly as he said. After a couple of bites I started to get used to the flavour, with the bread seeming to cool it down.

"Aye aye Fred, the lad's got a taste for it," said Wilf. "Give 'im some beer an' all."

And I had got a taste for it. After the initial shock, I soon fell in love with Fred and Wilf's curries. They always contained potatoes, onions and garlic they grew themselves along with a few scrag ends or bits of chicken from the butcher and any other vegetables they had to hand. Mr Singh, a tall, thick-set Sikh bloke in a burgundy-coloured turban, provided the curry powder and later on the coriander.

And after the curry, the beer tasted lovely. It was all smoky, sweet and almost soapy-tasting. The home brew was real beer of course, made in big buckets in Harry's shed over the other side of the allotment. For some reason he was banned from brewing in the house. Their womenfolk seemed to be dedicated to stopping them drinking as much as they wanted to drink so this too, like Wilf and Fred's curry, was an illicit little hobby.

I got told off for going home smelling of garlic and beer and my mam would no more cook Indian food than eat bricks, so Fred's shed was the only place I got this delicious 'gravy'.

Curry and beer were just two passions he awoke in me.

Castleford - in case you haven't looked at a map recently or are from the south - is technically in West Yorkshire, but for a town in West Yorkshire it's about as far east as possible before you cross into the East Riding.

The Romans came through Castleford and set up a base, the Vikings probably had a poke at it as well on a day out from York, but no invading force has yet established Castleford - or Cass as it's locally always known - as a football town. While the locals mostly split their support between Leeds United and Hull City, at the heart of sport in Castleford beats the rugby league team.

These days Castleford are the Castleford Tigers. This re-branding has happened right across rugby league, apparently to make it more exciting and appealing to kids, because of course simply calling a team Tigers is enough to make you interested in a game you never liked before.

Rugby league is also now a summer sport. To me, and I know Fred would agree, this is just plain wrong. Rugby league is a winter sport to be played in the mud, sleet and driving rain. Fred must be spinning in his grave. I know what he'd say:

"The rugby in the summer? 'Ave Southerners started playin'?" And of course they have.

Fred loved rugby league. He loved it so much he turned 'rugby league' into a verb.

"Come on John, we're going rugby leaguing," he'd say, or sometimes it'd just be 'leaguing'.

It was a shared love among the miners - they all seemed to prefer rugby to football. But none of them had any time for its posh relation, rugby union. There was much contempt for union. Bizarrely it was seen as a southern sport despite the fact that it was played in Scotland and even just up the road in places like Otley. This was probably more because 'southern' was used far more as the worst kind of insult than as a geographical description.

Fred told me he'd been to the first ever Castleford game in 1926, the year the club was founded. I remember him telling me about a player called Juicy Adams - "t'best scrum 'arf Cass ever 'ad". I thought a rugby league player called Juicy sounded a bit unlikely but I was happy to get taken down to Wheldon Road and get indoctrinated.

I wasn't yet ten but even at that early age I had a strong inkling that this was a quintessentially northern experience - from the smell of baccy and homemade beef tea made from Oxo stock cubes to the low cold mist that hung over the pitch on that midweek night in November. The beef tea was fantastic. My mam thought drinking beef tea was a bit too working-class so we never got it at home. It was a salty, slightly bitter and thin drink but on a cold Tuesday night, it was just the job.

Fred wore his usual burgundy checked wool muffler underneath his black heavy rough wool donkey jacket and I was wearing a duffel coat and an outsized rollneck jumper that mam had knitted extra big so that I could 'grow into it' - it still fitted me five years later. Much to my chagrin it was bright green, but back then, you wore what your mam gave you. I also had on occasion to wear a jumper knitted by gran from yellow, orange and brown space-dyed wool. "Bloody 'ell, it's a giant wasp," Fred would say as he made buzzing noises and swatted me with a rolled-up newspaper. It was character-forming.

Designer fashions were decades away and anyway, all your friends also sported crap knitwear produced by their arthritic relations on perpetually-clicking knitting needles. Back then it seemed that knitting needles were given to women at the wedding ceremony. Every woman I encountered in my first dozen years knitted. It was like a religion. And every single one of them thought they were a champion knitter and were quick to be disparaging of other women's knitting. Slagging off the quality of a woman's knitting was almost a sport for my mam and gran. They seemed to take great delight in it.

"She couldn't knit jacquard to save her life," they'd say and nod sagely at the disgrace of it all.

My gran just never stopped knitting. Not ever. She knitted everything from trousers for my Action Man to tweed socks. She knitted enough socks for the entire army and not one of them ever fitted anyone properly. Mine were far too long. Always. She seemed to keep making them longer and longer until, by age 16, she presumably thought I had giant clowns' feet. But of course, no-one ever complained. It seemed rude somehow. So she went on in blissful sock ignorance.

All the kids were in the same boat as regards knitwear though. And some dads too. Sometimes on a Saturday morning in town you'd pass a lad from school trailing behind his mam and dad wearing a new horrendous creation. You'd make brief, sympathetic eye contact and with a raise of the eyebrows you'd convey mutual sympathy for your humiliating clothing. You'd see dads wearing a bright royal blue chunky sweater 'fresh off the needles' as Fred would call it - so long in the sleeves he'd have to roll the cuff up to his arm.

Such a hand-knitted jumper was almost always far too long and looked more like a wool dress. But Yorkshire women were and indeed still are a tough breed and had the ability to make their husbands' lives hell if they dared to complain. So, like us kids, it was a burden they tried to bear with grace. Oddly enough, the knitwear grans and mams knitted for themselves always fitted perfectly, which suggests it was all some elaborate joke played on us poor menfolk.

Fred was no exception to the travails of ill-fitting jumpers. One rainy afternoon in front of the telly Gran declared another creation finished. It was an Arran-style sweater for Fred. Full of dropped stitches and holes, even I could tell Gran was a rubbish knitter.

Fred pulled it on anyway and paraded in front of us, arms out wide. It fitted where it touched, which wasn't in many places. "Champion," he'd say. Fred said everything was "champion", even things like this jumper that plainly were not champion.

Later on we went rugby leaguing, Fred still wearing the jumper under his donkey jacket as he left the house. As usual, we went to the club for a pre-game pint, or in my case a glass of RW Whites lemonade poured out of a heavy glass bottle with a rubber bung - the squeak of the rubber and the pop as it was pulled out was always a welcome sound to me as a boy.

Fred took the jumper off and gave it to the barman.

"Keep that safe till after t'game," he said. The barman laughed: "One of the wife's is it?"

They both laughed out loud. Being out with Fred was like being shown inside a secret male-only club where everyone understood exactly what everyone else was going through. It's like they all had the same lives and the same wives, and they conspired together to make the best of a bad job. Maybe women did the same thing - I don't know, I was never allowed in that club.

Fred never seemed to be more than a stone's throw away from someone he knew. It was remarkable. Perhaps it's living in the same place for so long and working in the industry which employed so many men in the town. Every third person you'd pass in the street would say hello or at least nod.

Anyway, the old fella on the turnstile knew Fred: "Narr then Fred...ooze this then?"

He looked down with bemusement at the head peeping out of the massive rollneck jumper like a pea wrapped in a scarf.

"It's our John...first time leaguing in't it John?"

"Bloody 'ell Fred. Poor lad doesn't deserve this, does he? Bloody 'ell," said the bloke again. He and Fred laughed the same wheezy laugh, clouds of breathy fog emerging from their mouths in thick streams. I didn't really understand why it was funny.

Fred toured the half-empty terrace - he seemed to know everyone who had turned up, probably because ex-miners made up most of the Cass crowd.

He introduced me in the same way to every group of men: "This is our John...first game!" They all laughed. The men's club effect again. Some cheered. They all smoked and smelled strongly of beer.

The rugby itself was unremarkable in every way. By the end of the match the players were indistinguishable from their opponents because they were covered completely in wet mud. I don't remember who won but I don't think it mattered much to Fred - he went for the craic and to get out of the house.

But while rugby league was Fred's first game, like most men, he also took an interest in football and he supported Hull City, who in the 60's were quite good, in a mid-table Second Division kind of way.

Boothferry Park was where Hull played and it was an impressive ground, even hosting England B internationals. I'd been trying to get my dad to take me to a game for about a year, which is a bloody long time when you're eight years old, but for some reason he always found a reason not to go. He wasn't mad on football.

Fred and my gran were staying with us for Christmas and I wanted to go to one of the festive games - Fred volunteered so off we went on the bus.

It goes without saying that Fred didn't have a car. Hardly any working-class people had cars. In fact, there were people who thought getting a car meant you were getting above your station. You'd be drinking wine and going to the theatre next.

"Who does he think he is with that car? Bus too good for him, is it?"

Inverse snobbery was probably a natural defensive reaction to the sight of someone escaping the bonds of their class but it wasn't something Fred had any time for - he rather typically saw cars as a free resource to exploit for his own benefit. Although he walked almost everywhere, if it started raining or he just wanted to get there quicker, he could get a lift effortlessly.

The first time I witnessed this was on a trip into town one Saturday morning to buy dried peas (I bought a lot of dried peas in those days for my pea-shooter gun, which was rarely out of my grip). We bought a large bag of peas from a pet shop. I don't recall why the pet shop sold dried peas - it didn't seem odd back then. Maybe peas were the food of choice for hamsters or iguanas or something.

We were just walking to the bus stop when a car pulled up and the passenger window was rolled down by a woman. She had the kind of posh Yorkshire accent of someone who had been born working-class but had spent a lot of their adult lives pretending to be middle-class. She probably lived somewhere like Pudsey. She asked Fred for directions:

"Do you know where Wilson Road is?"

Without pausing, Fred opened the back door of the car saying: "Aye, I'll show you. It's on our way. Come on lads."

Before they could protest the three of us clambered into the back seat and off we went. Even as a kid you can sense when adults are embarrassed and the posh couple in the front were clearly shocked that their innocent enquiry had led to these grubby working-class oiks getting into their nice new car. It smelled of leather. Leather seats seemed very posh to me.

"Nah then. Don't thee worry. I'll get thee theer," said Fred with a wink to us.

He then proceeded to direct the car all the way back to his house, where he got out, leaned into the window and said: "Nah then, take the third on t'right, straight on for a mile and first left. That's Wilson Road."

The car-owners were doubtless far too shocked to object to Fred freeloading a ride. The sheer cheek of the man was impressive - I thought it was brilliant and couldn't stop giggling. I did a lot of giggling in those days.

We were soon to learn that this was not the only way Fred got around.

It was half-term and we'd gone to Castleford to stay with Fred and my gran. This was great news because it meant lots of days out with Fred. One morning we got the bus into town, where he did a bit of shopping before we went into a small noisy cafe for a cup of tea. As usual, everyone in there seemed to know him. By this time they all knew me and my brother as well and most of them gave us a nod or an 'ello lad'. I always loved this. It made me feel warm inside and the smell of tea, toast and the steamy windows would stay with me throughout life as a comforting, almost romantic thing.

It was all so different from growing up and living in a new middle-class area where everyone kept themselves to themselves as though public social interaction was an unwelcome reminder of the working-class backgrounds they had all escaped.

As we were having tea and toasted teacakes, it started raining. To me it seemed to rain almost every day in Castleford.

A thin, bald man behind the counter called Eric said to Fred: "Rain's coming down Fred. Is thee gettin' a lift home?" He laughed and the woman making toast made a loud barking noise of amusement.

"Aye, we'll see," said Fred cryptically. We finished our tea and tea cakes and put our coats on.

"Right lads, you stay here," said Fred as we stood by the door. "I'll get us a nice drive home, shall I?"

He laughed a little to himself and his rattling pigeon-in-a-chimney lungs rasped. "Watch for the wave, now," he said as he departed.

We stood and watched him - he looked right up the road, spotted a likely car and walked briskly out onto the pavement waving his arms. He walked off the pavement and into the road still waving his arms at a sky blue Ford Anglia which pulled to a stop right in front of him. He'd have run Fred down otherwise. We couldn't hear what he was saying but soon enough we got 'the wave' from Fred and scuttled off to the car, getting into the back seats as Fred got in the front.

"Aye, he's not well," Fred was saying. "He looks alright but 'is doctor says 'ees not to get wet like. Well yi can't keep a young lad in t'house for ever can you?"

And so it went on. The bloke drove us to Fred's house. We got out without saying a word.

When the bloke pulled away Fred said, "say nowt to no-one lads", and winked at us. We knew this meant not to tell Gran, who would sure as anything tell our mam and he'd get a bollocking.

Fred was locally so famous for 'getting lifts' that eventually, as more people got cars in the early 70's, he could pretty much always get a lift without having to flag down cars in the street. But I think that was all too easy for Fred - he liked the challenge of blagging off total strangers.

At his funeral this unique ability was even mentioned in the eulogy.

If someone tried the same thing today they'd be arrested. It'd be thought of as the worst kind of invasion of personal space. Can you imagine? "He just got into my car officer, he didn't even ask, he just climbed in!"

Anyway, we took the bus that day to the ground in Hull, where to my young eyes there seemed to be thousands upon thousands of people. I remember the metallic clicking noise of the turnstiles and the thick clouds of fag smoke drifting across the terrace where we stood behind the goal and the excitement at seeing the expanse of green grass and brown mud that passed for a football pitch in 1968. Although Fred didn't know anyone in Hull, he was soon cracking on with the other blokes behind the goal, just as if he was in Castleford.

It felt like I'd joined a club and it made me feel excited and yet sort of cosy as well. It wasn't threatening or frightening in any way and everything seemed like an adventure. At half-time a bloke next to us shared a flask of tea with me and Fred - the only time I ever saw a flask was on a day out to Bridlington or Withernsea. It all seemed thrilling.

I was obsessed with the colours of the kits and from an early age, had memorised every team in England and Scotland's strip so that even now, I still think of towns as a colour. Hull were playing in their classic old gold and black. I was also a fan of Norwich City's yellow and green but they played in their away strip that day, which I think was a sort of dark green with yellow trim. This was back in the days when you only wore your second strip if you were playing away and your colours clashed. I don't know what happened to that principle, it served us all well enough for decades.

Hull City were in the middle of another mid-table season and lost 1-0 - that's about all I can remember about the game but that was the day football well and truly got its hooks in me and life would never be the same again.

Fred died in 1974, the coal in his lungs getting the old bugger in the end. The last time I saw him was about a year and a half before he popped his clogs - we'd moved from Hull to Teesside in the middle of 1969 and visits had become more scarce.

But we'd gone down to see them in the summer of 1973 and I was playing T.Rex and Slade very loudly on the radio, thus attracting the wrath of my mam and gran, who needed no excuse to deliver a bollocking.

By then, Fred wasn't that healthy, he was in his early 70's and had lost some of his energy but none of his spark. He'd also started arguing back with my gran, presumably knowing that the end wasn't far away so a few singed eyebrows was a price worth paying.

So when they shouted at me to turn the radio down, Fred wandered into the kitchen and said loudly: "Let the lad play it as loud as he likes. He bloody likes it like that. It's his music. You're not supposed to enjoy it. 'ees doing nowt wrong. It's supposed to be loud!"

It's supposed to be loud. Yes. That was a great lesson to learn. That went in deep and stayed in.

My mam and gran protested it was 'all noise' these days and you couldn't hear the words and tunes weren't like they used to be in their day. I dutifully turned it down. This served to really annoy Fred and it was the only time I saw him lose his temper.

"Turn it back up our John. These bloody old witches would be quick to take your money if you became a pop star; they'd not mind your loud music then! You enjoy yourself lad." He scowled at them, turned away, winked at me and went off down the garden to inspect a new barrel of blood that had just been delivered from the slaughterhouse.

He used it to feed his garden. I'm quite sure that would be illegal now.

More than anyone, Fred made me what I turned out to be; or perhaps more accurately he encouraged me to be what I was. Not because I spent that much time with him - I may have only spent the equivalent of a month around him my whole life - but because of his attitude.

He was, in his own sort of way, a rebel spirit. A rock 'n' roll granddad if you like. He showed me that having a laugh and a crack-on was worth more than any amount of social climbing or pretensions. I saw how he loved a few pints and a daft laugh and subconsciously thought, that'll do for me.

He showed me that just getting on and doing what you want to do, regardless of what anyone thinks, is the best way to live. He made me want to experiment and be adventurous when no-one else would even have thought that was something ordinary northern folk should think about doing. He showed up regular, straight people for what they were; a bit boring. And all of this in the last few years of his life.

I know that if he had been my age he would have been in a band, he would have been writing stories about pissing in sinks and shagging birds. He was just born a couple of generations too early but if he was here and I could say to him,

"Fred, what do you reckon about this book I've written. It's a bit dirty and it's a bit mad," he'd have laughed his pigeon-stuck-in-a-chimney laugh and with twinkling blue eyes say: "Aye lad, that sounds champion."

Cheers Fred. You auld bugger.

2. THE CODE OF THE ROAD.....AN EXCERPT

The Code of the Road is a full-length book due for publication in the first half of 2007. It's an account of the Beer Pigs' life on the road in California and Nevada in all its dirty, druggy, bare-arsed, low-rent rock 'n' roll glory and destruction. It's the book I've been asked to write for years. This is an exclusive extract, available here for the first time and is just a lick of the salty stuff you can expect...

We needed money and extra money with an added creamy layer of money on top and we needed it super-sized and with a side order of money to go. We had enough cash to get by for a week, maybe two if we restricted our drinking, which we all knew wasn't in any way likely; intoxication was a way of life when we were on the road and when we were off the road. It was who were and we liked it.

If we'd been in Britain, we'd have just picked up a phone and called around pubs and clubs until we'd got enough gigs to at least keep us in beer and food money, even if it meant sleeping in the van with your head in the bass drum. Here we didn't even know where anywhere was, and we didn't know where you could play, who to call or even how to use the pay-phones, but we had one thing in our favour; we were a team of charmers, brains and hard men and we had chatter chat chat and we had some ooomph muscle and we knew how to rock 'n' roll.

Ah yes. The holy rock 'n' roll; it flowed through us like an old-time religion; we believed in it 100% forever and ever Amen and when we were stoned we said there were rock 'n' roll angels watching out for us and it was like if we believed in it enough, everything would be okay. We used distortion units and wah-wah pedals for prayer and the noise that came out was our thing, it was the real thing. I love it, I need it, alright, I'm a highway star.

The non-believers, and they are everywhere, don't understand the immortal noise. To them it's just noise with words and that's all; they might like it on in the background sometimes and they might own a few records but it's not their lives, it's just a tune to hum on the radio to get through the day; it's not life and death and it doesn't hold the key to any great universal truths - but to us it was the Godhead where infinity and power and wang-dang doodle came from, you know, all the good stuff baby baby baby.

So what do a bunch of Anglo Bandidos do when they're in a new city and want to play some rock 'n' roll? We figured the only sensible thing to do was find a bar, use our slaver, get some people on our side and get some knowledge.

We had just one contact in LA and he was a man called Peter Belvoir, which is for no good reason pronounced Beaver. So they all just called him The Beaver, poor cunt. He'd got out of England a year earlier and was the friend of our sometime-roadie Spunky Monkey. Don't ask, it's worse than you think.

The Beaver had told us that we should report for duty at the Kings Head in Santa Monica and use it as a kind of headquarters. He said it was Brit Central and the Brits help each other out if they can you know, and it was all we had and it sounded like a start so we got a cab down there. The Beaver was a singer but we'd never met him and didn't know what he looked like or where he lived, only that he was out there somewhere in the heat and the dust.

We called a cab from the hotel - it turned up quickly and it was old and battered and dented and roared off down Santa Monica Boulevard with the engine coughing like a tramp with bronchitis. The plastic seats are torn and yellow sponge is bursting through and it's about 11am and the sky is a sizzling retina-burning lapis lazuli blue and it looks like someone has ordered blue and then added a couple of extra shots of blue. The date palms arc up into the infinite sky on this infinite July morning with the strength of the dawn of a new day and the

273

thick warm air wraps itself around us in the cab and all the windows are open and Lenny's long lank hair is blowing out of the window like he's a dog. The cab driver is from somewhere in the Middle East, Iran maybe.

"You boys English?" he shouted.

"Yes, we're English gentlemen," I said in my best foreigner-style version of an English accent. "Off for tea and sandwiches at the Kings Head."

He laughed explosively and he seems happy though his face looks hard like old leather and his black eyes look locked down forever.

"I tell you this...the Englishman he likes drinking...drinking comes before everything. I know this."

He raised an imaginary glass to his lips and sampled its contents with relish.

We all cheered. It was good to know our reputation had travelled 6,000 miles.

"Aye, that's true like," said Hunter, happy like a kid in the front seat as he slapped the bloke on his back. The driver smiled and went on: "And I tell you this - the Englishman he can hold his bloody drink too. Not like the American. He...he...he throws up, he can't take it."

He made a gurgling noise and laughed again - obviously had one too many frat boys throwing up in his cab.

We zoomed down to the coast from the strip, bouncing on the big pot-holes, wowing at all the sights of everyday LA and he pulls up sharply outside the pub and we all cheer again for some reason like we're on a school trip.

"Fancy a pint?" said Hunter, digging a handful of dollars out his pocket. "Y'seem like a nice fella like and I love yer shoes too mate. Are they slippers?"

He had on his feet some sort of beaded lightweight shoes all coloured patterns of glass beads and they were truly ace, but he shook his head ruefully.

274

"Oh no no no, my wife she would kill me with a knife!" He stabbed the air with the knife, like he knew what knife she'd use and how she'd wield it.

It didn't seem worth risking a stabbing for a pint so we tipped him five bucks and he swung round and sped off back the way we'd come.

I leaned on the door of the Kings Head just for a second, pausing to take in the moment, and I'm dry-mouthed and already sweating up the armpits of the Van Halen t-shirt I've got on and I'm happy happy to be going into a bar in the morning and the smell of smoke and fried food hits me in my clean day face like an old friend's embrace.

The Kings Head is Los Angeles' primo English-style pub and it looks like a regular bar except the walls are covered with famous Brits who've been there over the decades like Ringo and Paul and Freddie Mercury and Eric Clapton and the rest of the Anglo muso community up to and including Lynsey De Bloody Paul. No honestly.

I got a round in - Hunter spotted Newcastle Brown Ale and immediately felt at home but the rest of us were drinking the new pleasure that was Budweiser and it's easy to forget now but you couldn't get Bud in Britain back then. Hunter said it tasted like fizzy piss and maybe it does taste like his piss but to me it's always been the taste of the best of America; the taste of railroads and slide guitar; the taste of a '64 Mustang and Fender Stratocaster; the taste of the small town and the big city and I think I love it for that reason as much as the fact that you can drink a small ocean of the stuff without it weighing you down.

I told the bloke behind the bar our situation and where could we get some gigs? The guy sounds like he was once English but has gone native. Well you couldn't blame him, I imagine that the place just got its hooks in you deeper and deeper the longer you were there.

He asked what sort of stuff we played and did we have our own gear and Lenny, being the one who always carried pen and paper in case his muse descends and he has the urge to write his own version of Tangled Up In Blue, wrote down all the info. He went through names of band-friendly clubs and pubs and gave us a copy of LA Weekly and basically said to get on the phone and do some calling round, and we know that's just fine.

I think it was his pub and maybe it still is and I think his name was Phil and if it was, thanks Phil for the first step on a long road. He also said he knew some people who sometimes needed bands for parties and such and if we were any good, maybe we could get into all that and we said cool, it was exactly what we were up for, you know - we'd play for beer and bed and if that was too expensive we'd play just for the beer and we'd be thanking you mister or missus or Ms.

We said we were a cheap, reliable bar band that would play all night and okay, we were only one of about 45,000 and counting in LA, but not so many of them were English and we were quickly learning that being English set you apart and almost made you seem a bit special and who would have guessed that since we were nothing but twats in England? Rough-arsed fuckers. But here no-one knew and for all anyone could tell we could even have been royalty, if only we'd been more ugly, more inbred and worn more clothes that matched.

We put Tony on the phone to start trying to get us gigs and offer the deal of free drinks for the telesales girl. Tony, as well as being a lothario of gargantuan proportions, is also tight as a duck's egg vent and you could pretty much get him to do anything for free drink or food and so he sat his hairy self down by the pay-phone with a heap of quarters and started calling clubs and bars.

An hour later he'd arranged to see two people who he seemed to think ran clubs, although he wasn't really sure and he didn't know where they were even or how to get there, but if we showed up and gave them a tape or even maybe played a bit, they'd see if we were good enough and maybe we'd get a gig or maybe we wouldn't, but it was all we had and so we took it.

"What sort of coins on offer?" asked Hunter, but Tony hadn't even asked about that and when we looked at the addresses, one was in the Valley up over the hill in Northridge and the other was in fucking Newport down the coast! And we had no bloody transport and we were a bit pissed off at having to suddenly do some work and so we'd better get a van sorted out as well, but all we really wanted to do was sit and drink and suddenly it seemed like a lot of hard work, which we knew it would be, but we were still fucked up and jet-lagged, and even though we had a bit of what we liked to call velocity increaser to keep us going, we knew we were going to crash and burn.

So we had a couple of hours to get a van, get the gear, find this place in Northridge and see what was what. The van was easy enough, we rang up a place called Rent-A-Wreck - it's good to know your place in the market - and they let us hire this piece of shit for a couple of weeks that made a hell of noise while not going anywhere very fast. We paid the cash and found our way back up to Sunset and picked up the gear from the hotel and by now the heat is hot hot heat and it's in the 90's so we thought we'd better get a few cold beers. We pull into a liquor store and load up the van with Bud and Newkie Brown ale, which it turns out is brewed in 'Frisco, and cram them into two coolboxes and break open a few.

Northridge was weird. It was like it was nowhere really; almost like it didn't really exist at all because it was totally indistinct from anywhere else and you couldn't tell where it started or where it stopped if it wasn't for the signs and it's as though, like so many American towns, it's not meant to have any character because it's just purely functional. It's there and it has places you can buy stuff and places you can live and it does that job fine and that's all it's trying to do and it's happy that it's just another collection of strip malls and straight-out-of-the-box tract homes set below the wild brown mountains in the airless heat of the summer.

Tony had the Rand McNally map and for a pissed cunt he's a good map reader and Lenny's driving but he's feeling weird because he's on the wrong side of the road, which makes you lop-sided and a bit freaked out and it's going okay until the moment he turns left and, instead of taking the far right lane, he forgets he's not in England and heads left and all we can see is this big fucking truck bearing down on us like this big fucking evil thing and we think we're gonna die and really this is going to be a quick fucking death because this is a piece of tin we're in and this thing eating up the road is a cruise fucking missile and it's gonna make jam of us and in a flash of resentment at having got to LA but not getting laid before dying I feel resigned to my fate, what can you do, fuck it man. Then Lenny decides 'uh oh, not today for death, thank you' and like Steve fucking McQueen he cuts right across three lanes of oncoming and then weaves through two more lanes of vehicles going our way and slides into the inside slow lane like he meant it all along and the truck misses us easily by 20 feet - not even close ya fucker.

"I've shit meself," says Hunter. "You are officially a cunt, Lenny," but he's enjoying the madness and still being alive and he's laughing and Lenny is laughing and all our hearts beat beat beat.

"Just wanted to keep you on your toes big lad," he says and we all laugh again at being alive.

This is goo goo good and we crank up the radio as we sail down Reseda Boulevard with Stevie Ray Vaughan's 'Cold Sweat' as our soundtrack.

The club looks like a coal bunker. It's set back from a strip mall and it's got big boards with spray-painted names - presumably bands due to play - so we park up and bang on the door. Nothing. No fucker there. It all looks shut down and we wonder if it's the right place at all. Tony goes to the pay-phone and calls the number again while we open some beers and it's the same bloke he spoke to earlier who answers and says he'll be down in a bit with his daughter and he'll see us then, so we hang around and drink some beer and watch the cars cruise by doing their everyday Joe thing.

It's 100 degrees on the gas station thermometer and it feels like we're in hell and we've never been so hot in our lives and there's just no air; it feels like we're not on earth and humans shouldn't be trying to live on this planet because someone sucked out the oxygen. I've had four beers and I still don't need to piss because I'm sweating it all out. Rent-a-Wreck vans don't have air con unless you count the windows, and the valley - though we didn't know before then - is God's frying pan in the summer. It was killer heat and sweat ran in rivers down my legs so my jeans looked wet as though I'd pissed myself. I swear I hadn't.

When the bloke arrives he looks like Burt Reynolds' older spastic brother. He's about 22 stone, limping, wearing a Bermuda shirt, white cap and a pair of shorts that look like they were made in 1951. He smells like he sleeps in a cigar box.

"You boys the band?" he says like he's W C Fields. I think he's taking the piss but it's for real. He opens up the club and inside it's as cold as a witch's tit. He bellows out a laugh so rough it could have grated carrots.

"Bibbly Boy ain't no fool. We got air con to the max in here."

'Bibbly Boy'? Fuck. He flips on light switches. It looks like a shoe box with a stage the size of a mouse's fart with a PA and a drum kit. There's a bar and a couple of smaller rooms. This is it. It isn't the crustiest thing we've ever seen because the crustiest thing we've ever seen was a place in Billingham.

"So you're new in town, right? So you won't mind playing for free for me yes yes I like that."

"Hey mate, we never said nowt about it being free," says Hunter and stretches his 6'2" to 6'3".

"Okay, you get free drinks, I'm in a good mood. Gimme your tape and my daughter will tell me if you're any good."

279

We were still too hot and sweaty to argue so we give him the tape and a woman with big hair comes in and she's the daughter. She looks Greek and had apparently just started growing a 'tache. Either that or she's a guy with big tits. She's chewing gum and has hips that go wide and wider. She was okay but boredom was written over her like a love/hate tattoo.

We go through to an office and Bibbly Boy seems to have gone and we're pleased about that because he's an arsehole. She plays the tape, frowns and runs her fat little fingers through her hair, or she tries to but she can't get it through the curled knots, and then she smiles and says: "Yeah you'll do, the gig is next Friday. If you go down well you can do a night every week this month."

"What about money?" I asked.

"We'll see. We don't pay new bands. You can help yourself to the bar. You've got your own gear, yeah? You do two sets - start 10pm finish 3am-ish; there'll be another band on with you as well."

It seemed like a lot of effort for not much but playing rock 'n' roll on a Friday night was the holy gospel according to rock 'n' roll and we were happy to have the gig. So we got back into the van, pulled some more beer from the cooler and toasted our success such as it was, and that wasn't much, but you take your pleasure where and when you can in life and take off down the 405 all the way down to Newport Beach in rush-hour traffic moving at a steady 21 miles an hour bumper to bumper for the whole 65 miles.

Hunter's at the wheel and he's digging driving in California - he looks like a wild animal with his hair sticking up like a half-collapsed afro and he's drumming his hands on the wheel and nodding his head and pulling little faces with every beat on the radio and taking his hands off from time to time and letting the heap of shit van just idle forward without guidance while he plays air drums to Zep's 'Black Dog'. Classic rock fucking radio man...to us it was the most damn brilliant thing. We never heard our rock 'n' roll music on the radio except on the Friday Rock show. Rock on Tommy. And it is really is our music.

We slam down Pacific Coast Highway and take a left into Newport. This is our first sight of the ocean and we all shout like kids going to the seaside but it's not like the North Sea of our childhood - here the Pacific is an endless liquid miasma of shards of silver light and infinite dark blue depth and right in the harbour are hundreds of multi-million dollar boats all white and shiny and wooden and bobbing on the water.

Newport Beach is a rich dudes' gaff and is all big boats, pony-tailed women and guys in expensive versions of cotton Dockers. It's pretty bloody posh and it's hard not to be impressed even though you instinctively feel in that oh-so-British way that you shouldn't be so shallow as to be amazed by the wealth but hell-fire man, it was jaw-dropping and we were impressed and we didn't care who knew it.

"Any time after five pm she said," said Tony. "She said it was a bar and a diner and they do a rock night on Tuesdays."

The coast was much cooler and was in the high 70's and it felt like a cold bath after the heat of the valley and it felt like our skin was cool for the first time all day and it was like your body was drinking in the sea breeze and saying thank you. It was delicious. My brain is going fuzzy from the jet-lag again and I don't even know if I'm awake or asleep so I crank up the medication to keep going as we get lost.

"Fucking hell, look at that," shouted Tony as we went back inland. A sign points to John Wayne Airport.

"John Fucking Wayne Airport, that's a name to give an airport, not this fucking Heathrow bollocks, we should have Michael Caine Airport that'd be fucking right and Newcastle would have to be Jackie Milburn Airport as well and...." and Tony is racing on the stimulants and we're all feeling perky again. We see the bar eventually and park in its massive parking lot and spill out all crumpled and red-faced and hair everywhere.

This was more our comfort zone. Bar gig. Oh yeah baby. Barbara was the manager. She was middle-aged and lovely; all smiles, baggy linen pants and baggy shirts and baggy was good on a hot day and here she was and here we were and she's the first Southern Californian Rich Hippy with capital letters I've ever met and she's like all cool and hip but she's loaded; you can tell she's a bread head but also a Deadhead and I make this mental note that being a middle-aged Rich Hippy is a thing to aim for if anything is worth aiming for.

All is cool. She offers us tea, what with us being English, and we said 'how about some whisky instead if that was okay' and it was and she had a single malt for us with lots of ice and we sat at her bar and grooved on the colourful neon signs.

We gave her our tape, she thanked us and said she'd listen later and in hindsight she doesn't want to hear it with us there in case we're crap and she says that we should call her the next day and then she gets us all a sandwich and it's fucking delicious and we're all so high and so fucking tired that there's tears in our eyes at this kind gesture 6,000 miles from home where people are bad-mouthing Americans and here's Barb and here we are.

The trip to Newport seemed like a lot of fucking effort but we thought we'd made a good impression. We could have put the cassette in the mail to her and why didn't we just think of that? Were we stupid? Yeah we were stupid like the heat.

Back at the motel on Sunset we finally got some heavy sleep sleeping and slept that night deadbeat and drained and dehydrated. I woke up at 5am and the day felt like the first Kleenex in the box. No-one else was awake but I was restless and I like to get out on my own just to keep my head together. The Strip was cool and as quiet as it ever gets. A little mist hung in the air; the sun lurking with intent to fry the night-time moisture. I took a shower, pulled on a clean t-shirt and unclean jeans, finished a bottle of red wine and took a walk. LA felt like

282

a giant taking a nap between fierce extended bouts of partying. I understood.

I walked towards the lovely Mondrian hotel which I'd read about in guidebooks and here it is right in front of me painted up in coloured squares like Mr Mondrian would have wanted and I'm feeling like I'm a new man. The jet-lag wool-head had gone, blown away by the cool morning air pungent with eucalyptus, cinnamon, coffee and gas. From somewhere, a radio out there in the ether, just wafting in on the air, I can hear Nils Lofgren. Nils fucking Lofgren man. It's 'Moontears'. And I fucking love Lofgren and I'm already thinking Jesus, am I still on earth, and an electric zinger goes up my spine and discharges sparks through my cerebral cortex. Oh yeah. This is the City Of Rock 'N' Roll. That's what they said. No-one lied.

The Mondrian was open for breakfast already and I walked through the lobby and followed the signs to the patio out the back and it was empty apart from a woman in a thick coat like it was winter and a guy who looked like he was about to play tennis. I got a table and ordered peaches and coffee, eggs and toast.

The view was phew moma - LA spilling west to the coast spreading out below the strip and in the hazy distance the skyscrapers of downtown poked skywards. It was so green; palm trees and cypress trees and little houses scattered everywhere punctuated by telegraph poles and gas station signs; their neon plastic colour set amongst nature's green and urban LA's stucco coating; the 76 balls stood out like it was all one big pool table.

It all looked so beautiful and it's not like a city at all; it's more like a big Mediterranean village, a very big fucking village and I get to thinking how cities to me mean big, dirty, often ugly and aggressive jungles. Places like Sheffield and Birmingham and Coventry, or worse still London, which has great buildings and parks but feels like you're walking in an open-air toilet. By contrast this was like a garden. A big big big garden. It was awesome. I loved what it did to my eyes and to my soul.

A tiny bird purred through the air and darted in and out of some luscious cerise and white bougainvillea. It had to be a hummingbird. It really hummed too, this beautiful little thing doing its business, up early grafting hard with that long thin beak and I said good morning and wished it a good day on the nectar; yeah, you and me both birdy.

That morning, it was like none I had in my life before. It's all too much all too quick for my senses to take in but you know when you think a plant is dead and you water it one last time because you feel guilty about neglecting it for so long on the window sill and then within a few hours it's looking alive and by the next days it's upright again...that was me and I'm wide open to it and I'm thinking all the while that this is a big deal this LA thing and it already feels like a drug; like crack for the soul and I'm hooked on it from the first hit.

It wasn't like 'oh, this is nice but when are we going home'; it was 'right, this is how it should be, this is how life should be lived'. I was naive of course but it put a dreaming seed in my soul and that bloody seed set down some deep, deep roots.

The waitress brought my food and asked if everything was okay. I laughed and I said it was just fine thanks, the best fine thanks I'd ever had.

"It's a beautiful morning...gonna be a hot one," she said and looked out at the Los Angeleno vastness below and didn't go anywhere for a moment; even a waitress making small talk seemed like a new experience. It didn't happen at the Little Chef outside of Newark on the A1.

So I said, "Want to join me for coffee? I'm new in town from England", and I'm already thinking as I say the words, who the fuck am I saying stuff like I'm 'new in town'? Am I Joe fucking Hollywood now? But hell it feels alright. Jesus I feel immortal and it surges through me like a wave of electricity which comes with a cinnamon frosting. I am like a child again and all is new with the new and I have been reborn and all my old hard skin has gone and it feels corny and true.

She smiles, taken aback that anyone would pay her that much attention.

"I can't, I'm on duty 'til nine," she said and smiled again. "I always wanted to go to England - you know, for the history."

"Yeah we've got a lot of history in England; maybe too much history," I said and again did a double take on myself - what the fuck? Did LA make you talk like you're in a movie? This is some weird osmosis maybe but I liked that it was happening.

She smiled again. It was a soft smile, the kind that you could climb inside and sit next to in crisp linen sheets. She was blonde but not really. Early 20's probably and with a throaty sort of voice all dry and hoarse and bluesy like she needed some water and I'm grooving on it.

After an hour of delicious peaches that burst in my mouth like a fruit bomb, I left 15 dollars on the table for the nine-dollar breakfast. I hadn't worked out tipping and only knew that you were supposed to do it, but how much I had no idea - it was just another alien concept I had to assimilate in this new humanness.

I waved at the waitress through the glass as she scurried out the kitchen with a tray of food for more breakfasters. She wiggled her fingers at me nicely and I'm nodding oh yeah baby I'm coming back here. As I was leaving I saw a man who looked familiar. He's a big guy with a pudgy, sweaty face, for a few seconds I couldn't place him then I got it; it was Peter Buck from REM. I turned and looked at him walking out onto the patio - he was carrying a Johnny Cash album. I stood there in the lobby grinning, a zapping zing of adrenalin going through me again like my brain is having a multiple orgasm.

How damn cool this was and how LA and how new and the whole thing is a drug, it really is and man, I came away feeling so high. This shit didn't happen at a Travelodge on the A14 now did it? I was born for this place. It's like it was invented for me. And that's what everyone who falls in love with the City of Angels thinks. That is the siren song. It sucks you and it eats you and makes you grateful to be just another light snack.

I made the call to Barbara that night from the Kings Head and she liked what she'd heard and wanted us to play some blues and not too much heavy stuff and that's fine with us and that was the second gig in the bag for the following week. Ah, this is a piece of piss we thought and now we'd found the key to the door behind which lay gigs, money and women and that was a relief except it wasn't because we couldn't get any other work at all after that. Nada. We'd got beginners' luck. Tony gave up after calling fifty places and I must have tried at least another fifty and got nothing except three invitations to mail them a tape but it was just a way to get me off the phone, you could tell that.

We were doing it all wrong and we started to realise that but didn't know what to do because we needed money like now and we couldn't afford to wait for a month while someone listened to our tape. But there's no rule books for hairy arses like us to follow and we knew nothing ourselves. We were never going to get a manager because we had no money to pay anyone and never earned enough to make it a job worth doing anyway. Plus we didn't trust anyone but all the while the money is running out out out quickly quicker and soon it'd be gone.

I don't remember whose idea it was to call Mikey from the Rainbow but it turned out to be the best call we ever made because it got us work, it got us money, it got us laid and it gave us the life we'd been hoping for. Who would have thought that a little Mancunian ratter like Mikey would have been so important to anyone?

I got him at the third number on his list. It sounded like he was in bathroom. I told him we needed gigs and could he help us get any? Did he know anyone? He jabbered at me in his

Manc drawl, using words like little riffs in 4/4 time repeating words and phrases over and over and over.

"You gotta know the right people Johnny; gotta know the right people Johnny. Yeah, yeah, I know, I know, I know a few yeah a few yeah yeah let me think...," he rapped on all nervous and hyper from the speed. "I'll take 10%, 10% of anything, anything you're paid. Okay?"

Mikey was always on the money. I say okay like this is a real business fucking deal with a real fucking businessman and not some little druggy scammer because what choice do I have? We agree to meet in the Cat 'n' Fiddle on Sunset the next night.

For some instinctive reason I assumed Mikey would just come through for us, which was crazy because we didn't know who he was or what he was or why he was. All we knew was he was there. And that had to do. So we just relaxed and went round Santa Monica drinking and eating fries from Benitos on 3rd Street.

As night falls we slide into this little club. It's dark and quite small; like a long corridor with a band at one end. It's as dark as black velvet in there with just very low orangey lights and the band are playing 'Flute Thing' by The Blues Project I think or something like it and I'm digging it big, being a man who loves the blues in all its forms; the music takes me and makes me its slave every time; it's the father and yes it's the mother and the son and daughter and the fucking holy holy ghost and that's what I feel to my soul.

We get a table next to people who are smoking roll-ups and they look like they know high from low and so we get talking to them between numbers. They're locals, stoner sorts and are probably the kids of rich people, they had that look and they think we talk weird. Which we do.

And we're there for a few hours and we get royally fucked up and we're feeling good as this band is doing all sorts of bluesy jazz stuff; not rock 'n' roll but slick as you like.

"This lot can really play Tony," I said. "They've got all the fucking chops and we've got nowt compared to them. They can do all the suspended 9th chords and everything."

Tony grinned at me like he grins at everything in life; a big shit-eating grin, his chipped front teeth exposed and his swimming-pool blues eyes laughing at me.

"Aye, but we've got big balls man...," he said in his Whitley Bay accent, "...and we know how to rock 'n' roll. These musos couldn't rock their way out of a paper bag. It's not up here," he points to his head, "it's in here." He points to his heart: "Divvent forget that bonny lad."

Later our for-one-day-only friends invite us back to their gaff for a bit of recreational intoxication. It can't have been far because we walked there in ten minutes. The night folded itself around me like a warm bath. Hunter is singing something and I'm pissed out of my brain and here I am in southern California's navy blue night and the Pacific is crashing into the shore somewhere in the distance and sirens wail and the air is sweet and warm and all this is swimming before my eyes and in my brain and Lenny is writing something down, playing at being Jim Morrison probably.

Their apartment is fucking lovely, all wood floor and ethnic rugs and green. They had wooden blinds and I thought that was really a bit weird. They must have been loaded to live in a place like this.

I sit down on this big sofa chair thing and this woman with green eyes sits down next me, squeezing up real tight and says she's called Rachel or Raquel or something and I'm thinking 'you smell really nice', as you do when you've had a few tugs on herbal refreshment. She's like earth and roses and coffee all mixed together.

I'm probably looking a bit too much; like staring really I suppose; but you know I'm losing control and I'm happy to do so. Someone puts the Allman Brothers' Fillmore East album on and I'm flying and life is sweet. The girl lives there and she's

288

really something. I run a movie in my mind and I think she's the daughter of some rich Hollywood guy - maybe she was and while I'm wondering, she's getting in nice and close and I know it's on. Duane is stinging me with some salt-in-the-wound slide playing and we go to her room and I'm so drunk and so stoned that I'm almost tripping and I'm looking from outside myself as it all happens and I'm thinking this is a bloody good dirty movie. Christ, look at her on the bed underneath that long-haired guy with the shiny white arse.

As light begins to penetrate my blackness I'm aware of my head hurting and my mouth dried out and smooth like plastic. Fucking hangovers. The girl isn't there and it's quiet and the clock reads 11.30am. The bedroom is bare; nothing much more than the big double bed and a clock. I get up and find my clothes neatly folded on a wooden chair - a note written on orange notepaper with a flower print on the top says 'didn't want to wake you - some of us have to work!'.

Hunter comes in as I'm pulling on my jeans and laughs at me.

"You look destroyed."

"I feel like shit," I say, going sweaty and cold and knowing I'm going to need to puke.

"Fucking poof," he laughed again.

"Thanks for the sympathy."

I went into the bathroom next door and barfed a foul-smelling stream into the toilet. As I did so I hear Lenny's voice and he's cheering at every retch. Fuckers. I've always suffered from shit hangovers and throwing up is the best way to fix it. This is a good one, all out in two good pukes. Thank God for toothpaste.

"Right, I'm fucking ready for some scran and a drink." I am as well. You fall off the bike, you get right back on.

"Tony's humping a lass - we've got to wait till he's finished," says Lenny.

"That'll be all of two minutes then," says Hunter, who looks fresh as a daisy. He doesn't get hangovers; probably because he's not human.

From behind a door we can hear Tony doing his thing. Hunter opens the door, revealing Tony's arse nestling between two tanned splayed legs. The lass leans to one side and grins. I've never seen her before in my life but she looks great, as all of Tony's women seem to do.

"Howay Tony, shoot your load will you...we want to get off for food," said Hunter.

Tony doesn't stop, he just flips us the Vs and the girl laughs.

"Tasty lass her though," says Lenny as we sit down and wait.

"What was that one like last night then? Come on, we want details," says Hunter to me. "You were up her quick. You're worse than Hairy Boy."

But I can't remember much except she looked great and felt smooth and was peanut butter brown all over.

"Who was she?" I ask, a bit late probably.

Hunter shrugs and says: "Dunno, she lives here though and she was all over you, jammy get. Nic, you must remember something or did you just shoot your load before you got it in?"

I tried hard to remember. I couldn't even recall shooting my load.

"I don't even know if I did. I can't fucking remember anything, I was shit-faced."

Fifteen minutes later Tony emerges, pulling on his pants and saying: "Howay then, my work here is done."

"Dirty cunt," says Hunter.

"Nah, she was very clean actually."

We sat in the 3rd Street Deli and ate muffins, eggs, cheese, bacon, tea and juice and broke the night down, such as we could which wasn't much, but we agreed that on balance, weighing up what we could remember and the stains on our clothing, that it'd been a good night and if we ever ran across them again we'd buy them a few drinks if we had any money, which at that time didn't seem likely and while we were talking about money we had to get a cheaper place to stay - a cheap motel where we could afford to stay for a few weeks was ess-fucking-ential.

This turned out to be the Hotel Carmel in Santa Monica which is now fairly smart but back then was a budget hotel where you could get a room for two for something like $120 a week if you had a coupon out of this little booklet you could pick up at the airport. It didn't have air con but it had these big rotary blades in the ceiling and you lay there and it was like a helicopter was falling on you. It was all a bit worn but it was okay and it's on Broadway and 2nd right in downtown Santa Monica which we'd figured out was where we wanted to be so we were at the heart of the action. So we hauled ass down from the Strip and installed our jeans, t-shirts and beer fumes.

Then it was off to the Cat 'n' Fiddle to meet Mikey. We get there and it's another English style pub and it's got a dartboard and Hunter and Tony love playing darts. So we get some Millers and they play darts while me and Lenny go out onto this patio underneath the still blue sky to talk the business of rock 'n' roll. It's after 7pm and it's warm warm warm. The beer is icy tasty and takes less than a minute to drain. I go back to the bar and buy four more.

As I'm doing so Mikey comes in and he's in a red-and-black-striped 1970's-style Man City away shirt and a pair of army shorts and baseball boots. He looks like he's been awake for a month.

He sits down at our table and takes a beer from me in the manner of a man who expects everything to be provided. He's got a sheet of paper with names and addresses and he says he's almost there on getting us a few gigs. He keeps squinting and narrowing his fingers together in mid-air to show how close he is. He thinks we're great but he knows nothing about music so I discount his opinion right away.

Anyway, he's speaking to people who want to book bands for parties and it occurs to me that we could do that directly ourselves but that's me, always looking for the quickest way from A to B. But of course we don't know who books such bands so I shut up for now. Then he asks us for some money for expenses and we say 'fuck off, we're not giving you money till we've got paid for gigs' and he looks pissed off but he looks like he needs the money more than we do so he doesn't make anything more of it. We're not quite the bottom of the pile this particular day.

Later that night back in Santa Monica, I'm on my own having a late-night drink on 3rd Street. It's after 1am and it's still about 70 degrees and I meet a man called Dan and his wife Juliet. I like a man called Dan and as the turns of fate's wheels of fire would have it, I like a man called Dan who owns a bar in Sherman Oaks. He puts our tape in his Walkman and likes our noise and says why don't we play a couple of nights in the back room for $100 a night. I say yes as quick as it's possible for three letters to come out of a mouth and I buy him a Bourbon and write down the details and we're off and ready to rock.

The gig in the Valley at Northridge never happened and we later heard Bibbly Bobby had a heart attack and the place closed down soon after. Our first actual live performance was in the bar in Newport Beach on Campus Drive and I think it's called Hoagie Barmichaels now. Great name, you couldn't make that name up, except someone did so that's obviously not true but you know what I mean.

And so that's how we got started and this was before all the madness, the druggy woo-woos, the out-of-body things, the crazy parties, the crazy panties, the strung-out all night 'give it to me one more time' rock 'n' rollness that was to become who we really were underneath and it didn't take long for the Californication bug to bury under our skin. You give it an inch, you let it in the house and it immediately runs riot and takes over your life; but gives back much more than it takes.

It changed everything and made me different and it broke the cycle of regular life, it swept away the deck of cards life had dealt me and showed me that living better had always been nearer than I thought and that the view from out there on the edge was scary and magnificent...yeah it was really scary and really magnificent...